FUTURENET

SALLY RICHARDS

FUTURENET

THE PAST, PRESENT,
AND FUTURE
OF THE INTERNET
AS TOLD BY ITS
CREATORS
AND VISIONARIES

JOHN WILEY & SONS, INC.

"Luck is the residue of design."
—Branch Rickey, Brooklyn Dodgers
general manager

DEDICATION

There are quite a few men to thank for inventing the Internet, but there are many women I can thank for supporting me while I wrote this book. Writing a book is never an easy task—emotionally it takes a village. So, I want to acknowledge all of the wonderful women in my life who made this book possible.

A warm, loving thank-you to my mother, Hilda, who is and has always been an extraordinarily strong and loving source of support and encouragement.

A grand celebratory glass of cheer to the bright spirits of my grandmothers, Mary and Sally, who taught me always to endeavor and excel in whatever I choose to do in this life, and to hunker down, dig in, and spring up twice as fast when the going gets tough.

Special thanks to my agent extraordinaire, Margot Maley Hutchison (www.WatersideProductions.com), who is always a contributor to my enthusiasm, success, and coffers.

A huge debt of gratitude to my fabulously inspirational editor at Wiley, Jeanne Glasser, whose vision made this book entirely possible. Jeanne, your hard work in keeping this book on track is much appreciated—you have a clear mind, a sharp pencil, and a great deal of unfettered creativity.

Pat McCarron, thank you always for your sage advice in helping me make tough decisions; you are the best personal ethicist ever.

And roaring applause to my incredibly unwieldy weekly gathering of women called the Wild Women of Wonder

(WiWoWo), a group of Silicon Valley's greatest women ever and our West Coast version of the Algonquin Round Table (with special thanks to Donna Compton, Sue Cooper, Wahida Fazli, Jennifer Jeffrey, Nicole Kidd, Sylvia Paull, Carla Rayacich, Carol Sands, Loni Reeder, Deb Todd, and Mei-hong Xu).

And last but not least, to my niece Simonne, who loves her computer and supports her Aunt Sally with much love and wonder—I hope that one day there will be many, many more women engineers, programmers, and physicists who will make magic contributions to the Internet of your future.

With much love and gratitude I thank you all.

CONTENTS

ACKNOWLEDGMENTS   xi

PREFACE   xv

CHAPTER 1   WITHSTANDING . . .   1

CHAPTER 2   ADOLESCENCE   49

CHAPTER 3   ISSUES   77

CHAPTER 4   WHO WILL?   141

CHAPTER 5   FUTURESCOPE   193

INDEX   263

ACKNOWLEDGMENTS

Of course, I'd like to take this opportunity to thank all those who helped found the Internet as we know it today: the wildly creative Vannevar Bush (the future as he saw it was the science fiction of his time); the humble J.C.R. "Lick" Licklider; Len Kleinrock; Frank Heart; the intense and very honed Larry Roberts; the tremendously inspirational Doug Englebart; the determined Vint Cerf; Jon Postel (I wish I would have had a chance to have known you; your friends think very fondly of you); the dynamic Bob Kahn; Fred Baker, thank you for your saintly patience; the humanistic Bob Taylor; and the larger than life (and fabulous genius guy) David Farber. Also the ever-illusive, clandestine, and encrypted Ted Nelson; Tim Berners-Lee (wherever you are); Marc Andreesen; and the many, many others who didn't and did take part in this book; but who managed to pull together a fabulous legacy that will surely outlive us all.

Len Kleinrock, you have been especially generous with your time and resources, and an inspiration to me in all of your facets as technologist, realist, and dreamer—thank you!

I'm amazed to see how many of the above-mentioned guys still have skin in the game after decades of creating something so phenomenal—I'm in awe of the new companies, endeavors, and tools of power and imagination you're currently creating. I'm glad you're determined to continue in guiding the Internet's evolution.

Thank you for a space that has no center, no beginning,

and no end. And for the greatest tool of all—the tool to communicate freely with anyone in the world. You have given all of us a tremendous gift that you brought forth from your visions of a better day in technology and brought us something as magic as the Gutenberg press; you guys are a national treasure (make that a World Wide Wonder). You built something more powerful than the atomic bomb, an amazing technology with the power to tear down the boundaries of oppressive governments and prejudice of the human mind to bring the people of the Earth together as one small village having a town meeting; I dare say that this accomplishment should entitle you all to the Nobel Peace Prize. There is a Latin phrase that goes *crede quod habes, et habes.* Translated, it means believe that you have it, and you will have it. Thank you for believing. Now we have *IT* (as in Internet Technology) and we're having a fascinating ride trying to figure out what to do with it. I feel like a mesmerized kid with a wonderful creation every time I boot up. You guys rock!

Merci, Jim Hurd, you are a marvelous networker and truly a catalyst who fosters natural explosions—you were a great help in connecting me to some key people at a very serendipitous time.

Paul Hoffman, associate director Academic Technology Services, UCLA—you are *da bomb!* You managed to pull these chapters from the black holes leading to the netherworld residing on my Mac's hard drive (oh yeah, FYI this book was created—and recreated on a Mac G-4) and put them back into place. Thanks for your 13th-hour skills; your software tools are exquisite!

And Jerome "Jerry" Glenn (United Nations University), thank you for putting all of the pieces in place and tethering this gal's need for greater technology (at any price), and not letting up until it finally got into my head that we need to have humanity rest stops on our Information Highway (unless we want to end up in one of Philip K. Dick's parallel universes).

Thanks, Larry Kay, for finding that great Branch Rickey quote that I had been looking for—you are a very helpful friend.

And let me not forget, the forehead-smacking (metaphorically speaking) candor of John Perry Barlow. Bruce Damer, you have a great outlook on life, virtual and otherwise. Charles Ostman, thank you for pulling out all of the stops to make time.

I searched high and low for women to participate in this book but unfortunately didn't find very many who would return my calls. So, to the few who did, I treasure your thoughts and comments: the fabulously innovative Judy Estrin, the ever-confident Kim Polese (I'm very happy that you're still with us and creating); and the wonderful humanitarian, Lakshmi Pratury, who is changing—right here and now—the way and rate our children are learning to live in this world.

Thank you to everyone who participated in this book to make it a real story of the future, filled with enthusiasm and tempered with wisdom.

My gratitude is yours,
Sally

PREFACE

NO ABSOLUTES

There are some required lessons for us to learn as we endeavor in this life. One of the most relevant ones to our evolution is that there are no absolutes. Time and time again we move forward, only to get stuck, like a needle in the groove of a scratched 78 record, repeating the past as if it were our future . . . over and over again. These sticking points are usually produced by respected naysayer visionaries producing technology "laws" that are therein set as a standard that is repeated by an ever-present Greek chorus whenever a new technology is even imagined by some enthusiastic entrepreneur. In technology all laws are made to be broken, and we're lucky that visionary technologists exist who look at them only as challenges instead of boundaries to work within. There are also those visionary investors and organizations with grants that believe in early-stage innovation and reward it with cash, and the clients who will buy in early to the dream. Without these three elements there would be no forward movement in technology.

There are many people who would not have brought this visionary dream of the Internet forth had it not been for the path that Vannevar Bush chose and his pitch of a boundless future where communication and knowledge flowed effortlessly over computer networks. It took government funding from DARPA (the U.S. Defense Advanced Research Projects

Agency) to bring this contributed effort to a reality when the commercial sector wouldn't give it the time of day. *Who loves ya now, baby?*

Naysayers don't have a chance in our future, and I have a serious feeling that even our sacred Moore's Law, which did serve its time well, will be one of those absolutes that we'll be shedding some day soon. There are no absolutes in this life—least of all in technology.

I have a signature line on the bottom of my e-mail that I've had there for about two years. It reads, *I think there is a world market for maybe five computers,* said Thomas Watson, chairman of IBM, 1943, and *Computers in the future may weigh no more than 1.5 tons.* I hear a lot of people making absolutist statements about technology—and especially about their products—all the time, and I think, *Boy, I hope someone wrote that one down.* This is a fabulous time we live in and the only absolute thing is that this industry will look extremely (and wonderfully) different from moment to moment.

In these chaotic times, brilliance is bound to bubble to the top, now that all the rest has settled into the dot-com sediment. What many people don't realize, especially some VCs who are still feeling timid about going back and having to tell their fund's investors how much money they're still losing, is that an entirely new industry is now birthed from this burst bubble—one stronger than we ever imagined. This will be the era people will look back upon in 300 years and say, *Man, I was born too late.*

I was fortunate to have hooked up with the brilliant people who forged a technology from almost nothing but concepts, thousands of miles of cable, a need, and the audaciousness that comes from facing a new age where anything is possible. These guys created a technology that bloomed into an entire industry that changed the world. That is *changing* the world. This distributed technology was built to reroute communication if the network was damaged; it was vastly different from the telephone system we had in place then, or even have in place now, some 30 years later. It's odd both how much things change—and how much they remain the same.

I recently watched, as did most of America, the World Trade Center towers burst into flames and collapse into rubble live on TV. When I went to alternative news sources on the Internet, I found that there was quite a difference in the news I was receiving. I soon found uncensored accounts from newspeople not regulated by the commercial networks (and their sponsors and network chairmen), people in the know speaking freely, first-person Ground Zero accounts, streaming video . . . lists of the dead and missing. So much of this that was not available from my TV, and moreover it was immediate and interactive. And I certainly wasn't enabled to be interactive with the much-disheveled Peter Jennings.

Not only had the Internet made it over the hurdle of rerouting packets and surviving a national disaster, it was the only real source of news that was being delivered uncensored, and the only reliable communications tool. It was also a place where anyone could write whatever they wanted, so we got a real sense of close-to-the-bone stories from all over the world.

Being a journalist who was contemplating covering the war in Afghanistan, I was also able to rely on encryption software to reach people behind *enemy lines* to find out if there was any chance I could still get inside the country at a time when most communications were in danger of being intercepted and my contact was in danger of being revealed. Was this a bad thing for me to do? In sending the messages was I breaking any U.S. laws? Should the government be looking into my business? Did my business become its business as soon as the messages were encrypted?

Not long before I sent those messages to Afghanistan, I spoke out live on CNN against the Department of Justice's tactics against Dmitry Sklyrov and its controversial use of the Digital Millennium Copyright Act in jailing the Russian programmer. Not long after September 11, I became acutely aware that I had received a huge number of hits from U.S. government and military agencies, and strangely enough from mideastern countries. One government site hit every single web page and link on my home page; what they didn't know is that I have one hell of a backend on my site that allows me to view what they were doing (sans cookies). Either that, or they just didn't care and wanted to make their presence known. Probably the latter; I'm sure they have random AOL accounts they could use if they wanted to be *really* covert.

I made some calls of my own, and some due diligence was exercised on my behalf. I found that it was at first a random keyword search that had brought attention to my web site and landed me in the hot seat. Sure, I have a lot of controversial commentary on my site, but none that could be considered anything that would incite anti-American activity. Those same random words describing recent terrorist activity would have been found on any news site in the world. Nevertheless, I began to feel pangs of concern over the impending Carnivore legislation, a government program that allows "them" to use a software tool that peruses your e-mail by keyword scanning. Sure, I could put up enough security to even keep hacker Kevin Mitnick out of my web site (which is relatively easy now since he's banned from using the Internet as a condition of his parole, but you can see him in his guest role as an agent on the network show *Alias*) and e-mail. I could put up even more mechanisms to block keyword searches, but why? The more security you throw up on your firewall, the harder it becomes for the people you want to visit your site. But, still . . . you have to wonder if government eyes are the answer.

When I put up my web site several years ago, the last thing on my mind was the issue of government involvement in technology. Frankly speaking, I didn't think the government could afford to hire anyone who could possibly know enough about technology to make any trouble for your ordinary Jane or Joe journalist with a web site—after all, they were competing against dot-com salaries in their heyday. Now there are programmers practically sitting on the corners of Palo Alto's streets with signs: *Will code for food*. I recently photographed a group of entrepreneurs on Sand Hill Road (one of the areas in Palo Alto known for its VCs) for *Newsweek*, who were sporting picket signs asking for funding. Apparently the government agencies that are all chomping at the bit to help legislate technology have suddenly found themselves with very generous budgets due to knee-jerk reaction voting since 9/11.

Regardless, when I'm sitting there posting my random thoughts in the early morning hours, should my thoughts be of what's being added to my dossier? I really don't think so. Will the government censor me? No. Should this much power—actually much more—be given to the government? I remember how much time Mitnick was given for poking around where he didn't belong, I think one needs to decide whether the government should be given the equivalent for its hackers' free-for-all.

Back when the Internet was being developed, many of its creators knew what was about to happen—what a Pandora's box they were opening—and how it would never be shut again. The Internet was developed with government nurturing; it survived due to government-sponsored academic programs; and it withstood all of the curve balls that were thrown at it. Now, the orphan rejected by commercial interests in its infancy and the government that carefully nurtured its growth have come back to *leverage* and *control* the behemoth distributed Network; the snake without a mouth or tail; the never-ending loop of infinity that has worked just fine without boundaries, legislation, or enforcement. Now that 9/11 has occurred, all of that has changed. The flawed design of the telecom system was pointed out and underlined during this crisis, so you can bet the telephone industries are looking even harder at an Internet Protocol (IP) delivery system. The government is paranoid about how terrorists could use encryption and the Internet to plot havoc.

Personally, I feel that once the people in the government—those who would like to throw as many chains of control as they possibly can around this Pandora's Box—can personally write 500 lines of code and make a simple application work, then they can begin to understand the intricacies of what they're trying to build laws around. Then they can finally begin to write laws; but until then, they sure as hell better get a whole lot of technologists' input to help them out. They are on the outside looking in right now, and they are determining the restraints on technologies yet to even be developed; that, my dears, is the most dangerous proposition of them all.

As soon as the government sees that a technology is a major player—TV, radio, phone—it will try to regulate it. But normally not until the technology has proven itself effective as a tool of mass communication. Regulations—as we're starting to see with the Digital Millennium Copyright Act (DMCA)—have a negative effect on research and free markets. I'm guessing the Internet will probably be the central hub for all of the burgeoning technologies we're seeing right now in favor with VCs: Internet appliances (yes, some are still investing in this after the tremendous failures we've seen), nanotech, biotech, wireless, genotech, electronic "radio" ink. All of the incredibly great stuff to empower you in your everyday world. Powerful lobbyists paid by commercial interests influence government laws, even down to regulations that give the phone company the right to sell your phone numbers to solicitors or to use them for its own purposes. Or how about your credit information that companies sell that give people the ability to steal your identity? I know of this subject because I myself have been a victim of identity theft and a system that is not easily accessible to change fraudulent information.

Now we have the Internet, where, frankly, much of the value of a user comes from information gathered about that user and the ability of a web site to abstract that info, repackage it, and sell/trade it with other companies.

The laws will change; everything will change. We have a recently appointed head of the FBI, and we saw what happened at DefCon 2001—the arrest of 26-year-old Dmitry Sklyrov and the Department of Justice testing the judicial waters of the Digital Millennium Copyright Act. We are now facing a time when technologists and university professors are being threatened. This is not the world the Internet was created for. I think we're having extreme growing pains and have a long way to go. A very long way, indeed. Thank goodness there are people who are willing to work things out; people who are willing to protect rights that most of the people in America don't even know are in the balance.

I recently called Vermont's U.S. Senator Patrick Leahy for an interview for this book. He was, after all, one of the coauthors of the DMCA legislation. His assistant asked me for a letter explaining what the book was about. I said that I'd be happy to send it via e-mail: she said that their e-mail was not even close to being able to take individual requests that would get through because of the overwhelming amount they receive. So, their e-mail address was rendered useless, and they did not have another for press requests. I said I'd be agreeable to sending it via fax: she said it was the same story with the fax machine. She asked that I send a letter; I stifled a laugh. This was the man who was trying to legislate the Internet and his office could not find a way of effectively using it? This is a telling sign.

We're in a precarious position. We're in a recession where technology refuses to sleep, in a country at war, in a somewhat united land that continues to legislate—even if in a knee-jerk reaction, during a time when entrepreneurs and developers still smile in their dreams. The dot-com boom gave us a wild ride, and I'm glad to say I was there for all of it and got to see it firsthand. It taught us all a lot of lessons about the world and how much it was willing to pay for the privilege of any-time, anywhere, any device. Meanwhile, the porn industry grows; and we found out what people weren't willing to pay for. This is my ode to Webvan—the wonderful people who brought me my groceries when I was under the gun on dead-line for months at a time, but who couldn't find a way to keep their costs under control and the majority of their clients sat-isfied and coming back.

What would I say to the Internet personified? *You've come a long way baby!* What would the Internet say back? *I am still a baby, stop expecting so much—but you just wait until I'm a teenager—I can hardly wait until you give me the keys to the car!*

As I sat in Buck's <www.Buckswoodside.com> working on this book, kibitzing with restaurateur Jamis MacNiven about the deals he is still hearing being pitched to VC friends who have many of their meetings at his Woodside, California haunt (even in today's environment), we continue to ponder how anyone planned to make any money, and how any of us would come out of The Boom's Burst Bubble unscathed. Even as I sit at Buck's writing this book on my laptop in a cor-ner booth, with BBC correspondents Peter Day and Neil Koenig holding a microphone in my face and asking me, "Will Silicon Valley survive?" I never wavered.

We crashed and fell so damn hard. For a while there was more than a month-long waiting list to rent a moving truck because so many of the bespectacled, 23-year-old, bright and shiny MBA *dot-commas* were headed back home to live with their parents, their dreams shattered, their stock worthless, their houses and posh San Francisco flats on the Marina foreclosed, and their Hummers, Land Rovers, and BMWs repossessed. It's always taken more than a wish and a prayer to make it in this town; that's not ever going to change.

People with money mistook the Internet for a TV—a place to unload countless banners and pop-windows—and they expected them to work! They expected truckloads of money. I cannot tell you how many million-dollar startup parties I attended in the heyday of The Boom. I have a multitude of boxes filled with tee-shirts, baseball hats, keychains, boxer underwear, sunglasses, yo-yos, calculators, watches, glow sticks, lip balm sticks, paperweights, and even condoms with dot-com logos splashed all over them. A load of stuff I'll be able to auction off on eBay in 20 years as the legacy left from the careless spending of The Boom.

I went to a friend's house the other day up in the hills of Woodside. He's close to losing it, but he doesn't fret. He knows there's another deal around the corner. He's smart, and he'll land on his feet. He is a determined technologist who has made it through some cycles before. He had a new piece of furniture—a large piece of driftwood with two layers of glass on top to make a table. Pressed in between the layers are either near-worthless, or not worth the paper they're printed on, stock certificates from the companies he had jumped around from as he developed their technology, got them started, and moved on during the three years of The Boom. There were a lot of companies that I recognized . . . names torn from the dot-com obit pages. He smiled and commented that the wood was probably worth more than the stock, drank in the view of the Valley from his window, inhaled deeply, exhaled a few smoke rings, flicked some ashes into the ashtray that was balanced on the edge of the table, and smiled. "But, I'll be back," he said. I felt as though I was in some bad B-movie; one with an ongoing plot, but bad dialogue. I knew what he meant, and I had no reason to doubt him. Cycles are cycles, and he'd probably be having one of his extravagant Solstice parties soon, with the table being the centerpiece of discussion about The Crash that ignited a whole new industry. These guys don't give up easily—here what doesn't kill you, kills someone else. And if it's you that crashes then it's time for Plan B.

Yeah, we crashed. *What of it?* I ask back. The companies that weather this thing will make for a stronger industry. The people who survive will be the new pioneers in the next era. The fact is, something that began more than 30 years ago is just now picking up incredible speed—at a rate that we can't stop, and frankly why would we want to? Revel in this wondrous age we live in and sit back and enjoy this ride—if you have an Internet connection, you have purchased the ultimate "E" ticket. If you are helping to create the future; keep scope. If you are trying to legislate IT (as in Internet Technology); don't bother (Army-McCarthy Hearings proved that prosecuting creatives didn't work before and it won't work now). If you want the world at your fingertips 24/7, embrace IT and roll with the punches. One day you'll be able to buy your groceries online, and next time 'round it'll work.

IT is everything, and I say the future is so bright I have to wear shades (I am writing this from my laptop in the courtyard of the British Banker's Club <www.BritishBankersClub.com> near Palo Alto, so I *am* wearing shades—and the sky is soooo blue). I am connected; I have wireless capability, I have a PDA that allows the Internet to follow me (nearly) anywhere and any time (almost). We may have hit some bumps: three people I know in this industry lost their homes last week to the technology downturn. At least 50 people I know lost their jobs—and many, many more who lost their entire companies and the investments it took to build them. Are they pissed? Yeah. Are they despondent? Maybe a few are—but all they can think about is what they'll be creating next that will help build the next era. The future? Bring it on!

Safe journey,
Sally Richards
Sally@SallyRichards.com
October 31, 2001
From the Shores of Silicon Valley

FUTURENET

1

Withstanding . . .

I was reading late and doing research for this book during the early morning hours of September 11. I fell asleep with the TV on and a book on my face. I fell asleep feeling safe and lulled into REM by TV images of Valley icon Jamis MacNiven riding his neighbor's camel Omar during the Sand Hill Soap Box Derby Race, an event he created for corporate sponsors to donate money for schools to design some of the most efficient and sci-fi-looking cars to compete in an annual race. The documentary took place a year or so back when times were better, and I probably had a smile on my face when the sandman visited.

I awoke to something very surreal that I was only sub-liminally listening to as I emerged from a troubled sleep, removed the book from my face, and reached around blindly on my bed for my glasses. I soon understood that 9/11, 2001 marked the end of the world as we knew it.

I watched live from Silicon Valley as the second plane crashed into the World Trade Center. For a moment it didn't register; for one naïve moment I thought they were playing a replay of the first crash, which I was still only barely compre-hending. I started doing the math in my head . . . what were the odds of two planes crashing into The Towers by accident?

It was impossible. *Surely, it was impossible.* And then there was the news of the crash at the Pentagon. We soon knew the truth. I immediately booted up my computer; e-mail had already started to fly in: people wondering if I was in NYC that week, people wanting to know I was safe. People in NYC who couldn't get through on their phones. What I soon found out as I tried to make a number of phone calls around the country, most all were answered by that annoying recording: *All circuits are busy, please try your call again.* Strangely enough, I continue to hear that recording more often today as circuits continue to be overloaded. Alas, my e-mail worked, so I began the task of answering the mail I received and shooting even more off. I watched a CNN feed on my local network, turned on NPR, and listened as my fingers flew on the keyboard.

Although my long-distance phone carrier had failed me, the Internet kept right on rerouting. Packets swam confidently, speeding their way to predetermined destinations. Maybe it seems ghoulish to say it, but the e-mails being sent to most of the servers involved in the terrorist attacks would be routed to mirrored sites, many messages never to be read by the people they were intended for. The messages survived when most of the recipients did not. Messages that are probably still sitting on a mirrored site, some sys admin still having the task of deciding what to do with them. Encapsulated messages floating aimlessly. *Messages in bottles,* as Len Kleinrock would later comment when I mentioned this to him.

While I was sitting here on the West Coast trying to figure all of this out on 9/11, on the East Coast, Kim Polese, chairman of Marimba, was two blocks away from the World Trade Center in the Marimba NYC offices, about to head out to the WTC for a meeting. A meeting that not only would never happen, but one with people she has not been able to contact since.

"The World Trade Center didn't exist when it was time for my appointment," says Polese of that day's plans. "I was in midtown headed downtown; it was definitely a close call." Her offices have only recently (in late October) been able to receive power and water. Her only means of communicating with anyone that day, and those that would follow as airplanes were grounded, was her Blackberry PDA. "That's how I communicated. I asked my office to contact my family and let them know I was okay, because some of them aren't on e-mail. In a sense, it was a communication lifeline.

"My perspective is that the Internet has proven itself to be an incredible tool of communications for people around the world, so just the use of it as a utility of instant communication was underscored on 9/11," says Polese about her perspective of the Internet after the WTC incident. "I experienced a dramatic change in people's perception of the Internet; now it's clear that it's a standard part of where we turn to get information. One thing that's unique now is there's constantly breaking news. Almost every couple of hours you find yourself asking, *What's the latest?* because, unfortunately, it's still building and happening in real time. Even CNN can't have the speed immediacy that the Internet does by definition. It's not the novelty it was five years ago, or even less; it's a common part of our everyday life and where we turn to get the latest news."

The Internet, although put together with the idea of transferring technology data, was quite a humanistic element on that fateful day. And although a madman named bin Laden brought the United States to its knees for a brief time, I do have a feeling that it will be our technology that finds him and brings him to justice. Our technology will play a huge part in this war we're currently fighting. And even as I make these changes to this manuscript to update it due to 9/11, lobbyists are trying to push encryption laws through because they don't understand the technology and feel these applications are a threat to national security; a knee-jerk reaction made by politicians who don't understand technology and thus fear it.

But you know what? When the smoke cleared the Internet had survived, and the world was brought together as a village against a common enemy. It took a disaster of heartbreaking proportions to prove a theory thought out loud many times since its inception.

Scientists have always been the unsung heroes of wars; it may be brute force we first attack with, but innovations such as the Varian brother's Klystron, and the splitting of the atom are what really won wars. The geeks—and this word is not a slight, this is a moniker that technologists wear with pride (didn't you know the *ee* in geek stands for *electrical engineer*?)—are who won the war. It was brains over brawn (or should I say, science that aids brawn) that wins our fights in the end. It will be scientists who come up with vaccinations and early-warning detection aids for anthrax, the Ebola virus, and other biological threats that will keep us safe in the future.

In the years since those scientists got together in Los Alamos to work on the end-all solution of World War II, we've been developing an even greater tool; one of freedom, one that allows the free transfer of ideas—even if one lives in a communist country. After all, the Internet is U.S. democracy incarnate (or what we used to know as democracy). It offers us a one-stop shop for just about every amendment in our Constitution. The ability to publish anything we want anytime, anywhere, 24/7, in color, streaming, or just in plain simple text. The right to deliver that message completely naked (see www.nakednews.com, if you don't believe me), or even copulating while saying it. Has the world ever known such freedoms? Doubtful.

Knowledge can bring down governments; the Internet just

happens to be the medium of this messenger. There is no greater power than knowledge. There's a reason why China's government is closing down cyber cafés (by the thousands) that offer software Chinese citizens use to surf the Web and post messages anonymously. This Internet of ours is helping to spread human rights; making our world a global village where exchanges of ideas are a right, not a privilege. Yes, this war has been waging for a while and now our Western World is being streamed into the computers of people who will see there is another way—but frankly, not everyone is happy about this. Even some people in the good ol' U.S. of A. have a problem with allowing this much freedom.

Meanwhile, technology never sleeps, and we continue to make the Internet more of a ubiquitous part of our lives. I long for the day when a scientist splits my head open and places a beautiful little chip inside and the Internet becomes part of my biology; relatively speaking, that day is not far off. Not too long ago the writers of science fiction pulp fiction paperbacks imagined all kinds of things that were thought unbelievable science (thus, science *fiction*), but we've seen a whole lot of it come about. Who would have thought we would have videophones bringing the war live-time into our own TVs? Soon videophones will be no big thing; the prices will come down, and you'll be able to stream video 24/7 wherever you are, whatever you're doing, live to your web site, or phone to phone, to your glasses—or whatever that tool with an IP address may be.

The future is here; and it was *so* influenced by the imaginings of fertile, creative minds. Ask just about any developer or scientist what they read as a kid under the covers via flashlight and they'll tell you Isaac Asimov, they'll tell you comic books with guys with mutant powers, and they'll probably tell you they watched Gene Roddenberry's *Star Trek*. I'll never forget the day I was hanging out at Ask Jeeves in Emeryville when William Shatner dropped by the engineering department and all those geek code jockeys flipped out their butterfly cell phones and looked like they were about to ask to be beamed up. Tell me this was not a generation inspired by being amazed by speculative science fiction thought up by brilliant writers inspired by scientists with big dreams and a clear vision. Or was that the other way around? Regardless, someone had vision; someone had the science; and somehow they meshed.

And now, here I am talking about a chip being put in my head so that I can gain access to the Internet via some kind of bio/nano technology and wireless communication. Just remember where you read it.

But all of this is in the future; and I think before we can fully understand what will happen in *that* future, we need to get a strong grasp of what synergy of events and people happened in the past to make the vision of the Internet a reality. They were envisioning something grand—something that hasn't quite been realized. They didn't bring this network about so that we can sit here now with our PDAs and our computers and clog the pipes with annoying hoax petitions and sales spam. What could they have possibly been thinking when they imagined this future for us?

PARALLELS

There was a war to be won, and America was determined to win it. December 7, 1941, was a day that will live in infamy— and the day Japan made a fatal mistake; it gave America a reason to rally around a common cause with a single focal point—revenge.

President Roosevelt knew trouble was on its way after

receiving several reports from intelligence regarding inter-cepted encrypted messages from Tokyo to Japan's ambassa-dor to the United States. The message was decrypted and Roosevelt anticipated backlash from Japan's Admiral Isoruku Yamamoto for America's firm stance to not reverse economic sanctions and embargoes against Japan. Roosevelt remained clear in his demand that the Japanese first withdraw from China which it had invaded in 1937, get out of French Indochina, which it captured in 1941, and pull out of its alliance with Germany and Italy.

Although negotiations went down to the wire, the two countries did not come to an agreement. Roosevelt, via the decrypted messages, was in the know about the secret November 25 deadline that Yamamoto had established to attack the United States if its demands were not met.

Soon thereafter, Yamamoto gave the word and 360 Japa-nese warplanes, many on kamikaze missions, were launched from six aircraft carriers escorted by battleships, cruisers, and destroyers. It was a tropical, somewhat balmy Sunday morn-ing just before 8:00 AM when the first Zero was seen above by somewhat unbelieving eyes in Pearl Harbor. Many military personnel were sleeping in; none were expecting the attack. Although Roosevelt knew of the threat; none of the Pacific military had been put on Delta Alert.

The roaring engine of a single lead aircraft was soon fol-lowed by the thunder of 200 others, and the planes ripped Paradise apart—bombing and torpedoing the ships in the clear-blue waters below. Nearly 200 U.S. planes were destroyed on the ground and another 150 were damaged, leaving the defenders with only 43 operational aircraft. Even before the fires were put out and the billowing smoke began to clear, the somewhat futile rescue efforts to free the Ameri-cans sealed in capsized and sunken warships began. U.S. casu-alties totaled more than 3,400; the Japanese losses were fewer than 100 men, many of those giving their own lives as kamikazes—quite a coveted honor in Japanese culture at that time.

Yeah, America was pretty pissed off, and boy did the surprise attack serve to unify a country that was having its own economic problems. So why do I even bring this up? Because it was the war that birthed the Cold War, that in turn created the Internet. It's also because I need to dispel a myth. I've been told by many founders of the Internet, *Don't go there, it's a myth that the Internet was born from the concept that we needed a communications system that would withstand a nuclear holocaust.*

I start this story at Pearl Harbor because of the eerie similarities that make 9/11/2001 and 12/7/1941 seem like they're in parallel universes. In both cases another entity declared war against the United States; both were sneak attacks; and both were carried out by pilots willing to sacrifice their lives. In both instances there was some kind of connection to encrypted messages (in our current case it was only that encryption technology exists and was suspected, not that it was used). In both cases the American people came together to fight a common enemy. And, unfortunately, in both cases some of that zealous fervor was turned against American citizens and people who just happened to *look* like the enemy. Again, in both cases this thing now called the Internet became involved.

I contend that just as technology was funded and blossomed in the United States after the treaties were signed by all parties, so it shall be again. Okay, so maybe there won't be any treaty signed this time around, but there will be an end, at least for a period of time. And we will see this recession go away just as quickly as the Great Depression did after the United States entered WWII. I'm sure that the aerospace industry will be the first to experience the upswing from government purchases; actually, I've already seen stock go up at what are commonly called *war companies.*

Today I heard a report that someone in government is trying to pass legislation that will put electronic palm scanners into every airport in the United States, and possibly retinal scanners, and I saw another story about a company that is developing *black box* technology that will download a live streaming media of airline cockpit conversations via wireless technology to assure that a pilot's last words will always be heard no matter the circumstances. This is a very difficult time for the bad guys; we're pissed, we have motivation, and we have the technology. The technology will grow due to our need for stricter security, but it has also tempted many key government figures with the idea that our technology needs to be overseen, restrained, and boundaries drawn.

So picture, if you will, for the sake of my scenario, a much younger United States, one that before the war was barely making it through a depression. Then, unified as one, waving flags in the streets. Our soldiers are greeted, much worse for wear, with ticker tape parades; something our next generation of soldiers would not know.

Now picture a more sophisticated United States, one that is so technologically savvy that perhaps it's grown arrogant, fat, and lazy with the ability to rely on technology not aided by the human mind; a society lulled into complacency with automation. Every night her people come home from work to eat prepackaged, precooked, supposedly well-balanced meals directly from a box straight into microwaves to be heated and consumed. Four remotes per entertainment center as content of every kind is available and output at gluttonous rates. Our stomachs and minds are fed and satiated. Our kids play with some of the most amazing 3-D technology that exists: electronic video games where they see endless acts of violence in an evening's worth of entertainment. Game over until our next morning's commute.

A country where radar is so sophisticated it can detect and identify planes deviating ever so slightly from their set flight pattern—but one missing the vital policies and wherewithal to do anything about it until it's too late. Four planes were hijacked that September day, and probably others targeted for takeover but detoured because of the immediate orders for grounding of planes in the air.

So there we were with all of this technology, including the ability to have stricter policies in place to identify people who are a threat to national security, a way to identify objects such as box cutters through archaic X-ray machines; but really, no thought of putting all these technologies to use with the intelligent human aspect needed to temper technology and identify a bad situation. So many countries I have visited or lived in, including the United Kingdom and Germany, have stricter policies in place because they have so often been the victims of terrorism.

We're learning, we'll survive as a whole, and we'll thrive despite our lazy tendency to rely on automated technology manned by the complacent and governed by the clueless. We'll glean, we'll modify, we'll evolve. We won't be an easy target *next* time. I wonder if someone, somewhere said those same words after December 7, 1941?

■ DIGGING IN

Getting back to the past . . . Dr. Vannevar Bush, no relation to our current man at the helm, is where this story of Internet innovation really begins. Born in the late 1800s in Massachusetts, he would later teach at Tufts University until 1917. He developed the first submarine-detection research for the Navy, and before the age of 30 he became a faculty member at the Massachusetts Institute of Technology. He was one of the MIT research team members who built an automated network analyzer, a computer used to solve mathematical differential equations. It was no surprise to his colleagues when he was involved in building the first analog computers in the 1930s.

President Roosevelt saw Bush's genius and rewarded it by appointing him chairman of the National Defense Research Committee in 1940, to help win the war that America was about to engage in. In 1941, Bush was appointed director of the newly created Office of Scientific Research and Development, established to coordinate weapons development research, where he led nearly 6,000 leading scientists in the application of science to warfare; Bush oversaw Los Alamos and the Manhattan Project.

> "*This has not been a scientist's war; it has been a war in which all have had a part. The scientists, burying their old professional competition in the demand of a common cause, have shared greatly and learned much. It has been exhilarating to work in effective partnership. Now, for many, this appears to be approaching an end. What are the scientists to do next?*"
>
> —Vannevar Bush, in "As We May Think," published in the *Atlantic Monthly* in 1945

With World War II won, Bush served as chairman of the Joint Research and Development Board. Coming from academia, he knew the power of university research and brought together the U.S. military and universities via a commitment of research funding not previously seen in any administration. His unbridled enthusiasm for creating a techno-future would provide universities and think tanks with generous contributions to their coffers that would cover the costs of labs and hardware where the best and the brightest would conduct serious research without scrambling for funding. The only thing Bush asked in return? That the military would benefit from the research brought about by the funding. Bush, a true techno-Jeffersonian type, would become cofounder of Raytheon, one of the US's most prolific defense contractors, and then settle into a position as president of the Carnegie Institute of Washington research organization.

Bush's most remembered influence on the development of the Internet comes from his visionary description of *memex* referred to in "As We May Think," published in the *Atlantic Monthly* in 1945. This was where our visionary, Vannevar Bush, would reach across the world and touch fertile minds willing and ready to create the future by the sheer power of his words and clear thought when he wrote the first description of the potential uses for IT (Information Technology), that many technologists credit to inspiring the creation of the Internet.

Memex was the visionary's view of technology not yet delved into by the technologists of that era. With his visionary pennings, he spurred J.C.R. Licklider and Douglas Engelbart into action:

> Consider a future device for individual use, which is a sort of mechanized private file and library. It needs a name, and to coin one at random, "memex" will do. A "memex" is a device in which an individual stores all his books, records, and communications, and which is mechanized so that it may be consulted with exceeding speed and flexibility. It is an enlarged intimate supplement to his memory.

It consists of a desk, and while it can presumably be operated from a distance, it is primarily the piece of furniture at which he works. On the top are slanting translucent screens, on which material can be projected for convenient reading. There is a keyboard, and sets of buttons and levers. Otherwise it looks like an ordinary desk.

In one end is the stored material. The matter of bulk is well taken care of by improved microfilm. Only a small part of the interior of the "memex" is devoted to storage, the rest to mechanism. Yet if the user inserted 5000 pages of material a day it would take him hundreds of years to fill the repository, so he can be profligate and enter material freely.

—Vannevar Bush, in "As We May Think," published in the *Atlantic Monthly* in 1945

Vannevar's description goes on to tell of the ease of use which vast libraries of knowledge are stored and accessed. While Douglas Engelbart was serving in the U.S. military in the Philippines, he read the inspirational words of Bush that would hit home. Engelbart, who now lives in Silicon Valley, is far less well known than the next generation of technologists who would build on his technologies—the computer mouse, windows-style personal computing, hyperlinking, e-mail, and video conferencing, just to name a few.

Engelbart, raised during the Great Depression, had been attending a university to study engineering and then joined the Navy, where he received further technical training.

"I grew up during the Depression, so I mostly worried about keeping a steady job," says Engelbart of his career path. "I had more opportunities when the war came along; I had been working as a welder in a shipyard and also attending college for two years. Then I was drafted and ended up being trained by the Navy as an electronics technician. I spent a year in the Philippines, and I remember being on this island called Leyte at a receivership—that's what the Navy called any place they brought new people into before they were assigned. There were these houses up on stilts on this island that was pure jungle; we just mostly wandered around and did some kind of muster call twice a day and stood in line for chow.

"I looked up one day and saw this hut and it had a sign: Red Cross Library. I climbed up the ladder and it was this clean little room that had about 300 books, magazines, and some chairs; I was pretty much alone up there because most of the sailors and marines who were there didn't read much. But I found a magazine that had an article written by Vannevar Bush; it referred to all kinds of things that captured my imagination, including frames of microfiche and how you could go frame-by-frame and have some code on the top that would automatically refer you to something else. It sounded exciting as hell. So with my two years of pre-engineering school and a year of technical training around all of the oscilloscopes and radar—I could see that all of this electronic stuff was making it happen. You could really see where all of this was going."

Could it be that Bush's concept of the Internet and the vision of what it could become was just as important as Bush handing over the blueprints for this new technology? Probably even more so, because it was a vision that could only be honed with time and the experience of seeing where our society was going.

The end of the war was difficult for some, especially those who were deciding what to do with their lives after returning to a society that had evolved without their presence. For others it was the promise of a new future, a world on the threshold of creating new technologies that would make the United States a strong leader with a unified people and a limitless future.

When Engelbart returned he became an engineer and had a clear mission, one that took only a little prodding on his way to work one clear California morning.

"In 1950, I got engaged," says Engelbart of the promising future that lay ahead. "That next Monday I was driving to work and thinking about my job—I was going to be married and I was going to live happily ever after; that seemed taken care of. Suddenly, I got in to work and as I'm going down this long hallway at what is now NASA, in my job as an electrical engineer, I start to wonder about my professional goals.

"So when I got back to work that first day, I thought about what I was going to do and I proposed to myself—*Why don't I move into a career that benefits mankind?* Perhaps it was a little naïve for a country boy to ask this of himself, but I stuck with it. Month after month I would go into libraries and see the latest on what was being done and I wondered . . . *Should I become a biologist, a scientist, perhaps a teacher?*"

Engelbart began to think again about that article he had read in the Red Cross library kampong in a thick jungle so very far away from home. He hadn't forgotten about that article; he thought of it often as he wondered about where the world was going. That path led him to the Stanford Research Institute (SRI), where he would lend his vision to the future Internet.

Meanwhile, on the other side of the country, young Leonard "Len" Kleinrock had been having similar daydreams about the future. At the age of six he had been inspired by an ad in a *Superman* comic book, from which he ordered the plans to build a crystal radio. Kleinrock acquired all the parts needed to build it, including an earpiece he swiped from a public phone. It would be interesting to know what phone company had "donated" that piece of equipment and to see if Kleinrock's future work had any entanglements with that company. It was from his family's Manhattan apartment, where he spent his childhood hours flipping through futuristic pulp comic books with stories of superheroes armed with cool technology defeating the bad guys, that he amazed himself by getting that crystal radio to work. Music finally did come through the earpiece—no batteries or power required—and all at the hands of a six-year-old with great curiosity and a focused goal. Yes, Kleinrock's destiny was solidified that very day.

Time moved on for Kleinrock, and not being in a position to pay for higher education or having the leisure of not working full-time to earn a paycheck, he attended the tuition-free City College of New York. Ambitious from the start, he went to night school, worked hard, and received a full graduate fellowship from MIT in the Electrical Engineering Department.

At MIT Kleinrock found himself surrounded by peers conducting their Ph.D. research in information theory. Always one to forge his own path, Kleinrock chose instead to venture into the uncharted area of data networks. In 1961 he published the first paper on the subject of packet switching theory: "Information Flow in Large Communication Nets," in the *RLE Quarterly Progress Report*. This work would pave the way for Lawrence "Larry" Roberts to prove that packets could be used for the purpose of networking computers.

Kleinrock completed his research in 1962, and his work was published in 1964 by McGraw-Hill as an MIT book titled *Communication Nets*. His research created the basic principles of packet switching, and it laid the foundation for what we now know as the Internet.

OTHER MINDS AT WORK

In 1962, while Kleinrock was attending school and shaping his idea of the future, and Engelbart was trying to pinpoint which technology would best benefit man's interest, Jack Ruina, director of *ARPA,* appointed Joseph Carl Robnett "Lick"

Licklider as the director of the newly government-established Information Processing Techniques Office (IPTO).

The goal of that department? To carry on the research of SAGE, and specifically develop one of the first wide area computer networks for its U.S. radar warning system, and build a robust electronic network to interconnect the key military sites, the Pentagon being one of them.

In 1963, Licklider funded a research project called MAC, headed by Robert Fano at MIT. The project developed the potential for establishing communities of users on time-sharing computers, and monitored the interactions between its community by measuring communication, and found that the project nurtured the establishment of real human relationships based on long distance electronic interactions. This study had a long-lasting effect on the research community and underscored the benefits of wide area networks.

Licklider's future vision (I love the fact that he was so visionary he even addressed his memos to his colleagues as *Members and Affiliates of the Intergalactic Computer Network*) would greatly influence the creation of a DARPA-sponsored distributed network called ARPANET, that would seven years later become the Internet.

Licklider, like many who would follow his work, had a keen interest in the brain and in finding out how and why it worked. Before joining DARPA he was an experimental psychologist and professor at MIT with a focused interest in psychoacoustics. While at MIT Licklider worked on several projects that would nurture curiosity about how the sciences of human factors and computers of the future would converge.

While doing his research Licklider found that gathering data on psychoacoustics was incredibly cumbersome, and he went one step further from that conclusion to measuring *exactly* how cumbersome it really was. He clocked his own time to determine how much was being spent in gathering, storing, and doing his comparisons, in contrast to the actual time it took him to draw conclusions. His conclusion was that 85 percent of his time was spent gathering and analyzing, and that 15 percent was spent coming to a conclusion. This mental exercise had a way of reminding him every time he went to do research how there must be a better way; a computer technology that could be created to give him back the time he was losing by physically acquiring his research.

Before joining ARPA, Licklider had been looking at a way to solve problems at Bolt, Beranek & Newman (BBN) to carry through his psychoacoustics work, and had been given the thumbs-up on purchasing a PDP-1 from DEC—one of the first minicomputers that was equal in computing power to a mainframe. Even though BBN founder Leo Beranek wasn't quite sure how they would use the $25,000 minicomputer, he agreed to the exorbitant purchase because he had a hunch that it might turn out to be an important machine to the future direction of BBN.

The word *minicomputer* is used quite liberally in this context; although the PDP-1 was smaller than a mainframe, it still took up the space of two large stacked desks. What was great about this computer was that Licklider could be interactive with it; he could program the computer directly, instead of going through the ordeal of submitting punched cards and waiting for the data, and he could review the results via a live-time screen display. He saw where this industry was going.

Before he came to IPTO in 1962, Licklider wrote another paper that (like Vannevar's *Atlantic Monthly* article) envisioned the computer/man relationship and how it would be an important part of the future. His 1960 paper titled "Man-Computer Symbiosis" described an assistant within your computer (think of an efficient secretary rather than

Microsoft's annoying, animated paperclip assistant), and pre-dicted simulation modeling, graphical displays, and other tasks and features of today's computers.

Many people in companies and learning institutions were looking into projects that would further network technology. One of them was Paul Baran. It's fairly clear that the purpose of building a computer network that would survive a nuclear holocaust came from Baran, who wrote the first paper on secure packetized voice, titled "On Distributed Communications Networks, IEEE Transactions on Systems." He describes a network created by the military to withstand a nuclear war. Even though Baran's work for RAND was based on this idea, the ARPANET had no relation to his work. So, it's widely believed that this is the paper that somehow bled into the cultural media and the general idea that the Internet was built to withstand a nuclear holocaust.

In 1964 Licklider left the IPTO and went to work for IBM. In 1968 he went back to MIT to lead Project MAC, and in 1973 he returned once again to lead the IPTO for two more years and fittingly enough completed the life cycle of that project. He was one of the founding members of Infocom.

Following Licklider's 1964 departure Ivan Sutherland became the second director of IPTO/ARPA. Sutherland, like many people involved at ARPA, had a great interest in developing the computer graphics industry and created a sketch pad program for storing computer displays in memory where they could be modified. His program enabled the field of computer graphics that built the framework for the graphical displays available today.

Meanwhile at MIT, Lawrence Roberts had been working in the background. It was during a 1964 meeting between Licklider and Roberts that Licklider encouraged Roberts to undertake the creation of the Internet. Roberts claims that this meeting was the critical turning point, where Licklider's Internet concept was transferred to him to implement. In 1965, ARPA contracted its first network experiment, and Ivan Sutherland awarded it to Roberts at MIT's Lincoln Labs.

Sutherland saw the work of Robert Taylor, who was powerfully influenced by Licklider, was very interested in the man/computer relationship, and, like Licklider, was a researcher in psychoacoustics. In 1966, when Sutherland left and Roberts refused the job, Taylor was promoted to directorship of IPTO/ARPA and began the initial work of the ARPANET, but continued to try to lure Roberts onboard.

Roberts was very happy at Lincoln and was dead set against taking over the directorship of ARPA. In order to persuade him, Taylor leveraged the funding that ARPA provided to Roberts' lab at MIT.

"I was kind of blackmailed to go to ARPA," says Roberts with a smile as he thinks back on it. "Ivan was the one who brought it up initially; he had funded my experiments at Lincoln Labs. Ivan asked me to go to ARPA and I said, *No.* Apparently all of the principals at ARPA decided I should be the next person in line; Ivan asked me several times. So Ivan finally left the job to Bob Taylor. The community agreed that Bob Taylor should be in charge for a while, but that they should bring me on as fast as possible.

"Well, Bob called to try and get me to come on board, and I again said *No.* So what he did was go to his boss, Charlie Hertzfeld, and ask, *How much money do you give to Lincoln?* And he answered, *Well, we give them 51 percent of their money.* So Taylor asked, *Can't you do something to get Roberts here?* So, he called up the director of Lincoln and said, *Do something.* The director of Lincoln called me and said *I think it's in your best interest that you go to ARPA, and we'll pay your way and take care of everything—and it'll be good for your career.* I don't regret that I took the job.

"At that point I realized that I was so far ahead in research [Lawrence had been working in virtual reality]—so far beyond where graphics really were that I couldn't get commerciality out of it. We had head-mounted displays and 3-D projections; I did all that in my thesis. But it was way beyond what people were doing. It was going to be 30 years before anyone could use it. So, what I really believed was that it would be good to go out and do something that was closer to commercial reality. So I went to ARPA—and I have Bob to credit for all of that because he got me interested."

In 1966, Roberts joined the IPTO as chief scientist. Roberts began noticing some redundancy in resources to the ARPA-funded projects when he came on board.

> "*I* think about it [the pervasiveness of the Internet] most often when I'm driving down the freeway and see WWW. on a billboard—and no telephone number. I think, 'My god, the only way we're communicating now is through these web addresses.'"
>
> —Lawrence Roberts,
> cofather of the Internet

"There were lots of different computers with different databases and different systems that were not transferable," says Roberts. "For instance, if there was data on another computer, you couldn't just get it on all computers, and personally you couldn't store it all. Some of the information was coded in a way where it wasn't compatible and you couldn't move it. And the software at that time was mostly unique to a specific research site because they had developed it. So we had many, many incompatible computers, not at all like it is today, because Microsoft has changed that. We didn't even have word processing compatibility. The ability to get at other people's documents was difficult, and the best way to do that was across the Network. If you put in a standard ASCII communication mechanism someone could send the data and someone else could look at it. I realized that this technology was certainly better than circuit switching."

1967

Wes Clark suggests that instead of using the mainframe computers on the Network, minicomputers be used for Network packet switches. This puts the minds of people on the proposed Network to rest because they don't want any downtime on their mainframes.

On June 3, 1968, Roberts gave a report titled "Resource Sharing Computer Networks," describing the plan to build the ARPANET. A little more than two weeks later, Taylor signed the approval for the project. Taylor had the foresight and the authorization power to begin the wheels turning on the ARPANET project. Without this approval, things might not have gone quite the way they did. Although many individuals have been attributed to fathering the Internet, this first act of giving power (and cash) to the ARPANET project should by no means be underestimated.

In 1968 a call for proposals was raised by Roberts for the design of the ARPANET. He had done much of the overall network design, network economic analysis, line optimization, and the selection of computer sites to be connected. Later that year Roberts evaluated the potential paths, and with the ARPANET staff and a group of its contractors, they made a game plan. That same year, the Network Measurement Center at UCLA, led by Kleinrock, was given the contract to undertake ARPANET measurement. At that same time, the ARPANET packet switch contract was awarded to Frank Heart's group at BBN to create the ARPANET Interface Message Processors (IMPs), and the BBN group proposed using Honeywell 516 minicomputers for the IMPs. The BBN group had such icons as Bob Kahn, Severo Ornstein, Dave Walden, and many other key individuals on board.

1971

*R*ay Tomlinson, a principal scientist at BBN, popular for his work on early mail and file transfer programs, made a unilateral decision that sticks with us even to this day—many, many times a day. He meshed the file transfer protocols of one program with the send/receive abilities of two other electronic e-mail programs. To address e-mail Tomlinson had to specify both the machine and the particular user for the netizen for whom it was intended. He needed a single keystroke character that would separate the two in the address, but not be found in either the host name or a person's e-mail address. The @ sign fit the job beautifully.

Then, three years after Taylor had taken the baton as director, and well after ARPANET was on its way, he passed directorship of the IPTO on to Roberts. Taylor left to create the computer science lab at Xerox's Palo Alto Research Center (Xerox PARC), and in 1983 he founded DEC's Research Center in Silicon Valley.

The year 1969 was a very busy one for the burgeoning network. A paper written by Steve Crocker covering host-to-host protocol, the first output of the Network Working Group (NWG) was released and the much-awaited first node of ARPANET was installed at UCLA's Network Measurement Center, where under Kleinrock's direction it connected the IMP to their Sigma 7 computer. The second node of ARPANET was installed at SRI, where Engelbart's group connected it to its SDS 940 computer. In September 1969, the first ARPANET messages were sent.

A WHIRLWIND OF ARPANET ACTIVITY MOVES US FORWARD

Many people pushed the Internet technology further to develop it into the commercial Nirvana that it has become. An event took place in 1971 that directly affected the growth of the Internet: the first Terminal Interface Processor (TIP) in ARPANET allowed terminals to dial directly into the network. The next year Roberts created the first e-mail management program allowing responding, forwarding, and filing.

Also in 1972, FTP protocol specification (RFC 354) was released by Jon Postel and Abhay Bhushan. Another accomplishment during that eventful year was the first public demonstration of ARPANET, led by Kahn, a major milestone to showing the world what we could expect from the distributed network. Bob Kahn was hired by Roberts into

ARPANET. Xerox PARC was now moving into the picture, as Bob Metcalf's Ethernet design successfully expanded the ALOHA packet radio concepts and applied them to cable.

In 1973 Roberts left ARPA for commercial interests. That next year, BBN released a revised ARPANET routing after a complete rewrite by John McQuillan; this resolved many issues in the software and brought great improvements forward in the network's routing.

Bob Kahn and Vinton Cerf wrote a paper on Internet protocol, TCP, *A Protocol for Packet Network Interconnection;* and Kahn and Cerf began design in 1973. Two years later, ARPANET was transferred to the Defense Communications Agency. And that next year Vint Cerf joined ARPANET as the manager of the packet radio, packet satellite, and packet research programs, where he stayed until 1982. The next year, in 1977, the first TCP was in operation over ARPANET, Packet Radio Net, and SATNET (satellite network). During that year, Steve Crocker and John Vittal release e-mail specification (RFC 733).

The world was moving quickly in 1978, as Vint Cerf, Jon Postel, and Danny Cohen split TCP into TCP and IP, where TCP was the end-to-end process and IP was the network routing process.

The '80s mark the accomplishment of NSF organizing CSNET and increasing it to 70 sites by 1983 and integrating most computer science sites by 1986. The late Internet pioneer Jon Postel, along with Paul Mockapetris and Craig Partridge, developed the Domain Name System (DNS) to support the e-mail addressing space by creating .com, .edu, .int, .gov, .mil, .net, and .org. About that same time the NSF set up its NSFNET backbone to connect five supercomputing sites and network other Internet sites at 56kb; that next year NSF upgraded NSFNET to T1 speed.

ARPANET turned 20 years old in 1989—and then was

shut down. During the following months, node after node was taken off the Net, and the first commercial Internet lines were opened through MCI. By the mid-1990s ARPANET was only a part of a great legacy brought forward and spearheaded by a great many visionaries. In 1991 the floodgate to commercial use of the Internet was opened.

HERE, LOOKING BACK

Many of the founders of the Internet now look back with hindsight and also with the foresight they had when the pieces were beginning to fit together. We'll never know what Vannevar Bush would say about the Internet that embraces his original vision of vast amounts of knowledge available at a click, but I do have an inkling that he would be taking in its *adult* endeavors, one of the most successful segments of the Internet market, with curiosity and humor, chuckling about the nature of man and his computer.

HUMAN(ITY) AND THE COMPUTER

"I think that over the last two decades the Internet has been very important for humanity," says Lawrence Roberts. "Basically the Internet has made it very difficult for dictators and communism, because people get their information from all over the world and they didn't have to depend on restricted news sources. The Internet has changed the world—and I think it's what broke up the communist block, in large part because they couldn't control the news anymore. That's not true in every dictatorship; sometimes people don't have enough good Internet access to receive news, and even China is still trying to control the news. I think it will eventually topple that system because people are getting through and there's too much data—they can't monitor and control everything. I don't think they can live through it and control the news forever. Eventually their system will change—they're struggling against it, as you'd expect, but they can't win.

"As I was creating the Net, I very quickly saw that it could be helpful. What I was trying to do was establish a worldwide ability for people to get at information quickly. I thought that would change the rate of knowledge growth around the world. This was the next evolutionary stage where we could get information quickly and knowledge growth would grow very rapidly. Originally, I wasn't thinking as much about governments and democracy and freedom as I was later on. By the early part of the network operation, I saw the Net would affect that too, and that it would become a serious benefit. If you look at my first submission to Congress, I didn't say it [ARPANET] was going to kill communism, but I found that it would be valuable for the government, humanity, and the military. Later on I started realizing that was going to be one of the big impacts, and that it would in fact change the abilities of people everywhere."

"I went to Congress with the story about how it was going to change the way we communicate and our information transfer. There was nothing in it about military activity. Basically the military would benefit as much as anybody else. It was clear to Congress that if this worked it would work for the military as well as everyone else."

—Lawrence Roberts,
cofather of the Internet

"The first indication of this change was within months of it starting," recalls Roberts. "It was about '71 when we got the Network really working and got Hawaii online; people in Hawaii had very restricted news, and the people in Iowa were the same way. People we were involved with, educated people, were interested in what the gold market was doing, so they would watch over their systems, and for a lot of people that was their primary news source. Now, of course, that's normal, but back then some people didn't have good access to national news and started using the Network to find out what was going on in the world. So people started putting newsfeeds right on the Internet from the start. And people from all over found that tremendously valuable because they wanted to find out what was going on and search for what they were interested in instead of trying to read the local newspaper."

OLD CHALLENGES LINGER TODAY

With some of ARPANET's biggest challenges met and obstacles removed, the future was wide open and people began thinking beyond simply making it work.

"ARPANET had a real commercial advantage over circuit switching as far as moving data," says Lawrence Roberts of the early Net. "I also showed that voice was already economic on packet switching, but it wasn't even possible that it was going to move that fast because there wasn't a big enough benefit to move over to that method. People were going to stick with what they were doing for a period of time [the phone], but I predicted it would take around 20 years."

The greatest minds in the world began to ponder, research, and create what the future of this man and computer network would look like.

"When we started designing the Network the concept was

mainly to have high reliability," says Roberts. "The phone network was not sufficient or capable [for our purpose] for a number of reasons. One is that it didn't handle burst traffic, and second, it was too unreliable and slow to make quick connections. For data you need a very quick connection and you need to establish it instantly and be online all of the time. And you have to be able to burst at very high speeds and not pay for it all the rest of the time, so it's very different from the phone network. Getting that technology into place was the first thing for us and reliability was part of that process.

"The Network was a redundant, distributed system; it didn't have anything to do with disasters—that was Paul Baran's concept," stresses Roberts. "I was really worried about the reliability and stability of the Network so that it would do the job—the best design was a distributed design in general and it was reliable and economical. So I always knew it was going to be reliable; and as it grew it would become even more reliable because it would have thousands of nodes and you'd have to kill hundreds of them before it had any significant impact whatsoever. A few of them were actually hit in the World Trade Center; and it was a minor impact to the Network, so minor that the network didn't notice it at all. There were overloaded servers where you couldn't get anything off of CNN because they didn't have enough capacity and that was an individual server problem, not the Network's.

"The Network worked perfectly, in fact all the people I know were getting all of their information that way—especially those in Washington and New York where the phone networks had been affected," says Roberts, analyzing what occurred in the communications networks after 9/11. "The reason was because the phone network has a secondary problem—that we made sure we didn't design into IP networks—the problem is that as the load increases, the performance of the switch declines so that you have a curve that occurs. As load rises, the total capacity of the switch goes up and up and up, and then there's a point where the demand goes back down again. But if the demand becomes too high the switch can't hardly do anything. That's what happens in earthquakes and disasters with the phone network. The software and switching element is basically not capable of handling the call requests, so it can't deny them effectively and it goes into a mode and tells everyone to go away. It is a disaster all in itself because nobody is getting anything done. Whereas, with an IP network, everybody works slower, but it continues to get better and better until you peak out at the maximum capacity of the network and you're still operating and everybody is getting something done.

"In fact, during that disaster [9/11], nobody had any problem with the Network, it worked perfectly," says Roberts of the network that eventually evolved from ARPANET. "And that's exactly proving to people that the Net is a lot more reliable in that kind of environment. But the whole goal of the project was reliability in everyday operation; you don't want the failure of a piece of equipment to affect your net in any way. IP networks have been built with lots of redundancy anyway. I didn't think there was any likelihood of that being a problem and it wasn't. That's not saying that we have to get rid of the phone network, it's worked pretty well. Only in a case of disasters is the phone system a problem; and that's a big problem for the military, so they have to have their own systems. One issue comes up when you're designing a switch, and that issue is if you allow the control traffic, the stuff that is setting up the paths and the calls, to be the same priority as the data, then you can get into the same problem, and that's when you get into an overload and you can't get the control through. Then it gets slowed down until you can't make anything happen, so the network loses connectivity, because it's not keeping in touch with itself fast enough. If you give that a higher priority and dedicate three percent of your bandwidth to control, it works perfectly and there's never a failure and that's essentially what we've done," says a much wiser Roberts, who is now founder and chairman of Caspian Networks, a Silicon Valley Internet infrastructure company developing a new generation of equipment for the networks upon which today's Internet runs.

THE ORIGINAL VISION

Vannevar Bush and J.C.R. Licklider had a very futuristic world in mind when they went about writing their papers on how the future would shape up; envisioning people finally gaining control over the technology that would empower them. Super-intelligence powered by 24/7 availability to vast libraries of knowledge where one could click from window to window to obtain a deeper understanding of the world around him or her.

"When I sat down with Licklider in '64 he convinced me this [the Network] was important—that language allowed people to communicate, and that the printing press allowed them to communicate much faster," says Roberts about that fated day he had the discussion. "And my original thought was that we need to get to the third generation of information transfer where people can have all the information in the world. What we thought was that anyone in the world could get to a computer anywhere in the world and get any information. At that point we had all mainframes, so we weren't thinking so much in terms of personal computers; we were thinking about people at their terminals who were going to reach out to other people on the Network.

"When I first thought about it I was at MIT and I was thinking, *How do we change the state of the world?*" says Roberts about what was on the minds of a lot of people who would end up working together to build the ARPANET. That question hung in the collective consciousness of a generation of technologists who would reach out to find others with like minds.

"The second thought I had in answering that question was once you do this, the dictatorships, communism, and such couldn't exist with this massive flow of information in the world, not just what's under their control. My feeling was that it was very important for the speed of innovation, the speed of research, the speed of science, and commerce. There was no thought in my mind or anyone else's mind that e-commerce would succeed [as an industry]. E-commerce had failed on every front it had tried—people just didn't seem to want to buy from their TV set. If we had thought seriously about it we would have realized that there were things people could buy electronically with less work than they could go to the store to purchase. If it's something in the store that's really common it might not be attractive to buy online, but if it's something hard to find, and Amazon proved that pretty effectively, then it could be of major benefit.

"That was the first thing we missed," admits Roberts of the overlooked benefit. "The second thing we missed for years was e-mail and personal communication. Although very early on I did the e-mail handler, send mail and read mail, which gave me the basic file transfer, and then I said, *I can't use this,* because it is pouring out like teletype. So I built an e-mail library where I could save them and read them by title only, and choose to save them, read them, and respond to them, and it looked like it looks today; I can hardly tell the difference. That was in '71. After we built the Network and got the thing going, we quickly realized that all the communications benefits were major, and we'd be able to do voice and video later on and be able to virtually take anything on."

While Roberts was talking with Licklider back in 1964, Douglas Engelbart had already been inspired by Vannevar Bush's words that he read two decades earlier in the unlikely setting of a foreign jungle.

"The real thing that made the Net more dynamic was the emergence of the World Wide Web. What seemed to get that going was a free browser. If it had been just somebody who was saying, 'I have this product to sell,' then people may not have tried it. Tim Berners-Lee made it easy for everyone to try."

—Douglas Engelbart,
founder of the Bootstrap Institute

Engelbart found a home at the Stanford Research Institute (SRI) in Silicon Valley, where he settled into a research position, earning more than a dozen patents in two years while working on magnetic computer components, fundamental digital-device phenomena, and miniaturization scaling potential. In 1959 he'd been given the thumbs-up to pursue his own research. In the back of his mind he still contemplated Bush's words. He spent the next two years formulating a theoretical framework for a new discipline based on his thoughts that *complexity and urgency are increasing exponentially, and that the product of the two will soon challenge our organizations and institutions to change in quantum leaps rather than incremental steps.*

In 1963 Engelbart finally received the backing to start his own research lab at SRI, which he later dubbed the Augmentation Research Center. He began by developing the kind of technology he believed would be required to augment our human intellect.

During the 1960s and 1970s, his team produced a visionary project in hypermedia-groupware system called NLS (for oNLine System). In the spring of 1967, it was arranged that all the ARPA-sponsored computer research labs, including Engelbart's, would be networked to promote resource sharing. Engelbart saw ARPANET as a way to transfer NLS provisions into a wide-area distributed collaboration.

"Before ARPA came along, I was talking to my crew at SRI and saying that we just had to find a community of users for the project we were working on, and just how do we spread that community out? We knew it was going to be a challenge. Then there was this meeting in the spring of '67 at the University of Michigan. Larry Roberts and Bob Taylor were saying how they [ARPA] had this special project they wanted to talk to the group about. It was about computer networking and how they really felt that we ought to tie all the computers together. The way the whole thing was disclosed was that we could share computational resources and data.

"So the general idea was that we had to get it up and working and try it out. Well, we tried to get the Defense Department's computer centers to buy into it and they were all very skittish about doing something that would interfere with their productivity.

"So these prima donnas were talking about it—and one guy says to the other, *What have you got in your computer that I want?* The other guy says, *Don't you get my reports?* Knowing full well that the other guy doesn't. He answers, *Do you send them to me?* Knowing that the other guy probably has no idea who is on his list to receive his reports. So, they know they couldn't get anywhere shooting at each other, so they turn to Roberts and Taylor and say, *You guys are going to have to keep a database up that says who has what kinds of processes and who has what kinds of data, and how to access and exchange the information.*

"Apparently Roberts and Taylor had not thought about that, because they almost shriveled—they both had one secretary," says Engelbart, smiling as he remembers the moment. "So I said, *Hey, we are doing that kind of thing, and we could make an online information center that could hold that data and make it available to the Network.* We heard some sighs of relief, and that's when we got the commitment to be the Network Information Center [NIC]."

Because of Engelbart's quick reaction in meeting ARPA's need for a central directory, his site was the second host on the network. He saw NLS as a natural to support an online directory of resources, a project he continued to direct until 1977, when it was spun off.

Engelbart felt that the key to having the man and the future world's computer database, as Bush had described it, work flawlessly together was finally being actualized. While working on these theories, Engelbart became a pioneer in developing the following technologies: the mouse, 2-dimensional display editing, in-file object addressing, linking, hypermedia, multiple windows, cross-file editing, integrated hypermedia e-mail, hypermedia publishing, computer-aided meetings, formatting directives, and distributed client-server architecture, and the list goes on. He successfully garnered many patents, and concepts that would be leveraged into today's technologies, technology that would make today's technology icons rich.

In 1989 Engelbart founded the Bootstrap Institute <www.bootstrap.org>, feeling there was a great need to pursue researching and developing enabling technologies, best practices, and strategies to develop and deploy them. Engelbart now works with members of government, industry, and society to find solutions to the ever-growing difficulties that technology creates.

◼◼◼   HAPPENSTANCE?

This book opens with a quote from Branch Rickey, the Brooklyn Dodgers' general manager. It reads, "Luck is the residue of design." Could it be that the Internet is a creation of happenstance? A product of pure luck? A beautiful act of serendipitous chaos that brought the right people together at the right time?

"The technology hadn't been designed, per se," says Leonard Kleinrock, cofather of the Internet, professor of computer science at UCLA, chairman and advisory board member of TTIVanguard <www.TTIVanguard.com>, and chairman of Nomadix <www.Nomadix.com>. "It was very carefully thought out, but there was a lot of development, in the sense, the way software and systems are developed along the way, but it wasn't accidental. It was very purposeful, but it was new technology. *Accidental* says it was serendipitous, not planned, or strategic—and it was very strategic.

"One must never underestimate the proper attitude of ARPA for providing the funding, the flexibility, the freedom, and the testbed for the small number of experimental negatives to shake down the technology to serve the purpose they wanted; which was to share resources. They weren't intending to make a commercial powerhouse out of it. ARPANET had the time to mature in a proper environment of experimentation. The Network couldn't have started from day one because we were busy testing things, crashing things, not giving reliable service, or even intending to do so because we had to try new things all the time. The fact that ARPA made that available was a brilliant move on their part. I'm not sure they planned it to be so brilliant, but it was just the right thing at the right time.

"We had industry and government and academia all working beautifully together and a relatively loose governance on the other hand; ARPANET wasn't driven by milestones, it was driven by creativity and cooperation. It wasn't the hard-nosed sergeant in arms, it was that we all wanted to make it happen, and we did. As a result, it was a wonderful, wonderful experience."

Kleinrock, although a UCLA professor, is an MIT man at heart, and he has a theory about how some of the alchemy came about to make the ARPANET work. "I spent a number of years at MIT; it's a wellspring of new technology created by brilliant strokes of realization and newness. So it was not a new thing to Larry or me who had come out of this environment. Or to Bob Kahn, who also spent some time at MIT. MIT was really unique at the time; it was a Golden Age. Our classmates and our faculty were all coming up with these great results. I was able to prove that large systems dramatically improve performance. For a young kid coming out of graduate school to be thrown into that mix was fantastic; then you contribute, you turn people on, the creative juices start to flow, and you develop technology."

Again, in a mission to set the record straight, I posed the question of whether ARPANET was funded to create a mode of fail-proof communication in the case of a nuclear holocaust.

"There is an issue here," says Kleinrock, pondering the question. "Were there people deep in the Pentagon who were signing the checks who had that as their motivation? Maybe. We don't know. Was that the case presented to the researchers? By the researchers? Or by ARPA itself to the world? To the public? To us? No. Everyone whom I spoke with at ARPA who was involved in the funding process agrees that the idea was about resource sharing. I know what was motivating them—they were funding a bunch of principal investigators, and each time they gave somebody funding they would create a specialized resource out of it. The research resources dealt with the graphics, the databases, the machines . . . and every time the funding was given the researchers said, 'Go buy me a computer and I want that computer to have the same resources as all the other guys have—I want graphics, simulation, databases, etc.' ARPA said that it couldn't afford to give everybody everything, but if you, Mr. Researcher, were in the network and wanted to do graphics, you could log onto Utah, if you want simulation, you log onto UCLA—that was the motivation. That's the story sold to us and by us.

"We were not motivated by a network that would survive military or hostile attack," says Kleinrock of his initial involvement with ARPANET. "My design, which allowed those things [a network that would go undisturbed in an attack] to happen was predicated by very different things; that it should be scalable—and that wouldn't happen if there was centralized control. Once you have distributed control you've got redundancy, adoptability, flexibility, and all those other things that suit damage control because you don't put all of your eggs in one basket.

"If you look at the statistics of the Internet growth, it has been growing exponentially since day one, except it had to get really big before everyone else noticed it. A few events happened for it to accelerate some, like the Web."

Did Kleinrock expect the unprecedented growth of the Internet of recent years? In a press release from UCLA dated July 3, 1969, he gives glimpses of the challenge his department was then about to take on:

RELEASE: UCLA TO BE FIRST STATION IN NATIONWIDE COMPUTER NETWORK*

UCLA will become the first station in a nationwide computer network which, for the first time, will link

*UCLA Office of Public Information, "UCLA To Be First Station In Nationwide Computer Network," July 3, 1969, www.lk.cs.ucla.edu/LK/Bib/ REPORT/press.html.

together computers of different makes and using different machine languages into one time-sharing system.

Creation of the network represents a major forward step in computer technology and may serve as the forerunner of large computer networks of the future.

The ambitious project is supported by the Defense Department's Advanced Research Project Agency (ARPA), which has pioneered many advances in computer research, technology and applications during the past decade. The network project was proposed and is headed by ARPA's Dr. Lawrence G. Roberts.

The system will, in effect, pool the computer power, programs and specialized know-how of about 15 computer research centers, stretching from UCLA to M.I.T. Other California network stations (or nodes) will be located at the Rand Corp. and System Development Corp., both of Santa Monica; the Santa Barbara and Berkeley campuses of the University of California; Stanford University and the Stanford Research Institute.

The first stage of the network will go into operation this fall as a subnet joining UCLA, Stanford Research Institute, UC Santa Barbara, and the University of Utah. The entire network is expected to be operational in late 1970.

Engineering professor Leonard Kleinrock, who heads the UCLA project, describes how the network might handle a sample problem:

Programmers at Computer A have a blurred photo which they want to bring into focus. Their program transmits the photo to Computer B, which specializes in computer graphics, and instructs B's program to remove the blur and enhance the contrast. If B requires specialized computational assistance, it may call on Computer C for help.

The processed work is shuttled back and forth

until B is satisfied with the photo, and then sends it back to Computer A. The messages, ranging across the country, can flash between computers in a matter of seconds, Dr. Kleinrock says.

UCLA's part of the project will involve about 20 people, including some 15 graduate students. The group will play a key roll as the official network measurement center, analyzing computer interaction and network behavior, comparing performance against anticipated result, and keeping a continuous check on the network's effectiveness. For this job, UCLA will use a highly specialized computer, the Sigma 7, developed by Scientific Data Systems of Los Angeles.

Each computer in the network will be equipped with its own interface message processor (IMP) which will double as a sort of translator among the Babel of computer languages and as a message handler and router.

Computer networks are not an entirely new concept, notes Dr. Kleinrock. The SAGE radar defense system of the Fifties was one of the first, followed by the airlines' SABRE reservation system. At the present time, the nation's electronically switched telephone system is the world's largest computer network.

However, all three are highly specialized and single-purpose systems, in contrast to the planned ARPA system which will link a wide assortment of different computers for a wide range of unclassified research functions.

"As of now, computer networks are still in their infancy," says Dr. Kleinrock. "But as they grow up and become more sophisticated, we will probably see the spread of 'computer utilities', which, like present electric and telephone utilities, will service individual homes and offices across the country."

"What happened in the '60s," says Kleinrock, "was that it [networking] took a while to catch on because none of the researchers wanted to participate in the Network because they didn't want to put their computers on a network for others to share. They didn't want to do it until we went and told them [that] not only can they use yours, you can also use theirs.

"The original architecture of the Internet only had six bits of address. You could have at most 64, and it sort of flattened out until BBN expanded it. For two years it was very minimal growth because we didn't have a very good protocol. Until we developed the host-to-host protocol it was very difficult for you to use another machine; you'd have to learn the command language, get a logon, understand the applications, and they'd probably have a different operating system [than the computer they were trying to network with]. Until we got a transparent host-to-host protocol it was very difficult, but then it took off quickly. There was a blip when we did the first public demonstration of the ARPANET in 1972, a lot of people saw what was going on. That was not a major blip, it was a little blip, and then it just continued on growing.

"There were really three things I anticipated in the press release," says Kleinrock of what he pointed out in the press release. "I'm not counting the initial success of ARPANET where this technology proved that it would work; that was beautiful. In that press release I was basically predicting five things: that the Internet would have five properties. It would be ubiquitous, it would be always available, always on, anyone could connect in with any device, and it would be invisible like electricity. The Internet got the first three right, but it failed on the other two: It's very difficult for anyone with any device to get on—that's what I call Nomadic commuting. It's not invisible because if you call Windows an invisible, easy GUI, than I would agree, but I don't. I failed that part of the prediction. What I didn't predict was that my 93-year-old mother would be on the Internet today, and that it would penetrate so many aspects of our society; our government, our industry, our education, our entertainment.

"When did I see that? Well, in '72 when e-mail was introduced as an ad hoc add-on and it suddenly took over the network and I realized, *Ahhh . . . this is not about computers talking to each other, this is about people communicating*. That was the first insight I had—that's what was going to make this thing grow."

*"N*obody controls it, nobody can turn it off."
—Leonard Kleinrock,
    cofather of the Internet, and chairman
    of Nomadix and IITVanguard

"The second time I saw something was a few years later when newsgroups were the rage," says Kleinrock of his next epiphanous moment. "Newsgroups were created around the country by people with similar likes; be it recipes, stamps . . . everything. As a faculty member I was not engaged in any of that, and I remember one day walking into my graduate students' bullpen to ask one of them a question. And I said, *What's that?* [pointing to a screen], and he explained that he was signed onto a newsgroup and explained to me what was going on. I said, *Jesus Christ! There's an underworld of activity here. It's not visible but it's going on all over the place*. And that's what reconfirmed the idea that communities were going to form on their own and take advantage of the Internet infrastructure to grow.

"The third thing was when the Web hit and I began to see

the word *Internet* everywhere. I remember one day when I was flying, I counted all of the ads that talked about computers and/or networks in American Airline's magazine. More than half of the ads had something to do with those two things. And that number started growing very quickly. And that was the pervasiveness that I was seeing back in '72. Those were the epiphanies.

"Now, you can't turn the Internet off. The financial system would collapse for example: the transportation systems . . . automatic traffic lights, a whole bevy of things would collapse. Airplanes would not fly, when I say *the Internet,* I mean the automatic computer technologies on board an aircraft, or across the world."

REMINISCING

David J. Farber is one of the most outspoken people on the face of the Earth on the subject of technology and those sensitive areas surrounding it. He has an online newslist, *Interesting People,* where you can read commentary from the world's digerati 24/7 as it happens. He is currently the Alfred Fitler Moore Professor of Telecommunication Systems in the School of Engineering and Applied Sciences and professor of Business and Public Policy at the Wharton School. His latest claim to fame has been serving as the chief technologist at the Federal Communications Commission (FCC). But, going back to his roots, he graduated from the Stevens Institute of Technology in 1956 and began his 11-year career at Bell Laboratories, where he helped design the first electronic switching system (the ESS as well as helping to design the programming language SNOBOL). Then Farber headed west to The RAND Corporation and to Scientific Data Systems.

"While I was at Bell Laboratories in the early '60s until

about '67, I had been involved in communications and I saw the beginnings of packet switching. A bunch of us tried to convince AT&T that it should start a research project at Bell Labs on packet switching. We got rejected on the grounds that AT&T held that there was no real business for data," Farber says about the view AT&T took after being advised by some of the best and brightest in the industry. "The interesting thing here, if you talk about Xerox flubbing the future— AT&T outdid them. I then went off and ended up at the University of Irvine, where we were building what I believe was the first fully distributed operating system using a new LAN technology.

"As opposed to most people in the field, we actually built it and it actually ran. So when you read the literature in the field, you find a lot of people who talk about systems they would build if they ever built them. We actually built it and it ran. I was working in the networking area, and I got a call from a friend at UCLA, Jerry Estrin, who said he had a student up there who was interested in this new game—packet switching and real networks. They didn't have anybody up there to work with him, but he was interested in doing a Ph.D. in the area. I said, *I'll help him out.* That student was Jon Postel. That got me in, and it turns out another friend from Bell Lab days got involved in networks; that was Bob Kahn. Suddenly I found myself with a DARPA contract for some interesting stuff and an e-mail address on one of the very early networks.

"The most interesting thing was working with bright, young students at UCLA; at that point Vint Cerf and Steve Crocker were students there. I got involved in research and networking, then I left the University of California at Irvine and went to the University of Delaware, and a friend of mine was trying to start up something which would bring some network technology into the academic arena. At that point there were five universities tied into the baby ARPANET. That was the blossoming of university computer science programs, that was about when Sputnik went up. So then everybody wanted a computer science department [to be on ARPANET], and you had 400 computer science departments with two people in them. We made a proposal to the NSF to put together a network which would focus on bringing e-mail and some overall connectivity to the computer science departments; that was called CSNet. Much to everyone's astonishment the NSF funded it with some interesting caveats attached to it; one of them being that we had to break even in two years, which is not easy."

Farber and his team built the network and got it up and running, and made developments that would make it cheap for universities to connect to the very simple network. "We also went through all of the energy to come up with an agreement with Bob Kahn, who was at DARPA, for letting traffic flow to and from the experimental ARPANET. There were a bunch of big schools on that network and there was some talk about bringing computer science departments together so that the schools could communicate; so we built the first of the peering relationships. The other big thing that happened was that as we grew to maybe 50 to 60 schools we got requests from foreign countries asking if they could join in. We came up with this somewhat strange behavior of saying, *Okay you can join us if you create your own group like us,* because we only wanted to deal with one point per country—we didn't want to deal with 15 schools or 100 schools per country. So we basically sparked the development of national networks. We came up with a connection agreement which was, *You want to connect to us? You pay the bill.* As kids began graduating and having exposure to CSNet, they went off to industry and asked industry, *Can we keep our connection?* And industry said, *Connection to what?* They said, *CSNet,* and industry asked, *What's that?* So pretty soon we had IBM and a large number of companies banging on our door, asking *Can we use this?* and we said, *You can as long as it's for research and you can't use it for commercial traffic.* That was part of our agreement with the DARPA; that we wouldn't pass commercial traffic. They said, *Fine,* because they were trying to attract researchers. And we said, *It's going to cost you,* and then we sat back and thought about the largest amount we could get. So, we charged them an outrageous amount of money—the big companies paid about $50k a year—and we used it to subsidize the schools. The vast majority of the schools paid a small amount of money; industry paid a lot; and the big schools paid a lot. Everyone was happy. We knew if they were using it over and above just the research, but we closed our eyes. I chaired the NSF advisory board at that point, and it was clear that CSNet was a success, but what was happening was that other departments on the campuses kept coming to the computer science departments, asking, *Can we also use the network?* And we kept being bombarded with questions, *Is it okay to use it?* We always told them what we don't know won't hurt us.

"We went into the NSF with a proposal to expand the capability of NSnet into what was known as the National NSF Net NREN (National Research and Education Network). The proposal was accepted and we had the capability to expand the capability of the network to make it look more like the current network, so we started off down that track. But it was pretty clear that no amount of money or no management team we could bring together was going to give us the richness of the structure we needed for what was beginning to be an increasingly large network. So we came up with this brilliant idea of authorizing regional networks . . . northeast region, southeast region, California . . . which would run the network in their region for the universities. So you started getting things which rapidly evolved into ISPs—PSI Network, came out of New York's network. It was a rational thing. And part of the NREN activity was opened up to industry and made it much more of a commercial orientation; again trying to support the universities on the cheap supported by the commercial side. It just kept growing and growing and basically escaped the research control and you have basically the current network."

Farber is constantly on the speaker's circuit, and because he was able to make a viable business from his research, he is asked if he saw the trend coming.

"I'll show you an example of the industrial collaboration; about eight years ago, Bob Kahn and me observed that we were dealing with relatively small networks and yet inside the research labs there were really high-speed capabilities. But it didn't look like there was any way for that technology to get out of the research lab and into the hands of those who wanted to use it because there was no commercial driver. The whole thing was, *We can give you a lot of bandwidth but there is no market for it, so why should we give it to you?* So we started an activity called the Gigabit Test Beds. What that did was identify five test beds for operating at gigabit level. A very expensive game back then. We worked together with industry with this deal; industry will fund us on their own nickel, the NSF will fund the universities, and they'll fund themselves and give us the infrastructure. And that was a big, big win. We handled all the major corporations involved, all of the major universities, and some small ones, and we ran the first gigabit networks on the East Coast.

"Cisco came directly out of that network; as a direct result out of that effort we were looking for high-speed routers. A couple of other companies spun out of it; more important, the big carriers got a jump on when they normally would have deployed this technology. Again, it was a marvelous use of industrial/university collaboration because each one had something to gain."

So when asked again about the beginning—did Farber know a good value when he saw one? "One thing I observed out of this whole process was that none of us knew where this whole thing was going. I gave a talk at Microsoft a couple of months ago and commented that had we known where it was going at that time, we'd all be worth as much as Bill Gates. Anyone in the game from the start is worth nowhere as much as Bill Gates. People can say, *We knew it was going this way,* then you have to ask, *What happened . . . how come you're not rich?* Nobody knew it would explode like this. It took a couple of serendipities; the Web was a serendipity no one expected. The popularity of e-mail was something nobody expected. All those things that nobody could predict—it just took off.

"I knew the technology was valuable, there was no question about that; I knew it would replace things like the U.S. mail. We were swapping documents around through e-mail, and it was clear it was going to change the complexion of the way people carried on their research and their business. What we couldn't predict was the transfer over to a wildly growing popularization. We knew we would use it and that companies would use it; that wasn't an issue. But the explosion that took place with the Web was unpredictable, but of course that wouldn't have taken place if it didn't have a network to run on. So it's one of those serendipities. About four or five years ago the ACM [Association for Computing Machinery] asked me to write the predictions for its fiftieth anniversary—a projection of the next 25 years in networking and communication. I told them they were out of their mind; to do a five-year projection would maybe be accurate, I can reach for 10 with maybe some daydreaming, but this field is much too impacted by serendipity and it's very hard to predict."

CHAPTER 2

Adolescence

Once the Internet began gaining traction and with Tim Berners-Lee's contribution of the WWW. to the Net community, it began going through its awkward stage. You know, it's similar to that stage when you hit 13 as a kid. When you want to seem like you're a good student, and a good kid to your parents, but you also want to be accepted by your peers; you want to be everything to everyone. And one day you wake up and just rebel against everything to be your own person. Then you get caught up in what we know as hormones and you really go nuts. Well that's what the WWW. was to the Internet. Tim Berners-Lee couldn't have put any more excitement into the mix if he had dropped a scantily dressed Pamela Lee Anderson (no relation to Tim) into a high school boys' locker room. It was the beginning of real commercial growth in the Internet—a time to make mistakes, learn, and then move on to the next thing that would stimulate e-commerce.

E-commerce—such a strange thing when you think about it—the Web is a virtual mall that, no matter who you are, it can answer your every whim. But this chapter is not about recounting the past of CERN, et cetera, or how the Web is growing into economic elegance. It's about what all those downloaded cookies and marketing analyst companies can't quite put their finger on. It's the wild card—the human element, the synergistic synapse between man and his computer, that time and place that early developers guessed might happen on the way to man and machine becoming symbiotic. It's all about *You* and your relationship with *It*. The human factor that keeps you clicking.

One of the things apparent from the 9/11 fallout was that people needed to be with each other—even if only virtually. Even if the people you're virtually with are strangers. Thus many users, especially during times of war and uncertainty, gravitate to communities to find others of their own ilk; and never before have we had such a way of finding so many others like ourselves. Studies thus far have proven that we tend to purchase from sites we feel comfortable with, the sites we feel warm and fuzzy giving our credit card numbers to . . . Amazon, AOL, eBay. We feel we've grown up with them through their adolescent awkwardness. Part of that is brand, a great deal of it is because we feel part of their community. That's what this element means in purchasing power. What does it mean for humanity?

Right after the planes hit the World Trade Center, the Internet's use went up substantially. It was like major brain wave activity, a peak in the EEG of the collective consciousness of the Internet's users. What were we looking for?

"The day it happened people needed a lot of information about what to do and we responded," says Craig Newmark, CEO of craigslist <craigslist.org>, an online community that has managed to grab and maintain a watering hole feel. Craigslist achieved a very high profile with Newmark appearing on *Today* as one of technology's top 10 bachelors and it gained momentum with its nonprofit work. It's also famous, or should I say *infamous* for its *Missed Connections* listings, where people who see each other across smoke-filled rooms

(I guess not so much in California) or when passing someone on the street, can post oftentimes vague, provocative messages that actually end up with two people finding each other in the din of the modern-day world. A place where man and machine are connected by incentive and serendipity. You can always gauge what's going on in the humanscape of the San Francisco Bay Area by scrolling down the craigslist ads. You can feel the desperation of the people dependent mostly on their tech-supported jobs who are mentally cringing and waiting for the next shoe to drop. You can reach out and feel the tangible quality of the loneliness of people in transition. You can click on an ad and be offended by angry words that you weren't expecting. You can read poetry from the lovelorn and pining, and you can gauge the market by the job listings. Here, in this cyber world that Newmark created, you can keep your finger on the pulse of humanity.

Newmark, who started the bulletin board because his friends were having a hard time finding apartment listings, has made a policy of not charging a user's fee (the site does not accept advertising, download cookies, or sell user information; it collects money from job listings. Newmark had numerous chances to sell out to large companies that made him offers and probably would have left him one of those lucky dot-com millionaires instead of struggling in our *new, new economy,* but he did what he felt was right for the community he created. He also responded to what he felt was a need on September 11.

"Tuesday morning we had current and updated information, and that included where to give blood and relatively quickly to *not* give blood [because too many had donated]. We also put up 9/11 discussion forums in addition to the ones we already have. People had a tremendous urge to talk about what had happened, and what was going to happen."

As I scrolled through the 9/11 forum postings, some specifically from New York, I noted the urgent voice of the collected postings to reach out and be heard, even if only by strangers.

"The other thing was that for a couple of days our discussion board traffic surged, maybe to five times the normal amount. Our normal classified ad traffic went down substantially. Now a couple weeks later we're seeing that the discussion traffic has stayed at about double, but otherwise the classified ads have come back to normal. I think maybe people are heeding the fundamental lessons today which is, *Hey, get back to work, get back to your life.*

"The Monday before September 11, we had about 150,000 page views, that was pretty normal; on Tuesday we had 600,000. Now we have something around 300,000. Two things that were posted that Tuesday got to me. One was a picture of an abandoned baby stroller in a park that was nearby the WTC, and the other was a post that said *I Lost my Lori.* The message was telling people to let others who are important to them know that you love them."

So what is community and, in actuality, what does it mean to people? And can companies use community to leverage more e-commerce and build brand? Can it meet on both levels to be everything to everybody? The Pew Research Center (www.PewInternet.org) recently released a study in October 2001 about the numbers of people who were finding community via their keyboards. And although I am no stranger to the roll of communities on the Internet, I found its numbers astonishing. The Pew Internet & American Life Project, which this survey was directed by, is a research organization that studies the social impact of the Internet. The report is titled "Online Communities: Networks that nurture long-distance relationships and local ties."

"I like that we're in a post dot-com mode which I think is probably a cycle. There was a period in the '90s when in one month dot-coms suddenly outnumbered dot-orgs, and everybody thought that was going to be the end of the Internet—there goes the neighborhood. And then we had the dot-com bubble and then it burst. And people said, 'well that's the end of the Internet.' We're not even close."

—Stewart Brand, cofounder of The Well

According to the study, 90M Americans have participated in online groups—that's 84 percent of all American users! In use terms, that means more Americans have participated in user groups than have gotten news online, searched for health information, or bought a product. Twenty-six percent of the people polled have used the Net to connect to local organizations: church groups, kids' sports teams, charities, and community events. Fifty percent say that the Internet has given them the opportunity to meet someone they otherwise may not have become acquainted with. Thirty-seven percent say they have met people from generations other than their own. Twenty-seven percent say the Internet has connected them with people from different racial, ethnic, or economic backgrounds.

According to Nua Internet Surveys <www.Nua.com>, Lee Rainie, director of the Pew Internet & American Life Project, says, "For vast numbers of Americans, use of the Internet simultaneously expands their social worlds and connects them more deeply to the place where they live. Online groups are comfortable places for people to congregate and get to know organizations and people they might never have encountered."

One of the probably thousands of people this conclusion is a testament to is Liz Simpson <www.LizSimpson.com>, ironically, the author of *Get a Single Life* (Hodder & Stoughton), a book she had written before she met her *Mr. Right*. Simpson was happily going about her business as an author while visiting her friend in New York when the friend asked, because she was a writer, if she could help her write a personal profile for an online dating service that would draw the attention of a good man. Well, after the computer crashed twice while trying to post the ad Simpson had written for her friend (and could not save), they gave up. Upon her return home to Kent (U.K.), Simpson decided to give it a try herself. She searched the online profiles of a service called WebPersonals.com and found one man who caught her interest. As fate would have it, the company's software had a glitch and showed zero distance between the potential couple. In actuality technologist Doug Barnes was located in Oakland, California. The two met in person when Barnes had to make a trip to London to attend a technology conference. He made a second trip out and they decided to spend three months together over the summer in California. They married 18 months later, and are settling in as newlyweds in their California home.

"I had no connection with the *geek* community," says Simpson. "Looking on that service really opened up global opportunities to meet someone I would have never met otherwise. I mean, I'm the author of mind, body, and spirit books, Doug was going to be attending a digital money conference—I would have never attended that conference here in the U.K. What were the chances that if we had met briefly in the street we would have exchanged information? People tend to write very meaningful e-mails when they are getting to know someone, rather than the polite chat that goes on while they're exploring dating someone. Under normal circumstances we never would have met. We saw each other a few times and I spent the summer in California.

"We actually found out we had the same birthday and we decided to celebrate our birthdays in Guatemala, and that's when he asked me to marry him. I'm not the only one who has had this type of thing occur, I hear stories like this all the time."

So, okay, one *can* find everything online—not only love, but *anything*. As a society we're becoming used to 24/7 and impatient when we can't find something in the Real World just as easily.

Because we can have all of our needs met in Cyberspace, we're kind of torn about the use of this World Wide Web that gets piped into us anytime, via any device. Thus we've become as schizophrenic as it has. Do we view it as a pleasure dome; a one-stop shop to meet our every need, or as a great source of knowledge where we can gain access to every class of educational material to supplement our continued learning? Do we say, *Ha! This is the place where I can find anything I could ever want to purchase—watch out world, I have a Visa card and a need!* And what about all of us who actually use it for business? We keep in constant communication with the people we do business with and work with—and we actually send e-mail that has significant promissory value. And who's to say that the instant messages of people looking for *the right one* in a chat room have any lesser value than a business contract or critical e-commerce? So how much value can you put on curing loneliness, even if it's only . . . for let's say . . . a few minutes?

Adults will pay for *companionship*. One company that found a successful subscription model for the cure to common loneliness is Match.com, a company that really leverages its success stories to the hilt. I was told by former COO John Spottiswood that every time a press contact called the company (at least before it was purchased by CitySearch), the company searched through its database for the local success story for that publication or media contact. Think about it, there are so many success stories—hundreds of marriages brought about by this service—that they can actually pick and choose a happy ending to hand over to the press!

ONE MEMBER AT A TIME

Fifteen years ago, when we were all pretty much figuring out what to do with this bright, shiny toy called the Internet, two players were entering the market—one that would spawn forth tremendous amounts of creativity and value, and the other a King. The King, otherwise known as Steve Case, was named in October 2001 as one of *Vanity Fair*'s "Power 50: The Leaders of the Information Age." (Bezos was knocked down to 38 while his stock dipped another 25 percent last quarter.) They touted Case as the guy who oversees the world's largest media empire, *having access to more than half of all the American online households.* And, claiming that AOL Time Warner is *omnipresent— probably the first company that the average citizen will encounter every day of their lives. Hmmmm . . .* I wonder if they checked that stat against General Electric's, RCA's, Sony's, or Panasonic's widespread influence over the last 30 years? So what if Case purchased Time Warner with overinflated dot-com stock? Since when does that make you a King in this business?

I remember the campaign Case waged on the retail consumer market by flooding every checkout register counter with loads of free 25-hour free AOL CD-ROMs, and then it was 50 hours and 100 hours. Hey, as someone who had been paying full price for it all along I felt kind of ripped off. I was inundated in the snail mail with free CDs that I hadn't ordered, so I began hanging them in the fruit trees to keep the birds away. All I got out of it was a hot stick in the eye, a service that is difficult at best to dial into, customer service that takes me two hours to reach (and always to someone who needs to transfer me to a manager because they're dummer than a doornail), and no discounts whatsoever for being someone who has had the service practically from AOL's start.

Regardless, AOL and its chat rooms and Instant Messaging (*IMing* is now a verb) became part of that culture with hundreds of chat rooms for everything from health problems to fetishes of every kind. Now you can't even sit through a network TV show without being inundated by AOL commercials. Why? Because people get tired of the bad service, AOL has worked in a churn factor and probably has to sign people up at the rate it's losing people just to keep its numbers up.

Yet, there was a different type of online community bubbling up near the coastal shores of Sausalito, California. Two guys, Stewart Brand and Larry Brilliant, were testing the digital waters. They began their formidable effort called The Well <www.Well.com>. Both of these guys were pretty hooked into the counterculture movement that's made its base in the Bay Area. They found that they could give the Web a voice—actually lots of voices, individual voices that would give rise to trusted communities where, as in one very famous virtual bar pulled from our collective media past, *everybody knows your name.*

"One of The Well's online forums was called The Pub," says Brand. "The Pub was the kind of place where people would pretend to drink and make remarks; it was kind of a

Cheers online. When I first saw the term *World Wide Web,* I just kind of rolled my eyes, like, *Yeah sure, add it to the list.* The world is drastically different from what it would have been without the World Wide Web. It's much more of a global city. It's not a global village so much in the sense that Marshall McLuhan thought it was going to be, because in a global village everybody knows everything, whether they want to or not. In a city, especially a global city, there's a lot of freedom and a certain amount of danger, and people figure the freedom is worth the danger and they go to the city."

> *"The future isn't what it used to be."*
> —Marshall McLuhan

The Well was known for throwing great parties and having a real sense of community—where not only did many of its members know each other online, they were part of their Real World friend set, too. And with that community came a sense of closeness and intimacy where members could post their innermost thoughts to the rest of the group. Then, it became clear that the world was watching and you weren't in Kansas (or Sausalito) anymore, you were posting to the world.

"A few months or years on the Net and you get used to the idea that just about anything you posted could end up anywhere, including the front page of a newspaper. That's the way it is. My hope and expectation is that a certain amount of tolerance will come along with the loss of privacy. We simply know about too many strange practices to be able to view every single one of them with favor. I think that we'll know about them and exchange our forgiveness in order for others to forgive us.

> "*T*here's always been historical optimism around new technology, like there was around PCs when they came along. When some of that goes away, people tend to say that the optimism was sure wrong, it was incorrect—but it wasn't wrong. Because it enabled a bunch of stuff that did work."
>
> —Stewart Brand, cofounder of The Well

"There was one time in '89, after the earthquake, when a bunch of people were giving their accounts of the earthquake and one of the reporters at the *Wall Street Journal* who was on The Well asked permission to run most of that particular thread in a page-one article in the *Journal*. Most everybody in that discussion said sure, so he did, so it was our words and his byline. And that was an indication—an impact. That was pretty common, a lot of journalists were trolling The Well for news—and for a very good reason, we gave them free accounts. That was an indicator that the world is noticing. When The Well intersects with the *real world*. It's always very interesting, and when it intersects with the *broadcast real world* it goes to another level. So when you see that turning up, you know that it's having impact."

> "*I* have a son who is 24 and he's been on the Net all of his life. If it suddenly went away he wouldn't know exactly what to do."
>
> —Stewart Brand, cofounder of The Well

"A lot of people on The Well became professional writers," says Brand. "I watched people who had a knack for posting their opinions online who were instantly rewarded by the community saying how smart the post was, or responding to it in an intelligent way. People realized they were in fact writing. There were a lot of editors who would invite people posting to write for their publications. A lot of worthwhile things were started on The Well, including the Electronic Frontier Foundation [EFF]—John Perry Barlow and Mitch Kapor found each other on The Well. Mitch dropped in on Barlow from the air in Wyoming and put together the EFF in a matter of weeks; that would not have happened without The Well."

Brand finally felt that he had created something that transcended community when it came time to upgrade the computer systems and The Well didn't have the cash flow to do so. "We wanted to move up from a slow VAX to a faster unit; we didn't have the money, so the customers loaned us the money—so that was a sign. That sign was not only that *community* was not just a word, it was certainly an economic body as well as a social body because people stepped right up and said, *I'll pay for the next 12 months of my Well usage right now if I can have a faster machine, please.* And they did that in enough quantities that we could afford the upgrade."

I wonder how many people would pony-up advance cash for AOL if it was in a bind? Perhaps people would be lured away by MSN and Yahoo! with lucrative deals? I'd opt for a new ISP if Steve admitted he had wasted way too much money on marketing and not enough effort on retaining the customers he had—*and by the way, could you pay me a year in advance for your service?* Ha! I fantasize about moments like that.

Community was and is still very much part of The Well, but when Brand opened up that online world to people, what he hadn't realized right off the bat was that they would also be part of the real world, too. "Early on we had what we called The Well Office Party. Since what's online is almost entirely the postings of The Well, they figured *they are* The Well, and they expected to be invited to the office parties. And they were, and they came, and that face-to-face contact added a whole very important facet to The Well."

I'm sure by now you're getting the defining differences between a community such as AOL and The Well. I mean, when was the last time you got an invite for a party from Steve Case (even in AOL's early days)? For that matter, when was the last time you were able to straighten a problem out with AOL customer service people in less than an hour? The importance of community both virtual and intertwined with the Real World works for The Well. In the chat rooms on AOL chaos reins as people with aliases wreak havoc. Spam is a natural occurance on AOL, and my e-mails forwarded to Tosspam@AOL.com and SteveCase@AOL.com with the registration information of URLs sending spam out that I have personally researched go unanswered. Yes indeed, AOL builds a high churn factor into its membership numbers— that's why they have so many constant marketing campaigns. Never in the course of history has a company worked in so much of the unhappy customer factor; things have sure changed. I guess when you believe that you're the only game in town, companies can afford such arrogance.

SCRIPTING THE FUTURE

For many during this time of terrorism and retaliation, the Internet has become an incredibly important form of communication with people around the world. It's become *incul-turated* . . . ingrained into our lives—just as the radio did when it was put into cars as a standard feature, and then personal transistor radios, and then boom boxes, and finally onto our ears in the form of a rugged portable unit for jogging, and guess where else . . . the Internet. Hey, I'm listening to high-tech radio news <www.CNET.com> right this very minute off of my Internet connection.

I remember when I was five-years-old and my dad bought me a red pocket radio. Everywhere I went I'd have that radio with me. I kept it on a low volume, or with an earpiece in my ear for my entertainment only. Of course it was AM only, so signals were precarious at best, and I found myself touching the aluminum antenna to other pieces of metal to get better reception; drainpipes were great. I had very little idea what the newscasters were saying when they began talking about the day's events, but I somehow felt a bit superior to my kindergarden friends when I'd repeat them. I really felt I was in touch with the world. Today I feel like I have that little radio back—along with all of the wonderment that came with possessing it.

I recently discovered the amazing world of weblogs. Now people are using this concept to build their own means of radio communication that arrives in your mail, taps you on the shoulder, and says, *Hey, I'm here, this is what I think.* It's very cool because you can be very selective about who and what you subscribe to and even if you choose to read it or not. It is so much better than an Internet news bulletin board that you need to check every day.

Dave Winer, CEO of Userland Software Inc, publishes a weblog called *Scripting News* <www.scripting.com> and a very popular column called *DaveNet* <http://davenet.userland. com>. Just as Dave Farber's famous, or infamous, *Interesting People* list, it also has thousands of people subscribing to it, with digerati well represented in both cases. The difference between the lists? Well, both of them are e-mail-based: with Farber's list, you may get up to 20 e-mails on a busy day forwarded to you, while with Winer's *Scripting News* you receive just one. Winer's list is also supplemented with links and commentary to the outside world. Farber's list nearly all consists of e-mails from subscribers who are writing in to comment on the day's news—and they usually include either links or stories someone has cut and pasted into the e-mails forwarded out to the list by Farber. Both are a complete necessity if you want to stay in touch with what's going on—in touch with the collective political and technological (and they do intertwine a lot these days) collective consciousness. Given my druthers, personally I'd like to see Farber's list put on a more webloglike format, but it would take away the spontaneity to receive live-time postings immediately when the news is happening.

The software Winer uses for this very popular source of dispersing information to others just happens to be a product his company developed called Manila; it is one of the three most popular ways to disperse weblogs. I guess you could describe it as a text radio broadcasting system. Winer claims that based on the numbers of people writing weblogs on Manila <http://manila.userland.com>, Blogger <www.Blogger.com>, and LiveJournal <www.LiveJournal.com>, that there are now around 500,000 weblogs currently circulating, whereas last year there were only 50,000.

"So you can see that most of the weblogs started in the last year," says Winer of the phenomenon. "Two curves are going to continue to grow—the Web is going to become more familiar, and the tools are going to get easier to use. Scaling is going to work better. In a society where people say, *Hey, I should write that story up,* and it's no longer a problem for them to do it, the problem flips around, and now there are too many stories. How do you find the one you're interested in? And that's a very interesting problem. We love those kinds of problems; and that's all community stuff about getting all the data to flow through a certain set of scripts that turn out at the other end. There's DayPop <www.daypop.com>, which is a phenomenal new service where he's scanning all of the weblogs on a daily basis and producing top-40 lists of the most-pointed-to articles, and that in itself makes a great weblog, and he's got a great weblog search engine. And now Google is doing the same thing, it's now adjusting itself to the world of fast-changing content. There's been a lot of things happening since September 11, it was a total milestone in our world because it was the biggest story we ever had to cover because here was this dramatic, tragic event that happened—and there were all these eyeballs that saw it. It wasn't behind closed doors, it wasn't one of those subtle pieces—it was a big event and it shook up a lot of people and everyone wanted to hear what everybody else saw, and so the weblog world just kicked in on that one—and it kicked butt. If you wanted to see that story unfold—you'd keep CNN on, that's for sure, but you could do the whole damn thing with NPR on and reading weblogs; and you'd get a more interesting and deeper point of view—and that's what I want.

"What entertains me," continues Winer, "are different experiences, opening new horizons, someone teaching me new ways of thinking about things. Giving me new ideas. Perhaps one of the most astonishing things about September 11 is that it opened us up to see what was coming out of other places; that there were Pakistani weblogs and Iranian weblogs and lots of stuff going on in Saudi Arabia. . . . These are people and they had something to say and it wasn't familiar—and it was a phenomenal way to learn about other cultures. A way to learn and grow. My dream, my vision is that weblogs are the stepping stones of mankind; this is the elevation . . . the evolution. There is no doubt in my mind that we have to evolve as a species now, that's really what's going on, that we have to survive the challenges in front of us right now; and this is a leading-edge evolution—this is our minds growing."

WALKING AMONG US IN CYBERSPACE

Bruce Damer is a dreamer, an incredibly intelligent guy who spends a lot of his time physically—well, as much as one can—living and building in Cyberspace. When I say *in* Cyberspace, I don't mean in some AOL chat room, I mean in a multidimensional space where famous people actually come to play in his world. Damer is president and CEO of DigitalSpace <www.DigitalSpace.com> Corporation, director of Contact Consortium, and author of *Avatars*. He also codirects a research and development consortium bringing virtual worlds to the Net. He is a visiting scholar at the University of Washington HIT Lab, and through it his company engages in innovative projects with such partners as NASA and Adobe.

DigitalSpace is a commercial endeavor currently spinning off companies and acquiring companies to build avatar and peer-to-peer technologies to deploy into the commercial and B2B marketplace. The Contact Consortium is a nonprofit organization to further virtual education and technology that Damer founded with an anthropologist. Many people, and I mean *many,* believe that future communication on the Internet will include integration of 3-D avatar shells, and even perhaps the body gloves that users will wear that will simulate what is going on online.

I remember the first time I had such an experience. It was the early '90s, and I was strolling along the Pearl Street Mall in Boulder, Colorado. After spending a long, enlightening day at Naropa University with luminary beatnik types, my friend Pat McCarron and I came upon a storefront where throngs of students were lined out the door. We stopped and looked in the

windows where we saw people wearing electronic gear standing on small raised platforms enclosed by waist-high railings.
They had on headgear, sensors, and gaming guns. Whatever
they were doing, it looked cool, and we waited in line with the
rest. When it was our turn, we played in a virtual 3-D world
with multi-gamers, and it was a tremendous experience. We
dropped about a grand that night on the extravagantly priced
but well-worth-it experience of our first journey into a virtual
world. In the end, we had a problem with equilibrium for the
rest on the night; hopefully they'll figure that part out one of
these days. But I can definitely see a future where much of our
communication could be done in the *physical* 3-D world instead
of by phone or e-mail. I can also understand the allure of a 3-D
world to an online community.

"You need anthropology in virtual communities," says
Damer of the worlds he spends time in. For those of you who
don't know what an avatar is, picture your ability to create
your own 3-D identity, a shell if you will, with your imagination being the only boundary. Place this avatar into a world
that you have created, again, with your creativity being your
only restriction. Also add to that experience software that
allows others to find your world, and to come in and chat
with you via voice or text messaging. Picture hundreds, perhaps even thousands of people *teleported* into your world for a
conference, or to live in as a community. This kind of technology is the closest thing we have to organized Cyberspace
where people can completely alter their beings and go into
completely different worlds. You, as someone who has not
experienced this, may think of this as a waste of time, a video
game of sorts, when in actuality it is an experiment on a grand
scale delving into the future of online communities.

Some avatar conferences draw 6,000 to 8,000 people into
a virtual world to share experiences, hear speakers, share ideas
with those from across the world. I got a call from a friend

involved with COMDEX today, the same day that yet another commercial plane crashed into New York, this time in Queens. She said attendance is slim at best and many of the people heading out from New York had decided just to write it off. Many others are afraid of becoming a target for an anthrax attack in Las Vegas. With stock in webex.com climbing, and with webex taking the *PCWorld* 2001 World Class Award for Best Group Application, we can all see that the conventions of the future will have little to do with travel. You will simply put your goggles on and hang a *gone conferencing* sign on your door. The virtual conference space is quickly filling up after the events of 9/11; conference companies simply cannot continue absorbing the loss on low-attended conferences which have been decreasing ever since the bubble burst.

"I think we know why video conferencing failed," says Damer. "People don't want their real image projected, because we're conscious of how we look. And unless you're Dilbert and able to read magazines during long meetings, you want the ability to have a presence there, but not let it be known that you're multitasking—and that's a big reason why people don't use webcams—they show the horrible secret that you're multitasking. The ability to multitask is a closely held beloved right for a lot of people. So it really doesn't figure into things unless you're sharing pornography with a friend. So avatars give you more anonymity, and also give you more of a body presence. By plopping your avatar down next to someone, you can have this known presence and can still gesture and do the things that give you presence but don't force you to maintain eye contact, or contact with a camera."

Damer remembers thinking about Cyberspace when everyone else was still figuring out how to use Windows. "All those years at Xerox PARC were all about inventing the desktop metaphor—windows with documents in them—that was revolutionary for 1976 or '77, but it was stagnant until the

Mac came out, but all of the operating systems were the same metaphor with slight variations. For me it was—*Hey, here comes Cyberspace!* which was a telnet interface from the '70s until '93, and when Mosaic came out, it was like, *Oh, god, here they come—the documents.* Documents are inherently noninteractive media. You can put movie clips in them, but they don't represent human beings directly."

But how will the avatar technology make money? Everyone is asking where's the money? How does this medium support itself? In fact, it's a hallmark of any truly powerful new thing that no one has a clue and it just takes years and years of evolution until a medium becomes part of commonly used technology. Damer is ready to release a new enterprise product that companies will use for their employees to stay in touch. He feels that the idea will catch on.

"It starts with people getting used to instant messaging and gathering in workgroups online, and being able to tell if others in your group are available for quick meetings." Damer feels that once people get used to this technology they will become more comfortable with the avatar metaphor and voice messaging. "And as a generation moves up, they will get used to 3-D space—they'll demand it. They'll say, *Why do we have to be in this sucky thing that's just text chat—why can't I meet and do my work and actually see and talk to them?* It'll take a generation or so, but that will be what the Net is about—it will be Cyberspace. When you get online the Web will be a small thing—there's some pages coming up with the news and you'll enter a space, and you'll be part of this huge population. Millions and millions of people will be living in Cyberspace. It will be *Snow Crash* and the *Metaverse*.

"I think it's hard to say what it'll be like, but what it's all about is human presence. It doesn't have to have a graphical representation, it can be the fact that you carry around a device—a global positioning device—that tells you when someone you want to talk with is near you. The whole idea is everyone having needs and needing stuff constantly to keep themselves going—living in what's called the Interrupt Culture—Howard Rheingold's Brainstorm. It's not just about avatars, it's about everyone having their lives sliced up and having many, many tasks piled up all the time. It's a weaving together of humanity that's pretty unprecedented."

Although the idea of avatars is only now gaining in popularity, the idea of avatars as a metaphor goes back to the beginning of our shared time. "Avatars represent human beings in Cyberspace and allow people to put on masks and act out different personalities," says Damer. "It ties into very old human traditions from when we were painting on cave walls and the shamans danced around becoming other people—very, very old stuff. So, in a sense, the avatar movement is quite fundamental—everyone has an opinion about it. An opinion of how they would look in the world and very specific to culture and gender and personality types. And people want to build worlds that represent their dreams or their current lives; the things they design are sometimes a real reflection of their souls. It's about humans interacting."

It seems that until the time comes when business and society embrace the avatar as a medium, such as they did with e-mail and instant messaging, we will have to view it in a non-profit forum where we can look in awe on its knowledge-transfer abilities.

Damer is finding that avatar technology has a unique educational niche that two dimensions cannot fill. On July 20, 1999, a very special avatar event occurred in a small corner of Cyberspace—the reenactment of the Apollo XI and IX lunar missions, marking the 30th anniversary of the Apollo program <www.digitalspace.com/worlds/apollo/index.html>. One hundred people entered a special virtual world called MOON built by the CERHAS project led by Benjamin Britton at the University of Cincinnati. The virtual world includes a full museum to the past decades of manned space travel. Damer and DigitalSpace were instrumental in recruiting Apollo IX Astronaut Russell Schweickart to reenact and discuss his mission.

"Russell walked online in his avatar and told the story of the Apollo program and his flight while people climbed out and down the ladder of the lunar excursion model—the virtual one—and they experienced it personally. It was phenomenal," says Damer of the interactions of the people from all over the world who participated.

"I had trained him for two weeks. I was on the phone and he was on his laptop navigating around, and I'd say, *Come forward. Okay, go down using the cursor keys and now down into the hatch—I'll tell you when you're in.* I said to him, *Here you are, a fighter pilot, and you've done this for real in space, and now I'm training you how to do it in Cyberspace.* He said, *Don't worry about it.* So he came in and we had a few hundred people and he started talking about the mission and telling stories. One that stuck with me was that nobody at NASA or the contractors had ever worked out what was going to happen to the crew when they blew the third stage off. The crew of *Apollo IX* had loosened their shoulder straps to get more mobility so they could reach things; but the impact of the engines was so great that when the impact happened they were smashed forward. He said, *My face came this close to smashing on the instrument panel.* Houston saw their heart monitors going up and one of the crew said, *You tell the next crew to keep their seat belts fastened.* After hearing this story people were saying, *Hey, this is a real guy, not just a guy in a avatar suit with his face on it.*

"Then we flew out to the landing site with the lunar excursion module, and a little girl came up to him—she was about eight or 10 years old. She asked, *Mr. Schweickart, can I float my avatar into the hatch?* And he said, *Sure, just hold the shift-key down and you'll melt through the polygons, you'll go through them.* So she did and she got inside—and you can log on today and do this yourself. And she started to turn around and he said, *Stop.* She asked, *Why?* And he said, *Because you're coming out face-first. You have to come out with your rear end first.* And she asked, *Why?* And he explained that the suit is bulky on the top and that she couldn't get out of the hatch that way—there's a reason why the camera was pointed at the ladder and not the hatch. And I thought, *Oh my goodness, it would have been two billion people laughing at someone's rear end coming out of this very noble enterprise instead of seeing what they did.* And he said, *One small step for Julie* . . . Now everyone was standing outside of the module in their avatars, wanting to do it, and he said, *Line up and I'll help you.* She started to walk to him and they got closer and closer, until she just melted through him and he passed right through her. And later she sent me a telegram—a private message saying, *I have been touched by an Apollo astronaut.* I said, *No you haven't, his avatar walked right through you.* She answered back, *Yes I have, and I can feel it in my body, I have been touched by an Apollo astronaut.* That day a very human contact was made for Julie and she felt the reality of the historic event. Her connection to it was through a very powerful medium."

Just think if all children could have learning experiences *that* profound. Something tells me little Julie will grow up to be someone very interested in science and math. It seems as though young kids are not having any problems grasping the whole avatar metaphor and running with it.

Damer has another story about a boy in his teens learning some valuable lessons in a world he started in January 1996. "I was walking around in my world in my avatar, planting trees and putting a wall all around this area where people could build their town, and the trees would be cut down later so people could build their town. We created this place and we brought in about 60 people to self-organize and build a community structure. And these two boys showed up—two boys from Alabama—they were best friends, and built this place called the Bizarre Bazaar. About six months later, one of them, Brian, said they were going to build a floating city called Sky City because they had figured out that they could fly up to high altitudes and build as long as they owned the structures underneath. So, six months after that he teleported next to me and said, *Come on, I want to show it to you.* I said, *No, Brian, I can't right now, I'm doing with some other people In World*—that's what we call it when we're doing something not in Cyberspace, and he said, *Okay.* Six months after that, he came and said, *Okay, now it's really done.* So I said, *I'll come.* So I teleported over and there's this huge structure floating about 5,000 meters above the green plain below. It was great! There were pictures of all these different kids from all these different countries who helped build Sky City. Kids from Israel, Germany . . . everywhere.

"I said, *Wow, Brian, this is an amazing achievement—Now tell me, what did you learn by doing all this?* I thought he would tell me that he learned about network systems, or construction, or Cyberspace. Instead, he said, *I learned about people.* I asked what had happened, and he described a situation that occurred when they built the first version of Sky City. Two boys who were from the Quake Culture said, *We built it, now we trash it—we tear it apart.* The others had said no, that they had built it for posterity and to show future generations what they could do. What happened is when they weren't around, these guys would come in and start tearing stuff down. Brian said it was terrible; it was like blowing up a spaceship, and then I realized that these parts must have been floating all over the place. After they got halfway through ripping it down, he said that he had a hard time getting the other kids in the team back together again. So what he did was call a meeting with everyone involved and they talked in their talking circle—this structure they had built for meetings. They each put up their hand and voted on what the future of Sky City should be. The two boys came and sat at the edge of the circle in their avatars, and they probably hadn't realized until then that they had really hurt the others' feelings and that it wasn't a game—that it was important to them. The two boys left, and the community did rebuild Sky City. I asked Brian what else he had learned and he said, *I learned how to keep kids coming back, and how to decide when to build things and when to hold off. How to not put too much stuff all in one place. How to say 'hello' in another kid's language—not in English because it's not the language of everyone. And how to tell people about Sky City and to get visitors to come.* I was impressed; I said, *Brian—you learned how to live in the twenty-first century; you learned about something called global project management, where you did human resources, budgeting, kept the project on schedule, resolved a crisis—designed something beautiful and promoted it—you learned how to live in the future.* He said, *Cool.*

"His father sent me a letter—actually a *real* letter, to thank me for introducing his son to this world. It said: *He's met people from all over the world and it's changed our family.* I actually went to visit them and I asked, *How did it change your family?* It was because the older son, 17, is a hacker—the police had been to their house; he'd broken into Southern Bell computers and that was cool for him. And that was cool for him until Brian, who was in his shadow, did something creative that was productive and positive. Brian got his self-esteem in the shadow of his older brother. I saw his father last year on another trip back to Alabama and I asked, *What's happened with Brian?* He told me that Brian is now involved in producing theater in the high school and coordinates kids to build stage sets. He said that Brian had come to him one day and told him that either he could finish his English essay or he could work all night on finishing the show props. His father told him that he probably should finish up his English homework. So, Brian went away for an hour and then came back and said, *I just don't think that's right. If I don't work all night on these props I'm going to let 40 people down. If I don't do the English essay I'll let one down, my English teacher.* And I thought, *Wow! Maybe he had this innately in him—but the skills he learned in the virtual world have allowed him to do this very complex theater production work and make good decisions.* It showed us the medium was astoundingly powerful for learning. It's all about learning how to live in the world. The most important lesson is how do you work in a team—that's not often taught in schools, and people coming into the workplace are so uninformed and have little experience on how to work with teams—that's why big corporations have huge failings. It's because people don't learn about leadership ability and conflict resolution and motivation. You don't learn that in school and if they don't have those skills they're time bombs in companies."

CLEARLY

Clearly we can see from all of the Internet tools that have evolved over the last 20 years, the bulk of the successful ones have been the tools of communication and knowledge. The applications and hardware that enabled us to stay connected even when our physical world was falling down around our ears. We live in a time when most of us don't know our own neighbors, and our average job lasts 2.3 years, oftentimes leading us into a whole new industry with new contacts, and new friends. We live whole new lives with every evolution of ourselves and primarilly the only thing that stays the same is our personal e-mail address, if that. Perhaps you've found that some of the closest friends you've made in recent years are over e-mail. Now, during a time of war and terrorist acts, clearly there are many uses for community tools. Perhaps while we're all reaching out the world will become a better place to live in as well. I believe it's a time Vannevar Bush would have reveled living in. We have a long way to go before we figure out how to build these communication tools, how to use them, and how *not* to regulate them.

"People have a hard time reaching over conventional boundaries; they don't look at what could be; only at what it is now—only more so," says Alan Cooper, author of *The Inmates Are Running the Asylum,* and chairman of Cooper Interaction <www.Cooper.com>, a company offering consulting services to corporations and startups about user interfacing. "It's great to read science fiction of 30 years ago, it's an extension of the mechanical paradigm; and almost no science fiction writers managed to really see the age of the digital information appliance, and here we are with computational resources that were unimaginable then. I pretty much guarantee that you are not going to get a single correct answer to this question [about what the future will look like], not because the answers are not going to be correct, but just that the answers we're going to care about in 20 years aren't going to be visible today. All great inventions are completely invisible in foresight and completely visible in hindsight. So today the things that occupy us are our ability to communicate over the Internet. What are the things that are going to be conceived of in 20 or 30 years? By definition, they're something we can't conceive of today.

"The obvious thinking about the Internet is that we'll build one big intelligence," says Cooper of the future. "I think as an industry we're giddy with excitement over our new toy. . . . It's like a kid running around on Christmas morning with his new drum—just banging and banging on it. The adults are getting kind of antsy because it's just a lot of racket, and they're ambivalent because banging on the drum is a youthful thing and it's a good thing and it should be celebrated; on the other hand there comes a time to put the toys away and do something significant. I think that all of these personal and commercial web sites are just like that kid with the drum—making noise because it's just a joy to bang on that drum. So at what point do we stop banging on the drum and say, *it is time to build a symphony?* I don't think any of us see what that higher vision is. When you're six-years-old and you're banging on the drum, how can you conceive of a symphony?"

CHAPTER 3

Issues

Here we are 30 years after the Internet was conceived, with a very popular tool, indeed. So popular that it's of great legal and governmental concern to just about everyone and every organization involved—or even thinking about getting involved, or even those having no business getting involved. For some people it's almost like governing this mythical thing that they don't even understand—like the FAA trying to make guidelines for spaceship landings. I clearly saw this when I tried to interview Vermont Senator Patrick Leahy, and his assistant asked me to send a request for an interview. I asked for the e-mail address, and she said they really didn't have one I could send it to because they receive too much e-mail on it. I asked her for a fax number, and she said the same thing of the fax. Instead she gave me the senator's office address—a *physical* address. Come on, I haven't sent a real *snail mail* letter in over a year. I pay all of my bills online. For postcards I take a digital photo, and e-mail it. Snail mail in this day and age? *Pa-leeeze*. It gets even more ironic. Leahy is one of the major supporters of the Digital Millennium Copyright Act (DMCA)—the reason why a Russian programmer named Dmitry Sklyarov was arrested last year.

Researchers and scientists are being bullied by the Feds because of the freedom this law gives them to do so.

"*There were some good people involved in the DMCA, I just don't think they truly knew what they were doing. I mean there were some truly malignant people involved who knew damn good and well what they were doing. But you can't tell me Pat Leahy knew what he was doing. He's a really good guy, and had he known the consequences he never would have done it. Even Orrin Hatch, I think, never would have gone along with this. The majority staff counsel is now general counsel for Napster—and told me flat out that he read the 'Economy of Ideas' and that it changed his whole way of looking at everything. Unfortunately, he read it after he had an instrumental role in drafting the DMCA.*"

—John Perry Barlow, cofounder of the Electronic Frontier Foundation

With the almost daily introduction of antiterrorism legislation that broadens the jurisdiction of wiretaps to all forms of telecom formats, it seems as though every aspect of technology—be it to the user, creator, or distributor—is being threatened.

"Just as civil liberties are taken and given away in the name of national security, and as fighter jets fly over major metro-

"Yes, a coordinated team of hackers could take down the communications systems, the power system, perhaps the financial markets. But all of those systems would be back online pretty quickly—you can't really knock them out for an extended period. You could use those outages as a decoy though, to draw attention from what you are really planning."

—Kevin Mitnick, as read in *WIRED* magazine

politan areas, one begins to wonder. In a time of permanent war, can Cyberspace also become subject to martial law?" asked Heidi Brush of the University of Illinois at Champaign-Urbana, who presented her paper titled *Electronic Jihad* at Internet Research 2.0, the second annual conference of the Association of Internet Researchers. "Once the Internet is defined as a potential battleground, or as a haven for suspected terrorists, will the U.S. insist on a loss of privacy online in the name of national security? Does Operation Noble Eagle enable the inauguration of an era of electronic martial law? I think so. I definitely think there's more of a security focus. The Internet has always had elements of the military, but now I think it's become quite express."

People have the misconception that the DMCA was passed under the current Republican Administration, when in actuality it was passed under the Clinton Administration. Some claim letting the DMCA ride was a payback to the entertainment moguls who contributed large sums of campaign money to that administration's coffers. I can understand Clinton not being too involved in rallying the troops against it, but Gore is very knowledgeable about technology, rights, and legislation. Former Vice President Gore was not available for comment for this book.

"It's the same thing we've been fighting all along," says John Perry Barlow, cofounder of the Electronic Frontier Foundation (EFF). "By this time in the Clinton Administration I had already realized that they were not our friends, they were our enemies. I don't know if that's the case with Bush, I think he's probably too clueless to have any sense of what's going on. It's a generation of old men running this government—they're not wired; they don't know about this; they don't care about it. The only statement Bush made on the campaign about the Internet was that's where he thought the Columbine killers got the idea to go out and shoot their friends."

The politics of copyright, patents, encryption, and governance have been hot issues over the last few years with the growth of the Internet and the realization of its economic potential (despite the burst bubble). Ever since September 11, nothing has been the same, including your right to protect your privacy. Of course there were other issues that were hotly brewing before 9/11 came along—encryption, the disappearing *Fair Use Act*—the list goes on and on. And instead of this period of time when technology was finally getting to the point of developing into an excellent communications tool, we're tying ourselves up in copyright knots and forgetting about the beauty of what was created for us via the original Constitution.

"*I* don't think there's any silver bullet for the issues we're facing about today's Internet."

—Stewart Brand, cofounder of The Well

We've come a long way in the last two hundred years, and many of the copyright laws have evolved significantly as technology changed, but now we're at war in the courtrooms of America. I remember when I was at Stanford studying media law in the '80s, I never even saw a footnote about how the Internet was going to affect the laws. I mean, hey, truth be told, I'm a writer . . . and that means, as a writer, the only means I have of making a living is protecting my copyrights so I can leverage them into income. So I understand this issue from both sides of the fence—as a person who's living off of keeping her copyrights valuable and from the user standpoint of wanting to use the Fair Use Act for writing this book and in my private life.

"The bad guys' goal is to prove that our system is broken and that all of this freedom is just a façade. That the U.S. is just the same kind of dictatorship that they live under, only that theirs is approved by God and ours isn't. The more we restrict freedoms in the country, the more the bad guys win."

—Bob Young, chairman of Red Hat and founder of The Center for the Public Domain

The Internet has been developing at an incredible rate for the past four years—so fast that the people and agencies that have been put in place to solve its growing pains seem to be having a difficult time making mandates that make sense to everyone involved.

"There are a great many issues that the Internet is raising," says Vinton Cerf, senior vice president for Internet Architecture and Technology at WorldCom, regarding the problems many people and organizations are grappling with. "Concerns over privacy and over the protection of transactions over the Net; protection of intellectual property—these are major challenges. There are problems with people who abuse the Net, people who spam, people who send out viruses and worms. Finding a way to deal with these problems that's coherent and works on a global scale is a challenge. I expect to see continued arguments over taxation on transactions that take place on the Net; that's going to require some clever thinking on a global scale. So we have a lot of policy challenges ahead of us, and I think that not only ICANN, but the Internet Society and many of the other organizations that cater to various network interests are going to have to engage in finding solutions to these very complex problems."

We have issues now about technology—and real or not, we're going to have to deal with them, either by complying or fighting. A day does not go by when I don't get 20 e-mails with pointers to media stories on encryption, copyright, or patents. Yes, now that we're beginning to bloom from our technology adolescence, we now have other issues to deal with. Issues that are tearing this country apart because technologists and legislatures are drawing lines in the sand and saying, *bring it on!*

ENCRYPTION AND COPYRIGHT

The next part of this story is about a cryptographer I met named Dmitry Sklyarov, who allegedly wrote a piece of software that soon became the test case for the DMCA. Sklyarov became the poster boy for programmers all over the world who feel their rights to create software are being trampled when he was arrested at a hackers' conference. I met Sklyarov shortly after he met bail, and after having several discussions with his legal dream team and e-mailing with his wife in Russia, who did have an opportunity to travel here with their two infants and await the decision of the Department of Justice as to whether Sklyarov would be facing the trial of his life. So before I met the 26-year-old I had a pretty good picture of who he was, a braniac kid, and a prisoner of circumstance.

I met Alex Katalov, CEO of ElcomSoft, a Moscow-based company founded in 1990, who claimed to be a vendor to the U.S. government. We met while Sklyarov was transferred to San Jose and released on bail. We met at a Software Developers' Forum <www.SDForum.org> meeting in San Francisco where Phil Zimmermann was speaking. A few of the facts that haven't come to light about this case are that Adobe supposedly licenses with software partners to do basically the same thing ElcomSoft's product does. Basically, provide eBook users with a key to unlock Adobe's software so you can load your legally purchased eBook from its text-based format into a speech-based program. Basically, if you're blind you can now hear a mechanical voice read your book. It's not like you have a pristine copy of Peter Coyote reading pros, it's whatever synthetic voice your software provides.

According to Katalov, ElcomSoft received an order of cease and desist from Adobe, which he claims his company complied with after only selling a handful of copies. I was told by Katalov that Sklyarov gave his talk on encryption at DefCon, what is known as a hackers' conference, after being switched to that conference from another at the last minute. Apparently, ElcomSoft had no power over the switch and attended the highly profiled hackers' conference, where Sklyarov was arrested while giving his talk about how he broke Adobe's eBook encryption. Katalov stated that Sklyarov's wife was questioned about her husband's activities somewhere in the early morning hours Moscow-time, after being told that U.S. Federal agents had her husband in custody and it was in his best interests that she answer their questions.

Sklyarov was held in a Federal prison for weeks until he could be released, after finding a U.S. sponsor to take responsibility for him while he awaited trial. He was eventually charged with several Federal offenses, including violating an anti-trafficking provision. The complexity of this case is that it tests the DMCA, which was essentially influenced by many lobbyists for the entertainment industry who see the Internet and digital publishing as threats to their copyright protection. But, copyright infringement is not an issue in this case. ElcomSoft claims that its Advanced eBook Processor software cannot be used by anyone except those who have already legally purchased the right to view the eBooks from book retailers. Instead, this case hinges on provisions added to copyright law by the DMCA. The provisions do not address copyright violation, but rather the distribution of tools and software that can be used for copyright infringement.

The major point of contention is the following: Section 1201(b)(1)(A) prohibits manufacturing, importing, offering to the public, providing or otherwise trafficking any *technology, product, service, device, component, or part thereof, that is primarily designed or produced for the purpose of circumventing protection afforded by a technological measure that effectively protects a right of a copyright owner under this title in a work or a portion thereof.*

Meanwhile, I heard that programmers from all over the world began sending their Adobe products back, and a boycott was leveraged against the company. Adobe did finally try to drop the charges, but once these things get rolling, you can't stop them. The Feds are off and running, and it's now out of Adobe's hands.

Funny thing, I saw Sklyarov and his wife at a *WIRED* magazine's Rave Award party where he had been nominated in the Tech Renegade category. Believe me, this guy is quiet, polite, and has a great sense of humor when he comes out of his shell. At the time of his arrest, Sklyarov was completing his Ph.D. through research in testing the security of the eBook technology at ElcomSoft. Then he was snatched from a conference, dropped into a Federal prison, and all of a sudden was wearing a neon orange pantsuit and slippers and standing in front of a Federal judge in San Jose, California.

"I would never have thought they would have done something as stupid as arrest Dmitry in the first place. Now that they have, I don't know what they're likely to do next. My primary objective is to help a young man who has no business being caught in this situation—and as much as I would lick my chops and make asses of these people very vividly in court—I'd rather just send him home. This case is muddied with jurisdictional issues.

—John Perry Barlow, cofounder of the Electronic Frontier Foundation

The courtroom was packed wall-to-wall with Sklyarov's supporters, mostly programmers who had taken off for a long lunch to lend their presence to the crowd picketing outside—hundreds of people carrying *Free Dmitry!* signs. Oddly enough it was all happening under the towering building of Adobe in downtown San Jose. I could see Warnock's balcony from a different perspective that day, where I once stood with him—where the huge A in *Adobe* touches down from the roof—talking about the future. I wondered what he was thinking that day.

Having lived abroad and being involved with the technology industry, one thing I've learned is that programmers have empathy for each other. Because programmers have learned a higher type of communication—languages that have no physical borders, although they do come with their own set of prejudices. Programmers seem to have a strong bond with one another—even if they have never passed an e-mail between them. Sklyarov, whose primary language is C, has found many kindred spirits coming forth on his behalf.

The son of two computer engineers, Sklyarov felt the worst thing for him (after not having seen his family and they were able to join him in the U.S.) was that he couldn't work because of the visa restraints and the enormous amount of time spent with his attorneys trying to strategize. As he said to me, "I like to use my brain; this is very difficult not to be able to work."

"In Russia there is a phrase—the 'wild Russian soul.' It means that a man could pull away his shirt and give it to another man, for nothing—just to help out. There are many good people out there helping me who this phrase describes."
—Dmitry Sklyarov, cryptographer

When I first heard about Sklyarov's arrest and transfer from the DefCon show in Las Vegas to Oklahoma, two thoughts entered my head. The first was poor guy, being in another country and being arrested for something as lame as this. And second, who wants to end up in Oklahoma? Per-capita, how many technologists are in Oklahoma?

In the early 1980s, when I was 17, I was arrested in East Berlin on a trumped-up littering charge. I had the wherewithal to give the two machine-gun-toting soldiers (who didn't speak English) $300 in traveler's checks to have them forget about me long enough for me to get on a train headed to West Germany, where I promptly reported the checks stolen. I knew the pitfalls of suddenly ending up in a confusing situation; alone, in another country, not knowing my rights, or *their* limitations. I really felt for the guy.

"I don't think being a programmer in jail is different from other people in prison," says Sklyarov, only able to comment on-record about his emotional state, not anything pertinent to the trial. "I think that in one cell dorm you could have anyone, from a man who stole a glass of beer, or a man who stole 10 million dollars. I saw no conflict at all in prison. It didn't matter what color your skin, what you did, everyone was just trying to help everyone out. In Russia, it's not this way. There was no fighting [in the American jail], probably because if you did, there would be penalties and it will be not be better for you. And, if a black man has some food he'll give it to a white man and vice versa, without asking something back. All of us were in the same frustration. There are laws in this country, but nothing incredible like a brick falling from the wall on my head and killing me could happen in jail. I wasn't scared because I knew I would be transferring to California and people were working to get me free."

When I was asked to speak on CNN News about the Sklyarov case, I had said point-blank that the Department of Justice (DOJ) would lose this battle, I said it was like taking a knife to a gunfight. I knew they wouldn't be able to hold Sklyarov for long, or be able to prosecute him. Last week (in December) he was released on the contingency he would testify in the DOJ's case against ElcomSoft.

How did the DOJ ever expect its charges against the programmer to stick? It was akin to going inside of Napster and arresting the programmers instead of taking the company to court. It's all a bit heavy-handed. As time goes on in this case, I have a feeling that the Fair Use Act will prove to be more important than the entertainment industry's rights to *protect* copyright by throwing programmers in prison.

I was also there in the heyday when investors asked my opinion on Napster and if they should invest—I said the company would not survive for a number of reasons, one of them being that you can't make a living in this country off of stolen copyrights. What ElcomSoft is doing is not aiding in copyright theft, it's assuring the purchaser of the copyrighted product to make their copy under the Fair Use Act. In my world that is a higher order than making arrests on behalf of the entertainment industry to protect an archaic encryption code that has outlived its usefulness.

"The problem is how do we get the average citizen's outrage going on this when the average citizen reads all about viruses and computer security and it all seems like black magic? The average citizen thinks that Dmitry Sklyarov is some Russian who is stealing valuable American property."

—Bob Young, chairman of Red Hat and founder of the Center for the Public Domain

"Freedom is a very strange word, you can use it in so many different contexts and it will mean different things."

—Dmitry Sklyarov, cryptographer

"I was very glad to see all of those people in the courtroom and to know that all those people support me," says Sklyarov. "I don't want to be a cult figure or a star. I want to be with myself and not to see a lot of eyes on me, although it is very good that people are helping me. I want to work—I need to work . . . to do something. It's very difficult for me not to use my brain. I don't think it's really important for me to be part of history [as in changing the DMCA] or becoming famous. It may be good for me in the future, but who knows? If I ever had a chance to take it back and never be famous, or be where I am now, I'd choose to never be famous."

Sklyarov has left sunny California and is back in Russia awaiting the time when he will be called back to the U.S. to testify in the DOJ's trial against ElcomSoft. He was facing 25 years to life [if his prosecutors could have pushed through retroactive legislation] in prison and up to $2.5M in fines—*does anyone realize how much money that actually is in Russia?* Others are currently facing the wrath of the DMCA, including researchers, professors, scientists, and technologists. My question about this whole situation is, why didn't the Feds choose a more straightforward test case than this? Was it that Adobe, a well-respected technology company, was willing to press charges? Was it that at the time of Sklyarov's arrest he was speaking at a hackers' conference when anti-hacker sentiment was running high because of the amount of worms and viruses being unleashed on companies and individuals at the

> "*It's all about protecting the big interests, it's not about protecting the infrastructure from diabolical attack—I could support that. If somebody wants to bring down the whole goddamn Internet, I would be just as incensed as the next person. And if law enforcement has the capacity to find such a plot and stop it, I'm happy to have my tax dollars go to that. Now, if what law enforcement is really doing is protecting the interest of Time Warner—that's another matter altogether. And so far I don't see any of the former and plenty of the latter.*"
>
> —John Perry Barlow, cofounder of the Electronic Frontier Foundation

time? Were they playing the anti-Russian card? Were/are there other forces at work here? All I know is that this is going to be a trial that sets some real precedents. I hope they don't drop it like they did the case of Phil Zimmermann, creator of Pretty Good Privacy (PGP). At least this way everyone will have their day in court and the DMCA will be challenged.

Philip Zimmermann, <www.philzimmermann.com>, is the creator of Pretty Good Privacy, PGP, freeware that eventually boosted him into techno–cult hero status. An icon to the masses of programmers who, once again, the U.S. government created with its heavy-handed zealous ability to do so. The U.S. government charged that U.S. export restrictions for cryptographic software were violated when PGP was spread throughout the world via the Internet following its

"I expect to see much better technology for public key infrastructure, and that will, in many dimensions, help us because it will authenticate people on the Net. This could eventually lead to democratic voting processes that are enhanced by being online; again we have the challenge of authenticating the voter while keeping his ballot secret."

—Vinton Cerf, senior vice president, Internet Architecture and Technology, WorldCom

1991 publication as freeware. Despite a lack of resources, Zimmermann fought the good fight against the government for three years until they dismissed the case. PGP went on to become the most popular e-mail encryption software in the world. When the case was dropped in 1996, Zimmermann founded PGP Inc., a company that was acquired by Network Associates Inc. in 1997, where he stayed on for three years as Senior Fellow. Zimmermann currently serves as chief cryptographer at Hush Communications, and is a consultant to companies and organizations throughout the world on issues of cryptography.

Zimmermann won that fight, but not without a hard battle that nearly drove him to bankruptcy. "I thought of creating PGP in the mid-1980s, when I was a peace activist," recalls Zimmermann. "At that time there was a lot of political tension between the Reagan White House Administration and the peace movement. I felt that grassroots political organizations needed to protect their data. I didn't have time to start writing

"*I think people also understand communication mediums are used by both good guys and bad guys and so are telephones, cell phones, and pagers, which are all such valuable technologies—and they're all used by bad guys to do their business. You can't take it out on the Internet. There's been a lot of talk about how the terrorists used the Internet to communicate. They're going to use whatever efficient mechanism they can. I just think it is a very hard problem, and we need to be careful not to have knee-jerk reaction to things. The whole issue of exporting encryption— just because you don't export it doesn't mean it's not there.*"

—Judy Estrin, CEO, Packet Design

code then, but that's when I got the idea. I was a software engineer in Boulder, Colorado, and I wrote parts of it starting in 1986 and in 1988 and at the end of 1990, when I began working in earnest on putting everything together and working full time on it—without funding. It was about six months of full-time work, just me, 12 hours a day, seven days a week.

"There were laws in place, export laws, and I knew about those, and I thought by releasing the software domestically I wouldn't have any problems with those laws. It turned out to be more complicated than that. The source code was put out on newsgroups, but in 1991 I really didn't know what a newsgroup was, and I actually thought you could control where newsgroups went. I was told that the mechanisms for newsgroups allowed you to specify whether it would be U.S.-only or not. It turned out that it has little effect, because all it does is put a little tag on it that says if you're interested only in U.S. news you can read this. In other words, a computer in Europe could look at it and decide it would like to look at U.S. news only. It went completely out of my hands. Later on I learned what had happened."

Zimmermann had his first contact with the government in what would turn out to be a long three years in 1993. "In fact, I didn't realize what their agenda was when they first called me up. A special agent from U.S. Customs started asking questions about PGP. I thought she had just run into PGP in some other case and needed some advice. I was telling her stuff about PGP and she said she'd like to fly out to Boulder from San Jose and ask more questions, and that's when I thought maybe something else was going on.

"Two agents flew out—and nobody flies out to Boulder unless there's more than an academic interest," says Zimmermann of the meeting. "So I contacted a criminal lawyer and we decided to let them interview me in his office with him present. It was surprising how ignorant they were of the general concepts of their idea that there was something wrong."

That was the beginning, and it became increasingly apparent that Zimmermann had a tough road ahead. "There was a mixture of worry and despair about facing prison, and I was very much aware of weaknesses in my case that could be exploited by the prosecutor, so I thought there was a good chance I could end up going to prison. Also, there was a kind of folk hero thing going on and I was getting a lot of support; so it was a hot and cold sort of mix—there was just no middle ground."

"The founding fathers laid down a structure that has persisted for a couple of hundred years; it seems to be the right model."
—Len Kleinrock, cofather of the
Internet and chairman of Nomadix

"As soon as I was told that I was really the target of a criminal investigation, I immediately started a criminal defense fund and people from all over the world contributed to it. Most of my legal team was *pro bono;* my lead counsel was not because he didn't work for a big law firm and didn't have a regular salary, so I paid him, but there was a lot of time he didn't charge me for. Early in the investigation I remember talking with an Israeli cryptographer at a crypto conference, and he said asylum could be arranged in Israel. Maybe he thought I was Jewish; regardless, it was a nice offer and I thought about taking him up on it. Then, I thought that if I did, I'd never be able to fight this thing.

"Once it started getting closer to a decision from the Department of Justice people began really aligning behind me and said, *Hey, we're ready to go.* To them it was a big First Amendment case. I kind of felt—you know, it was like that final scene in *It's a Wonderful Life.* The scene where everyone comes into the room and dumps the money on the table to bail him out because he's in trouble? It felt like that. A lot of people did help during that three years and the journalists had a huge impact on the case. There were about five stories a week for three years, and every single one of them was positive—not just 99 percent of them, every last one of them. That is what really gave me the idea that there was something really wrong with the case. We all know that sometimes the law doesn't make sense; but if you have a law that is so disjointed from what everyone's moral sense is—so completely opposite—then the law has to go. There was already a law that said you couldn't export munitions; that isn't a bad law, that's a good law. There was a munitions list that the State Department had and most of the things on that list were things that should be on the list—missiles, helicopters, guns. One of the items on there was encryption software. They finally took it off of the munitions list, they didn't change the law, they just took it off of the list—and it was done by executive decision rather than legislation. It felt good, we kicked their ass."

"These are issues that aren't going to be solved on one side or the other any day soon. And, anyway, they're probably not supposed to because the textology keeps changing, the possibilities keep changing; the important issues keep changing. September 11 changed the chemistry—how far it changes and in which direction we're still sorting out. After we're done sorting that out, something else will come up and we'll have to figure something else out. I don't think it'll ever stop. Some issues are basically paradoxical—whichever way you decide, it proposes the opposite, and with complete logic and good reason, and then you have to contemplate the opposite. So, some of the issues having to do with freedom and privacy and being able to hide and unhide will keep issues fresh for a long time."

—Stewart Brand, cofounder of The Well

Now Zimmermann is dodging bullets of other types. Instead of from the Feds, he's catching flack from fanatics sending him messages asking him what it was like to kill the people in the World Trade Center. The big fallacy is the line of thinking that encryption was used anywhere. It seems as though most of these guys were using free accounts, nothing as complex as encryption software. It seems that in this game of legislation, just when you've won a battle, there's another behind it, and they all usually have something to do with the lack of knowledge. Code itself is not a crime; it's the actions people take with the code—as in actually committing illegal acts that in a fair world would *really be* illegal acts—when they should be held accountable.

Many people who were around since the beginning of the ARPANET feel that the government isn't well-informed enough to be making a call about encryption, or people's rights to use it. As a matter of fact, I really don't know anyone in technology who feels that government should have a final say in technology, especially not without a fair amount of technologists being included in on the vote.

"*The government does things that are in the wrong direction, and other times in the right. The control over encryption has been a stupid thing they've been doing—you can't control encryption. The government has no benefit from controlling corporate or individual privacy at this point by saying you can't have it.*"

—Lawrence Roberts, cofather of the Internet and chairman of Caspian Networks

"The fact that someone can tap into a phone line or a cable is no different than their ability to listen to a wireless transmission," says Leonard Kleinrock, one of the cofathers of the Internet. "You have to protect it at a higher level, so you either encrypt the data itself or support the tunnels. Wireless exasperates the problem because I don't have to be physically in your environment to gain access to your communication. Security has always been the stepsister of computing, and people are basically unwilling to pay money or make efforts to bring it about, so security has not been designed into network infrastructures. It's been added on after the fact and that's always the hard way to do it. The fact is that we do have an infrastructure and we're not going to tear it up and put a new one in—that's why the RSAs of the world are there—their certificates and their digital signatures. It's a question of, *How much effort do you put into the encryption versus how much effort the enemy is going to put into decrypting it?*" Obviously encryption and your ability to use it are big issues coming into this next era of technology and communication.

"I chaired a committee that wrote a National Research Council Report in 1994 called 'Realizing the Information Future: The Internet and Beyond.' Dave Clark, Bob Kahn . . . quite a few people worked on that project. We addressed issues such as ethics, security, technology—there are some great insights into what role the government should have in all of this." This study can be downloaded directly from Kleinrock's personal home page <www.lk.cs.ucla.edu>.

"I think our rights are constantly being attacked—I think there are lots of folks resisting technology; it's especially our current administration that worries me," says Kleinrock of the current governmental climate. "There seems to be a lot of want to govern or control technology. This can be a real danger and I frankly don't know the solution. I find myself coming down on the side that government should act as a forum and not a governing body. This forum should enable people to have a place for discourse, to meet, and discuss these issues—not impose regulations or authority on technology. It does worry me that in an economy that's not so great, we have a conservative administration, it is worrisome."

"Our infrastructure critically depends on being able to use encryption. The DMCA makes it illegal to even touch that, or research it for other reasons—and we're going to find ourselves on very weak ground when only the government has good encryption, and the commercial sector has none."

—Dave Farber, former chief technologist of the Federal Communications Commission

Apparently Kleinrock isn't the only one who thinks that government intervention is not the appropriate thing to do. "I just hope that people will keep their eyes on the opportunity that's here. We really have a very special moment right now where if we do things right we can assure liberty for untold numbers of generations of human history," says John Perry Barlow, founder of the EFF and a product of the Civil Rights Movement. "And if we don't, we've probably assured increasing capacities for enslavement and darkness. I also think it's a time where if you understand the economics and aren't trying to understand them through the assumptions of the past, that this is an excellent time to do good, and do well. You have to understand what's going on, which means opening up your mind and listening and watching and seeing what's working instead of simply assuming this is the way it should work because this is the way it always has."

Bob Young, chairman of Red Hat, also feels strongly on the subject. I remember meeting Young at a Garage.com Bootcamp conference back in 1999. You see, I used to be a proprietary software kind of gal until Young and I were walking back to our cars in the parking garage of the hotel where the conference was being held and he got me thinking. I think we must have talked for a while and he put the seeds of doubt in my mind. Then I called him and we talked for over an hour about the virtues of open source. By the end of that day I never looked back. I also began to fully understand why Apple only has single-digit numbers in the market.

Now, as we talk about the government—the American government—there is something very ironic about Bob Young lecturing on this subject. You see, Bob is a Canadian. Funny thing, I learned something new from Bob about my own governmental heritage that I never knew before. Frankly speaking, I have known many scholars of American history, but I have never known a single one who has the flair and passion for telling the story of the American Constitution that Bob has. In other words, if I was on *Who Wants to Be a Millionaire,* and Regis happened to pull out a question about the history of American copyrights and patents, Bob would be my *lifeline*—thank goodness I have his cell number.

That's why when he told me that he had founded the Center for the Public Domain (www.centerforthepublicdomain .org), I thought it was only appropriate. As I said about Dmitry Sklyarov on CNN—it's going to take a Russian to teach the American government a lesson about copyright (because it is the copyright underlying the protection that's been broken). And it will take Bob Young, a Canadian, to remind Americans about why our original laws and rights were written the way they are. The organization's mission?

"When you actually get into the politics of it and see it from our perspective and see the effects the DMCA is going to have on the technology industry, the conclusion is that these guys are either ignorant, or, in fact, in league with the publishers. When in actuality it's simpler than that; they are simply uneducated about the issues, as are the majority of voters."

> —Bob Young, chairman of Red Hat and
> founder of the Center for the Public
> Domain

The Center for the Public Domain is a nonprofit foundation supporting the growth of a healthy and robust public domain by establishing programs, grants, and partnerships in the areas of academic research, medicine, law, education, media, technology, and the arts.

As a writer, I'd like to think the copyrights protecting my work are something of value I can pass on to other people once I'm six-under; although Young has caused me to take a closer look at this. I'd like to have these rights even go on after that, and left to whomever people want to leave them to and so on. In America, copyright is good only for the life of the author and a limited number of years thereafter.

Recently when I went to Alexa.org and saw my site in all of its incarnations recorded—*recorded, copied, stored, and accessible*—for posterity on The Internet Archive. Well . . . I was slightly stunned when Brewster Kahle showed me this over the Internet during a phone call. I have a strict copyright warning posted directly on my site, with links to the U.S.

Copyright Office, with a statement that I will prosecute for infringement. Yes, I was a bit anal about copyright, because as it's written, if I don't make an extreme effort to protect it, I can lose the right to hold it. But, both Kahle and Young had an effect on me on the subject. I suppose that sometimes you just have to let some of it go (as in copyright control) and see what comes back.

"We can start out with the government," said Young when we last spoke. "I'll start out with the old adage, the two things you never want to see made are sausages, or laws. Basically the government responds to two stimuli—money and votes, and so if they don't see any votes at risk they will respond to money. You can have all the money in the world, but if all the votes are on the other side, the guy with the money is still going to lose. All the original antitrust laws were written to address the fact that the billionaires at the turn-of-the-century were using their financial power in ways that the populace clearly didn't think was in their interest. Unfortunately, what we're seeing is that through a lack of understanding in our society, and largely around our electronic and digital issues, is the guys with the money influencing our legislators to address laws in ways that are not in the citizenry's best interest. And because citizens don't really understand the issues, they're not really paying that close attention.

"So the legislators are paying attention to the money," says Young of how he feels technology legislation is put into action. "So when all of the big publishers march up to Washington and say this whole Internet digital society we're building is going to destroy my business by making it possible for any 16-year-old to steal my intellectual property—you get good legislators listening. These are people I'm very impressed with as legislators—you get guys like Leahy in Vermont sponsoring legislation like the DMCA and being completely oblivious. All he thinks he's doing is solving a

"You can't turn it off now, but you can sure change the architecture so that it's a lot more easily controlled. The current libertarian quality of the Internet is a condition of its original architecture, but not necessarily its eventual architecture. Which is why Mitch Kapor and I and the EFF have been very focused on issues that would affect the architecture. I'm much happier to have it be governed by some general consensus—uncodified, unlegislated, and ethically rather than legally maintained way. Maintained by all of us rather than by some very mechanical system of control. I think we all have to rise to the occasion; I think this is a very strong incentive for all of us to be stronger people."

—John Perry Barlow, cofounder of the Electronic Frontier Foundation

commercial problem for Disney or Time Warner, when in actuality what he's doing is reducing rights that are currently held by American citizens, and awarding those rights to these small groups of multi-national publishers. But because no one is standing up for the citizenry on the issue, it looks to Leahy, and to all of the other legislators, like a very reasonable, logical set of paths. For those of us in the industry who have been following the issue, you look at this and go, *What are these people thinking?* They were elected to serve the interest of the voters, not the interest of Disney and Time Warner."

Young points out the dangers of what he's seen in the past with conservatism and liberalism—cycles that move to and fro. Movement somewhat like a razored pendulum in some old horror movie, when the drama is cranked up and the hero only has barely enough time to come in and untie the heroine before the pendulum slices through her and scrapes the table. One message that comes through when talking with Young is his sense of immediacy, of the here and now.

"What we're seeing is the pendulum swinging," says Young. "This is why you're seeing such consolidation among the publishers and major technology companies. It's because they have all the money to buy up all of the copyrights and patents and as they get bigger they can squash more innovation, which gives them even more power. And that will continue to move across until it starts becoming obvious and you will start to see the momentum, and the noise will start to grow through educational effort, and eventually when all of us start pushing hard enough, we'll get the ol' pendulum swinging the other way. You can be certain by the time we win the pendulum, it will be swinging so far in the other direction that the problem will be too little property rights. That's probably going to take 40 years. In the meantime, the pendulum is already in the danger zone."

Until that time, the DMCA is a constant reminder of the point of contention that remains between the technologists and the legislators. "I had the opportunity to debate this point with Leahy," says Young, "because he was the bill's primary author—at least he gets credit for it, but I doubt that he wrote so much as a sentence to the damn thing. What he was unaware of was that it doesn't make the *behavior* illegal; it makes the *technology* illegal. It's kind of like making the ownership of screwdrivers and hammers and crowbars illegal because they can be used to break into houses. The DMCA isn't about making the breaking and entering illegal, it's about making the tools for breaking and entering illegal. There's two problems with that. One, the problem is that it never works because the only people, as a result of that law, who don't use those tools are law-abiding people. The people who are going to be crooks and breaking and entering—well, it wouldn't occur to them *not* to use those tools. And what happens is that all of the law-abiding people suddenly can't use screwdrivers and crowbars for legitimate purposes. That's the way technologists read the DMCA, because there are a whole bunch of legitimate uses of the technology you can't use it for because the very fact of owning the technology makes it illegal. It's like a society shooting everyone in the foot because there's been an increase in snatch-and-grab purse thefts, and that way no one will snatch and grab."

> "*What* we should actually be doing is making behaviors illegal, if we actually care about them—not the tools that allow these behaviors."
>
> —Bob Young, chairman of Red Hat and founder of the Center for the Public Domain

"Why are we shooting ourselves in the foot to put the bad guys in prison?" asks Young. Let's write laws that make the behavior illegal if we actually care about it, but let's not shoot ourselves in the foot. Let's not restrict entrepreneurs from coming up with new technologies or applications that they can't bring forth because the government has arbitrarily said that copyright used for copying is illegal, period. It's amazing how broadly worded the DMCA is; the way that it's written it says that any code and technology used to get around copy protection software is illegal, and it doesn't define what copy protection software is. Not only does it define technology that does exist, it defines technology that hasn't been used widely in our industry in the last 30 years.

"The problem is Adobe's copy protection that these guys had written the work to get around is primitive. The DMCA was meant to address people who had really written complex copyright software, and they wanted to stop the hackers on the Net from using very sophisticated technology to get around the copy protection, but the fact is there's no problem. If these guys implemented decent copy protection, virtually no one would be bothering to try to get around it."

The technology is there to build good copyright protection—and if Disney or Microsoft wanted to protect their technology, software is out there that would allow them to do it. It makes their lives easier not to have to use it, so they get Leahy to pass a law that says we can use really primitive protection and throw you in jail for writing software that's written to decode anything. They can get the FBI to throw you in jail. All the entrepreneurs understand it's a bad thing."

"*If* you really put in the privacy security rights management from the environment cradle to the grave, privacy becomes less of a problem, and all those kinds of things just kind of go away. But that costs money and it's much easier to pass stupid laws."

—Dave Farber, former chief
technologist, Federal Communications
Commission

As you can tell, Bob Young is very passionate about this subject, but I ask if it ever scares him to think about what will happen in a future where technology is ruled by the DMCA.

"It is a problem, but the reason why it's not scary is because our system does have checks and balances and as a result some of the DMCA stuff will get overturned by the Supreme Court and they will just say, *This is not compatible with our founding fathers' vision for the country—go back and rewrite this because it's too flawed to support it.* It could take 10 years. I tend not to look at it in emotional terms or you could get discouraged too easily. You treat it like an economic problem that needs to be solved and keep plugging away at it. The thing about things happening slowly is that in another 10 years the guys who are 30 will start running for Congress; the 30-year-olds today are a hell of a lot better educated technologically than the 50-year-olds currently representing us.

"There are a lot of smart lawyers out there working in technology, and a lot of lawyers have political aspirations. Something like 90 percent of our legislators are lawyers. I don't think it will be the guys who are writing the software who will be running for Congress, but I do think it will be the lawyers working at IBM and Oracle who are going to run. As a result of writing all of these contracts and working in this industry, they'll end up with getting a good enough education so that when they get to Congress and the next generation of Bill Gateses and Larry Ellisons comes marching through, saying, *You must pass this extension to further the patent or software copyright acts,* they'll say, *No we don't and thanks for mentioning it, because we meant to roll some of those rights back.* Eventually we'll get there, but there's a lot of educating of both the legislators and the voters before we stop coming up with flawed legislation like the DMCA."

So do people in positions of power in D.C. listen to what technologists say before they decide where their money or votes will go? The outspoken Dave Farber is a fountain of information. His Interesting People list (www.interesting-people.org) has its finger on the pulse of the world's technology and thoughts pertaining to it. Farber has held many positions in technology over the years; more recently he was chief technologist at the Federal Communications Commission (FCC).

"The largest part of my responsibility was to take ideas and explain them to the commissioners and the rest of the FCC staff in terms they could understand," says Farber. "To lay out policy alternatives based on an understanding of technology. Many of the things the FCC has to address have a technological base, and you run into troubles in two ways at the FCC.

"In general, the commissioners are good people but they're lawyers; they're just not programmed to think about technology, so to give them a technical talk about something does not do any good. They want to understand what the technology does to the subtle alternatives they have to consider, so you have to unascend technology, but be sensitive to the political, legal, and congressional processes and package that up to get the ideas across and give them the alternatives. You have to try to predict where the next problems will be so they aren't a big surprise. The rest of it is the normal playing the politics of getting things done—basically educating The Hill and helping other agencies.

"The Hill has very few technologists, especially on The Floor. The White House had very few, and they get their information from the lobbyists—and they're there to present their view. You see a lot of bills introduced and you look at one and at who introduced it and you know that person had no way of even reading that bill. I've seen that time and time again. I'd go down there and talk to a senator and staff about the Internet; basically Internet 101, and the next day they'd introduce this incredibly complex bill about ISPs. I'd say, *Okay, that must have been Verizon or some other company that wrote that, because certainly their office couldn't have understood that.* They have very few mechanisms for getting a good understanding of what the policy alternatives are. Nobody on The Hill ever goes to the formal testimonies. It's a near-miracle when you see a senator or a representative attend those meetings. Their staff reports to them, but usually that has very little real impact on anything, and it's the lobbyists that have the influence. My prediction [on legislating technology] is that it's going to be a catastrophe. We saw that in the crypto game; the danger is that you create more of a problem than you cure. Getting that across to The Hill is not trivial, and they could kill the goose that laid the golden egg. Even though the egg is a little bit sour, it's the only goose we have."

What are Farber's views on the danger of encryption, and does he feel that it can be controlled? "Criminals don't care if they break the law," he says. If you can detect them [encrypted messages], you can get at them. Detecting encrypted traffic can be a very, very difficult thing to do because there's too much traffic; and you can hide encrypted messages inside music files and all kinds of places. You could maybe detect it if you say the only things you are allowed to send are English words, but that would destroy things. You could say that we're going to make sure you can't buy the *crypto gun,* but in fact, as with real guns, does that really stop anybody?

Crypto is an open sport and there's no way to bottle the genie back up. Nasty people tend to have the resources to get stuff; I used to think for years that if it wasn't for the fact they'd throw you in jail, the best business would be servicing the illegal part of society. A lot more money on that side of things, and there's no competition. The only technicality is that you get thrown in jail.

"The big headache that's been caused now by this Dmitry Sklyarov case is that people will not come to this country, they won't expose themselves to something that's legal in their country but that gets you in big, big trouble here. The industry pushing those things is just bad behavior. I remember sitting at a meeting at the FCC—I won't say who the particular parties were. They were proposing that the FCC mandate a particular encryption scheme for protection of high-definition video. I looked at the scheme they were proposing and—Mike Powell used to say that *the nice thing about having Dave around is that it stops them from lying to us*—I looked at it and said, *That scheme you have doesn't seem that solid, how long will it take to break? Maybe a year before some kid breaks it?* And they said, *Yeah, that's about right.* Why standardize something that will be broken in a year and then use the FBI to enforce it? Not smart. Their mentality was to use something not so good so they could save a nickel inside a set-top box. If you add it up that's a lot of money for them, but the cost to the country is irrelevant to them. We continuously do that, and we will continue to do it as long as we keep the election system we have where you're nice to your favorite contributors."

1999

Special Prosecutor Kenneth Starr's report on the Clinton/Lewinsky affair was published in its entirety on the Internet. Ironic thing, though, by doing so it violated the Child Online Protection Act [signed by Bill Clinton and later proven unconstitutional].

"I think as soon as things calm down a bit, assuming that things calm down, I think there's probably enough problems with the DMCA that Congress will take another cut at it," says Farber. "In the Senate, where at least they're not so busy running for election every five minutes, they understand that the bill has a lot of problems. Whether they succeed or not depends a lot on what the courts do. If the courts outlaw parts of it, this industry is smart they'll come back and rewrite it, and during that process it will lose a lot because people will realize that things weren't what they should have been."

Will America's laws cause the nation to shoot itself in the foot when developing new technologies and go somewhere else because of the restrictions here? "I think we'll lose opportunities for certain technologies to develop in some fields," says Farber. "If you have laws like this, good scientists will not leave the county to work in that area, they'll just work in another area. You'll sort of chase a future technology offshore. We've done that with crypto; it's now fostered in Germany and other countries that don't have our restrictions."

One person whom I know is always working on concerns relating to the future of technology is Kim Polese, chairman of Marimba. Polese is dedicated to participating in organizations to solve the rifts between technologists and legislators, and she was also part of a group of entrepreneurs Former Vice President Al Gore consulted with on technology policies.

"The technology industry has some valid concerns about over-legislating, especially when it comes to something like content digital media protection," says Polese. "There's a real legitimate concern around artists and content distributors that invest time, energy, and money in their work and should be rewarded for it. The issue is certainly valid and one that we need to address and come up with a solution for, but legislating or creating a chip or a hardware or software solution to do that is a slippery slope. For one thing, government involvement tends to slow down progress or innovation when it comes to trying to legislate something this complex and fluid.

The way I feel about it is that there should be an open standard for content protection, which the technology industry creates together with the content and entertainment industries. It's actually starting to happen and I've seen some recent discussions between members of the two industries to really try to work together. They're trying to create a solution that will make it possible for not only the big media companies to protect their assets, but also the smaller players and not stifle the development and acceleration of this industry."

"*I* think that eventually we'll find the Network simply disappearing and performing functions for us through software. Tasks that we'd just assume not have to do ourselves in the same way that vacuum cleaners and dishwashers do work that we just assume not to do. I think it will become quite casual, and I think privacy will be quite preserved as we get better and better at cryptology and quite conveniently managing the keys that are needed to manage it."

—Vinton Cerf, cofather of the Internet and senior vice president of Internet Architecture and Technology, WorldCom

"The foundation issue [about regulating encryption] is one of great concern to every citizen and should not be taken lightly," says Polese. "Especially when you start trying to legislate protection for certain types or degrees of encryption. Unfortunately, someone can always top the latest encryption, and other governments and people in other countries can get hold of technology and through their own innovations be able to trump whatever the protection is we try to maintain. In other words it's not an easy issue where there's one simple solution by which the government has the capability of having a certain level of encryption and implementing it, and companies and citizens don't. I think the issue is complex enough that one solution alone would not be effective, and would be fraught with all kinds of downsides having to do with competitiveness, personal freedoms, and individual liberties.

"My feelings on these issues are that they are not only worthy topics for focus, debate, and action, but also collaboration between government and industry when it comes to digital content protection, and participation by citizens when it comes to personal liberties and freedoms."

One of the grand old guard who stands firm in his determination to protect the rights of people—both creators and users of technology—is John Perry Barlow, cofounder of the Electronic Frontier Foundation (EFF). Barlow is a hippy from way back, when, writing lyrics for the Grateful Dead and learning about the Web, in his role as a participant on The Well. He saw events that progressed around him and that finally ended up at his front door in Wyoming.

"I don't think founding the EFF was a decision; I think it was a natural process. Being a weirdo as early as I knew that there was such a thing, I've always had an affinity for weirdo rights—the right of the underdog to express her- or himself. I've always had a suspicion of authority, which was intensified and vitalized during my experiences in the '60s. I was involved in the Civil Rights Movement and the anti-war movement, and I managed to stay on disciplinary probation throughout most of my academic career. I became involved in the online world because mostly I was thinking about what was going to happen to community; it seemed that *generica* was taking over, and I tend to think of community as a necessary human spiritual nutrient. So I started looking for other kinds of community, because the ones that I was used to were going out of being. I noticed that the Dead Heads, the followers of the Grateful Dead—which whom I was pretty familiar because of my role as a songwriter—seemed to have something that looked a lot like a community. It also was lacking some fundamental things such as continuity and random interaction on a continuous basis—and a physical location. And I was wondering what they did for *that*.

Someone suggested that I should check out what was called the ARPANET and The Well <www.Well.com>. Both of these things were very abstract to me. When they said I should *check that out*, I asked, *What does that mean—where is that?* I already had a computer, I had a Compaq that looked like a suitcase and weighed about 40 pounds. It was just a matter of getting myself a modem and making it work—back in 1985—and getting online. As soon as I got on The Well I checked out these Grateful Dead communities that were there. I certainly felt I was *in* something that had a lot of the characteristics of a small town, and certainly the feel of a community—certainly of a pub, or the courthouse steps type of thing. People randomly communicated within this community. I became very excited about the possibility that whatever that place was—and it certainly felt like a place—and it would become a substrate for the formation of a new type of community.

"So I became a very vocal part of it—the various Dead user groups and even branched out and became a part of others. In 1989, after I'd been at it a while, *Harper's* wanted to do an online forum, very progressive of them considering how much any of us knew at the time. They wanted to do a forum on freedom of expression, hacking, security. There were a couple of editors there, Paul and John, who were way ahead of the game. They decided to do it as an online forum and they went around to The Well to look for the pithiest of posters, and they asked me if I wanted to join the forum. I told them that I really didn't know anything about the issues—although I knew something about civil liberties, but I didn't know anything about hacking and cracking or any of those things and they said, *It's all right, you'll figure it out.*"

"Most of the initial rules on The Well worked out fine. One that I should have caught at the beginning was that I put in that the users would own their own words. Well, I should have said, 'you're responsible for your own words.' The ownership idea became a complete distraction for a long time. Because people thought their words had commercial value and they could sell them and protect them from being copied and so on. That was a mistake. It eventually got worked out as the community realized that it didn't care about selling the words, but what they did care about was that people were responsible for what they said. The reason I put that in was that I knew people were going to say terrible things about each other and I wanted them to sue each other and not The Well."

—Stewart Brand, cofounder of The Well

The Well is where Barlow got his first taste of the under-culture, a part of the site that was important to the alchemy of its legendary success. "I got involved in this online forum and I had my first encounters with computer crackers—there were a couple of kids—*Fiberoptic* and *AcidFreak* and their colleagues, and Emanuel Goldstein of *2600 Magazine* who is still currently being defended by the EFF against the Record Industry Association of America [RIAA] today. My first reaction to these kids was kind of a standard old hippy reaction to the younger generation who didn't seem to have any values and they were like a bunch of nihilists. I was being really kind of absurd and making disparaging comments about them, including one that I think was painfully true—which was if someone took away their modems and gave them skateboards it wouldn't make a nickel's worth of difference. This irritated them so much that they downloaded my TRW file into this conference—and said that they were going to change it permanently if I didn't pipe down. Actually, they couldn't do that, but I didn't know they couldn't.

"So I responded by sending an e-mail to *Fiberoptic,* saying I think we've fully used the bandwidth of this medium, I would appreciate it if you would give me a phone call and I won't even insult your intelligence by giving you my number. I was listed, but he didn't know that, so just to demonstrate his hacking prowess he called me inside of 15 minutes. Then all of a sudden when he got on the phone everything fell into place. Here's this pencilneck kid whose voice hasn't changed yet, and I realized that he wasn't very different from the way I was at his age—he was basically a good kid. He was just seized with the usual male adolescent urge to violate the forbidden—not to do any malice, he just wanted to go where he wasn't suppose to. It was no different than me breaking into a variety of things I broke into just to say that I had been there. So I felt this kind of affinity toward him, and over the course of the conference kind of became the scoutmaster to the legion of doom."

Barlow was a fixture of The Well and from his home in Wyoming became part of the culture that had moved from Haight-Ashbury to Cyberspace. But there was soon trouble in the place they called home away from home.

"A series of events took place that caused me a lot of concern. First of all *AcidFreak* and *Fiberoptic* and some of their buddies got busted hard, really *brutally hard*. AcidFreak had a 12-year-old sister who was held at gunpoint—literally the muzzle of the gun to her head—for two and-a-half hours before he got home, while all of these Secret Service guys hauled out every electronic object in the house including a clock radio, and all of the audio cassettes, which sounded awfully harsh to me. Then I thought, *Well maybe these kids are a lot more dangerous than I thought they were for the government to come after them like that; maybe they're doing stuff that is really a large threat to public safety.* I don't know why I still had any faith in the government because it had been dashed numerous times before.

"I guess you like to believe because it makes you feel safer. I also heard where the Feds swept down on a role-playing game company in Texas and took all of their files and basically came within an inch of putting them out of business because they had a game that the FBI thought was a handbook for computer crime. And I heard about an online crackers' magazine called *Crack* where the editor had all of his equipment seized simply for possessing a Bell-South document that you could actually get from Bell-South if you asked for it, but which Bell-South was claiming was stolen. I was hearing about all of this stuff and getting more and more concerned, but somehow none of it fit yet. Then in early '90 I got a phone call from an FBI agent and he sounded terribly nervous—and that I hated. And I asked, *What do you want to talk to me about?* and he said he couldn't tell me—and that I hated even more. We were kind of like friends and he had investigated livestock theft for me and he had a pretty good handle on it, and a friend of mine had been appointed head of the Fish and Wildlife Service and he had come and talked to me about my friend's background check, so he wasn't a total stranger—but he was acting like one."

"The new thing is being born and it's so young—it's made up entirely of people like Dmitry who don't have a lot of credibility yet, but by the time they're 40 they will."

—John Perry Barlow, cofounder of the
Electronic Frontier Foundation

"So he turns up in Pinedale, and he's in a very confused and agitated state and it takes me a long time to figure what he's going on about," says Barlow who was trying to put the pieces together carefully for the FBI agent. "It turns out that somebody—or *somebodies* had taken some of the source code from the Macintosh ROM and was shipping it around on the Net in an apparent protest against Apple's proprietary policy. And they were calling themselves the New Prometheus League [in Greek/Geek mythology, Prometheus stole fire from the gods and gave it to humankind], and the agent kept calling them The New *Prosthesis* League. I had to spend two hours with him to just explain to him what the crime was, before I could explain to him why I wasn't the perpetrator. That's when I saw the tip of the iceberg about the government's cluelessness in this area. Everything he had was wrong. Here you have a slightly insecure guy, well-armed, walking around, and knowing something would follow. The whole thing was straight out of *Alice in Wonderland*—very disturbing."

"I don't think there is any question that the forces of copyright and patent are so frightened that it's not beyond their capacity to try to erect a police state to protect themselves with. That's not hyperbolic; one of the conditions we imposed on China to get them Most Favored Nation trading status was that they would make copyright violation a capital offense—so that's the real deal."

—John Perry Barlow, cofounder of the
Electronic Frontier Foundation

Barlow found The Well a good place to sound off about the frustrations toward the government that he was feeling. "To make myself feel a little better about it, I wrote something about it and posted it on The Well where it was read by Mitch Kapor, who had started Lotus. He had also had a visit from the FBI regarding the New Prometheus League because Mitch was one of the people to whom the software was sent directly. The reason why they had come to me was because I had been attending something called the Hacker's Conference—which Apple told the agent was a complete hotbed for anti-Apple sentiment even though one of the founders of it was Steve Wozniak. You get the picture. They had a lot of goofy stuff—they believed that John Draper, the original Captain Crunch, was working on very sensitive defense technology for Autodesk. Well, Mitch read what I posted and suddenly he felt like he had a support group, so he was going across the country the next day and he called me up and said, *I understand you had a visit from the FBI. I did too. I've been troubled by this and I'd like to sit down and talk to you about this if you don't mind. Is your airport there big enough to accept my jet that I'm flying?* I said yes, and he literally fell out of the sky and I spent the day going over the other things that I knew and he got more and more agitated. We decided to call up a civil liberties law firm and get them to start investigating some of these cases. I don't think we even thought we were starting up an organization; we were just starting an investigation. But that was the beginning of the EFF right there and over the course of the next month or so as we started assembling cases to go to court with. Steve Wozniak came along and asked to join us, which he did for a while. John Gilmore showed up; I got this e-mail from Gilmore saying, *I really appreciate what you're doing. Would $100,000 help?*

"Now we're battling the most powerful forces there are with the most money—and a large body of what I think is misconstrued law," says Barlow of the forces at work. "Nevertheless, the institution has managed to get a lot of laws passed on its behalf. For instance, Dmitry Sklyarov . . . that we can arrest someone in our country for what he did in his country, which was not a crime there, is preposterous. I see absolutely no justification for it. It shouldn't be a crime here. The judiciary knows as much about PDF files as the FBI agent who investigated me knew about the New *Prosthesis* League. I think the amount of information that a Federal-sized government has to be able to assimilate, collate, and digest is now so huge that the chances of them actually being able to come up with any kind of rational policy is very small, so I don't worry about that so much as I do when I see it thrashing around like a dying dinosaur. Just because it's dying and thrashing around doesn't mean you're safe from it.

"We have to get the anti-circumvention provision out of there and demonstrate legally that it's a clear attack on Fair

Use and free expression and frankly what I would like to see us do both legally and through our various pronouncements is to get people thinking about the legitimacy of property in Cyberspace, and the utility property of Cyberspace as an economic matter. I'm thoroughly convinced that if we want to harvest the economic potential of the virtual world the last thing we want to bring in there is property—because it's not about ownership, it's about relationship. And if you put it in terms of ownership, you diminish the role of relationship. It's fundamental. You go from a condition of continuous flow to one that is kind of chunked up in a way that mercantile transactions always are, and it's not about the chunks."

Brewster Kahle's name may not be as familiar as some of the luminaries in this book, but he was then and is now quite instrumental in his contribution to mature the Web. Kahle was the creator of WAIS and, more recently, The Internet Archive. The Internet Archive is a place, such as the Library of Alexandria, where you have a continuous snapshot of the past and present Web, so on the site you can use the *wayback machine* to go back and view the entire Web as it was in 1999, for instance. I was taken aback when I first saw my personal web site in its different iterations over the years. I had no idea it was being copied and stored—*none*. I hadn't signed anything to the contrary, and despite having a huge copyright infringement policy posted, there it was. I was somewhat speechless. All of a sudden I was saying to Kahle that it's a great idea, and then he said, *Look up your web site*. Then I saw copies of the site going back to 1999. And there it was: how was I going to deal with it? The problem is, as someone who considers herself the rightful owner of the copyright of the content on my web site, if someone were to come and steal it from their site—and I'm just thinking of his in the terms of law—and I have no contract or licensing agreement with them . . . well, where does this leave me? Has the site diluted my copyright property? Or because it's a nonprofit archiving for the future, does the law overlook its duplicating of copyrighted property it doesn't own?

If you look at it in terms of a library, then if one library in your county ordered a book and made Xerox copies of it to store in its library branches, would that be copyright infringement? Undoubtedly there will be some precedents set in the future. Okay, so I'm torn on the whole *letting go* thing, but Kahle got me a little closer to understanding it.

"If you look at the bigger picture about what we're building, it's something tremendous and great—it is of historic and momentous ability," says Kahle. "It's not just the development of the fax machine or the VCR tape; we're talking about something that humanity could go through a major step in terms of how we even think about who we are as people, how we communicate, what it means to be in a family, in a company— we're seeing a lot of those changes happen because of the Internet. I guess it shouldn't be too surprising that the old guard feel like they've got something to lose and they're going to do everything they can to stop change. Having people be afraid of change is not the biggest surprise. We've got something just too important to lose, although we've got a lot of people who are going to try to stop it. The opportunity that we see is one of universal access to our cultural heritage. The universal access to our cultural heritage is a dream that has been only a dream forever."

Kahle feels that the Internet Archive is a safe place to store the whole of the Web and make it accessible. I look at it kind of like a wild animal reserve I visited in East Africa—I was so fortunate to see so many animals that are disappearing, and I have the recorded experiences of those animals on video and I'll be able to archive them; unfortunately that tape may last longer than the species I saw. My point is, they *are recorded*—no matter what happens to the animals, I have a record that they

"There's no question though, you're now going to see a whole set of stupid legislation go through, because people will perceive that it's going to protect us from this dangerous technology [encryption], when in actual fact they don't understand the technology. When you understand that there are legislators who don't understand the difference between binaries and source code, you can have a little sympathy for them and their inability to write good legislation in the digital age. You don't have to be able to write code, but they do need to understand concepts like source code versus binary."

> —Bob Young, chairman of Red Hat and
> founder of the Center for the Public
> Domain

once existed. It was a magnificent, humbling experience. And I have to tell you, to be able to look back on the Internet Archive at webvan when investors thought it was the best thing since sliced bread . . . I remember those days fondly, and it was nice to go back in the *wayback machine* for a quick visit. After all, who will believe what happened during the dot-com bubble?

"People think the Internet is here forever and it's not going to go away. *Nu-uh*, if we don't fight like hell, the counterrevolution is going to win," says Kahle. "If we have universal access—our opportunity is not just to have it in one place, in Alexandria—this time around we can have the thoughts, ideas, and dreams of millions of people in a public sphere and universally accessible, and that's a beautiful thing. You talk to professors now who are requiring their students to come up with one source of information that is not from the Web so they continue to use the old paper technology. The answer to that is, *Good luck*. There's no going back. You talk to a lot of librarians and they say, *This Web is a fad; they'll come back to our library*. I think the answer is, *No, they won't*. But their accusation that the Web doesn't have the good stuff on it is also true. So don't think people are going to go back to the stacks, but we don't have a lot of information up on the Net that we need to have up. That's our challenge and that's where, even more, the counterrevolution is making huge headway. We have to find mechanisms for filling out the library. Right now we've got the most fertile authoring environment ever created by humans. There are worries that we may lose the entire twentieth century because it will be basically wrapped up in old-fashioned copyright law and not worth trying to untangle from very-well-represented-in-Washington publishers. We're trying to build permanence into the Web. We're trying to build the library, and libraries have past copies. A lot of the best works are out of print, and without libraries we would have lost the ancient knowledge. Our opportunity is unbelievable, and it's just because of digital technology."

Not only is it the past we have to think about, and the future of copyright laws and legislation, we also have to think about the future as applied to the past. With live characters . . . in a 3-D world. Life is going to be even more complex very soon. Bruce Damer, author of *Avatars!* [Peachpit Press], and one of the leading avatar experts in the field, has a story about what happens when the past visits the future and how that will look from both the copyright or trademark owner's perspective and the avatar user.

"*Our biggest danger right now is that a combination of legal and technical copyright constraints will make it so nobody can have anything they don't pay for. Nobody can share anything, nobody can pass information on. And every time information changes hands a royalty is based on that. Our second-biggest threat is that the architecture is going to be altered in ways that will make it far more susceptible to a position of local or global control by the usual suspects.*"

—John Perry Barlow, cofounder of the
Electronic Frontier Foundation

"Richard Dreyfuss contacted the William Morris agency some years back and asked his agent, *Avatars . . . virtual worlds . . . it's going to be a new performance venue—where are my residuals coming from?* And the agent said, *I don't understand what you're saying.* And Dreyfuss said, *Go find out, I'm paying you people enough.* So we did an investigation with this person from William Morris and told them what will happen is that you'll have these huge worlds that people inhabit and they'll contain characters from our cultural heritage. So what is our cultural heritage? It's the *Brady Bunch,* it's TV shows, that's our cultural heritage—it's made up of TV and movie characters. In a sense, in the twentieth century one could argue that it was their right to participate in and shape that thing from your cultural heritage, but it happens to be owned by studios. So what happens? What's happening on standard web pages currently is that people are making their own devotional sites and the studios come in and shut them down, or work with them, or whatever. When you build a virtual world it's something different because there's a free speech component—if you made a virtual world where you were Captain Picard talking to William Shatner's avatar and it was a parody of *Star Trek,* it would be allowed—you'd be protected under the Constitution to do that. If someone's trying to make money on it, well that's another question. Will the studio system ever understand the idea of the public wanting to inhabit characters they consider their cultural heritage? Probably not. The conclusion we came to at the end of this long dialog with this fellow from William Morris was the system will never be able to accept an environment where they don't control everything."

PATENTS

The reason why patents are so controversial right now is because there are a lot of lobbyists funded by big money trying to get extensions on technical patents. What does that mean?

"The problem of all this expansion of intellectual property rights is that it doesn't threaten IBM and Compaq because both of those guys can hire enough lawyers and have a big enough patent portfolio themselves that they sort of have a mutually assured destruction strategy," says Bob Young, chairman of Red Hat and founder of The Center for Public Domain. "In effect all the big technology suppliers trade their patent portfolios with each other. IBM and Compaq have a deal which says I can use any of your patents and you can use any of my patents because they know the costs of legislating and protecting each other's patents is more than its worth, and at any one time they're bound to be infringing on the other guy's patents. So that works fine for them; they can afford to sign agreements like that.

"The problem is that the next generation of entrepreneurs—the guys in college today—are going to graduate and launch a product, and the first thing that's going to happen to them is that instead of getting a call from a customer they're going to get a call from a lawyer saying, *You are infringing on our patent and we're going to shut you down,* says Young. "The reason why this is going to happen is because the IBMs and Compaqs are no fools, they understand that the biggest threat is not going to come from each other, it's going to come from the *next* Compaq. It's a fear that some kid in his garage is starting the next Compaq and changing their business. Whatever that innovation turns out to be, they want to own it. They're all in favor of vastly expanded intellectual property rights because it gives them leverage over those bright young kids starting out today. This happens over and over again, where innovative little companies are being put out of business because they can't afford the legal bills to defend their technology offerings."

One of the things that has changed in patent law is that you don't have to produce a working prototype to file a patent. Imagine if you had an idea and all you needed was the money to file it, and not the wherewithal to actually invent it.

"The fact is that you can get patents on things that are not actually inventible. You can get business method patents and 1-Click shopping patents," says Young. "This goes back to the Jefferson/Franklin debates; this was Jefferson's concern at the time of writing the U.S. Constitution. He said that ideas should not be patentable; the compromise was to make inventions patentable. Which is why the rule was that you had to deliver a working prototype of your invention if you hoped to get a patent. Today, you not only don't have to deliver a working prototype of the invention—you can get a patent on what

"*The reason why we called it the 'Electronic Frontier' is that it would always be a frontier. Because of changes in technology and changes in society, there were always going to be tricky questions for possibly hundreds and thousands of years. There will always be tension between established patterns of social behavior and what controls those patterns.*"

—John Perry Barlow, cofounder of the Electronic Frontier Foundation

is essentially an idea. So Amazon gets a business methods patent on 1-Click shopping on the Internet. 1-Click Shopping isn't an invention—there are 106 ways you could write software to enable your web site to offer the ability to buy something with one click. Essentially what you do is allow your customers to register all their information online, and with the proper cookie he can go into your site and with one click order something.

"Given this award, Barnes & Noble had to add a second click to its shopping experience," Young says. "It's not that Barnes & Noble had stolen any software code from Amazon, or had used an algorithm that Amazon had invented. Barnes & Noble had invented a completely unrelated code that simply implemented that same idea, but in fact it was Amazon's patent on the idea that forced Barnes & Noble to add another click to their shopping experience. You look at that and say, *That's just wrong.* There was no economic, moral, or any other justification for giving a government-enforced monopoly to Amazon on that idea."

"The Patent Office is giving people patents on products where there is no way of knowing if they are manufacturable, or if one will actually execute the way the patent says it's executable."

> —Bob Young, chairman of Red Hat
> and founder of the Center for the Public
> Domain

Can Young see it from the other side of the table? Although he has a company, it is a company based on open source code. I mean, can he see the advantage of why a company like Amazon would want to patent 1-Click?

"In all of the businesses I've started, all of them could have benefited from business method patents, and I could be sitting here arguing the exact opposite point of view, but I didn't need to stop my competitors. I was able to build a 20-million-dollar-a-year business around one-week computer rentals. I could have been awarded this patent and been able to get the FBI to shut down my competitors, but I just couldn't figure where the value was in doing such a thing. I can't figure out how our society is enriched by having the government award 20-year monopolies around business ideas—there's no justification to it."

Do foreign countries look favorably upon American copyright laws? "Microsoft may have a big amount of support in the United States compared to the amount of criticism it gets in England; there, Microsoft in not a hero. In France, Microsoft is not perceived as a wonderful corporation, it's just another big, evil, dominant American corporation. Microsoft can go to Washington and get a relatively friendly hearing, compared to what it gets when going to Brussels or Paris.

There's already a growing gap between intellectual property rules in Europe and America over things like the ability to slap patents on genes, which I thought Clinton and Blair had gotten together and said they weren't going to do certain things. But I guess there's still some controversy around a breast cancer gene that some American medical company has the U.S. patent on and is going around extracting fees from anyone trying to study this gene to build breast cancer remedies. That's not what the patent system is for; it's supposed to accelerate research, it's not supposed to give some company the right to reduce the amount of research going on."

Patenting software is a strange balance between the world of copyright and patents. Having written code, and having written books, language *is* language and creating laws that make it work and flow is an essential part of both.

"Software borders on speech and engineering and it's got important aspects of both in it," says Dave Winer, CEO of Userland Software Inc. "And they comingle, and it's really hard to know when you're writing and when you're engineering. So patents are kind of a weird thing, in the context of writing. Imagine as an author, I had written a book where the theme was boy meets girl, and I get a patent on that, and from that point on nobody could write a book about boy meets girl—you'd have to write about something else. But, of course, practically every book that's been written has been about boy meets girl. No matter how you want to disguise it, that's what's going on. Software is littered with things like this; the whole profession of writing software involves resynthesising techniques that you have used many times before, and other people have used many times before. You don't know where the idea originated and it's impossible to know who did it. There's a lot of people who are looking at it as, *boy meets girl is my new idea, I'm going to patent that.* As opposed to, *my new idea is boy meets girl.* In the early '90s the

U.S. Patent and Trademark Office started accepting software patents, and they began granting them in the mid-'90s—and it's starting to become very clear that some very boy meets girl stuff is owned by people who didn't invent it.

"It's a crazy situation, and it's impossible to know how it's going to shake out. It means lawyers are invading technology—basically the software is being developed by lawyers, and although lawyers may be very good at filing lawsuits and getting court orders, programming is a different profession than being a lawyer. Programmers don't like to ask for permission to do things, so we're going to have a hell of a fight over this."

Another component of the patent issue is the open standards issue; when a company builds its software to standards that have been set by the industry so that competition is healthy. Winer has been in the game for a while and says open standards are a necessity to the growth and usability of Internet software.

"I think open source code always has had a place in the development process. When you want other people to adopt your way of doing things, giving them free source code to implement that goal is considered part of the deal. Most standards have worked out that way. A lot of people think open source is something new. It's not terribly new; it goes to the generosity of programmers who do it because they want to create new toys and work group stuff—I mean, it's no fun to have a walkie-talkie if you're the only one to have one. So that's the premise; it's always worked that way.

"At the same time, there's always been commercial software, and that is a different kind of thing, so each has its place. If your software plays well with other software, it means you shared something with other developers and didn't get paid for it. That's the way it works."

Winer is outspoken but still diplomatic, and he has been

able to walk the fine line and be partners with both Microsoft and the open source communities. Because he's able to pull and give value to all, he won the *WIRED* magazine's 2001 *RAVE Award* for Tech Renegade of the Year.

"*We* need to look out for proprietary protocols, control, and ownership in places where we've had freedom before. So the underlying genius [of an open Internet protocol] was Vint Cerf and Bob Kahn and TCIP. The Internet is defined by its protocols, not its code; and there are people who are in the position to be able to control the Internet now."

—Brewster Kahle, cofounder of
The Internet Archive

"We're building our product completely with open standards. In other words, if you have an outliner you prefer, then you'll be able to be part of this network using your outliner—you don't have to use ours. That's because we're committed to doing that, we don't think customers should have to buy software where there's the extra hidden price or you can't switch if you don't like where they're going. That's also been the philosophy behind the Internet, going all the way back to the beginning—that's also the philosophy of programming. That, *Hey—my software is so good, I don't need to lock you in, and if it ever gets to not being that good then you should switch. And I'm going to give you that extra value in my software right up front by saying if you ever see me doing anything that makes it impossible for you to switch, you have to call me on it. My job is to make sure*

*you not only get a great user experience, and it performs well, and
it gets improved quickly enough—I also have the feature that you
can switch when you want.* Then we're all free."

ICANN

Remember all of those URLs you registered in the heyday of
the Internet? Well there's some voodoo of sorts that goes on
after you register a URL with Register.com, or other registration companies. Then it all ends up sorted out at this organization called The Internet Corporation for Assigned Names
and Numbers (ICANN), based in Los Angeles. The nonprofit's charter is to assume responsibility for the IP address
space allocation, protocol parameter assignment, domain
name system management, and root server system management functions previously performed under U.S. government
contract by the Internet Assigned Numbers Authority
(IANA) and other entities.

Before ICANN became just about one of the hottest, most
controversial topics of the Web for the year 2001, there was just
one person who did what ICANN is grappling with today—
holding it all together. It is true that one guy, the late Jon Postel,
was fairly amazing and responsible for a good many things during his lifetime, including working on the early development of
Internet protocols, the creation of the TCP/IP documenter, and
was the codeveloper of many of the key Internet standards, including TCP/IP (basic Internet protocols), SMTP (e-mail
transfer), and DNS (name servers). He also founded the IANA,
and made many other crucial contributions to the Internet, and
he was also a tremendous advocate of conservation of protocol
and port numbers. Postel died in 1998, without seeing much of
the dot-com Gold Rush and the tremendous amount of change
that would take place in only a matter of years, and the com-
plexities those changes would cause.

Now, ICANN, with such luminaries as Chairman Vinton Cerf, Alejandro Pisanty, Amadeu Abril Abril, Karl Auerbach, Robert Blokzijl, Ivan Moura Campos, Lyman Chapin, and Jonathan Cohen on its current board, seeks to find ways to meet the new challenges. Some of the biggest challenges it faces are the essentials of any new organization—deciding, for example, how to vote and who should be allowed to cast a ballot. It does have an arbitration system for URL disputes, but it has been viciously attacked recently about its alleged favoritism of corporations. The decisions it makes are not binding, so there is little use of taking a claim to ICANN. When I was in the San Jose Federal Courthouse waiting for Dmitry Sklyarov's arraignment to begin, I listened in on a case having to do with the ownership rights of a URL. The company said that it had received the award of rightful ownership from ICANN, and the judge didn't blink, didn't ask to see it, just moved right along and established another date for the case to be heard in its entirety.

In 2001, ICANN and VeriSign Inc., formally entered into revised agreements under which the Internet's .com, .net, and .org domains will be operated for the next several years. Although I'm not sure of the exact deal cut, ICANN will receive several dollars from each domain name registered to keep its efforts moving forward. All domain-naming companies will filter their information through VeriSign. Before the new agreements, VeriSign operated the Internet's .com, .net, and .org registries under agreements with ICANN and the U.S. Department of Commerce that could have been extended to 2007. Under new agreements, VeriSign will retain its right to operate the .org registry until 2002. The .net registry agreement will expire in June 30, 2005, and prior to that time will be opened for competitive rebidding, unless market measurements indicate that an earlier expiration date is necessary for competitive reasons. VeriSign will continue to operate the .com registry until at least the 2007 expiration date, and agreed to enhanced measures (including annual audits arranged by ICANN and made available to the U.S. government) to ensure that its registry operation unit gives equal treatment to all domain name registrars, including VeriSign's registrar business. Under the 1999 agreements, the U.S. Commerce Department's approval was required for the replacement agreements. On May 18, the Commerce Department approved the agreements, after VeriSign agreed to a shorter term for the agreement concerning .net.

All of this may change. It seems that ICANN is one of those evolving organizations that is going through conflict and struggling with its power and conflicts inside and outside the organization.

As ICANN grew into its own over the last few years, the domain registration landscape changed as Network Solutions was acquired by VeriSign, one the world's most visible companies when it comes to security, encryption, verification, and electronic signatures. With this acquisition, VeriSign also takes on Network Solution's reputation for heinous customer service and all that means. From personal experience, I can tell you that it is no piece of cake to try to change anything at Network Solutions. I long for the day they have a verification system in place that makes more sense than staying on hold for an hour and faxing personal documents such as my passport and my driver's license to who knows who there.

The following story is that of Gary Kremen, a very colorful character from Chicago and a computer science graduate who has an MBA from Stanford Business School—not your average proprietor of porn. Kremen, founder of Match.com, director of Sex.com, and chairman of Grant Media LLC, the entity that owns the equity in Sex.com, is one of the people speaking loudest about having issues with ICANN. Kremen says that he registered the URL Sex.com in 1993 with Internic, the domain-name registration body that is now controlled by Network

"I'm seriously skeptical that there will be many more big stories about people being paid large sums of money for their [URL] registrations. I could be wrong about that, but eventually people will figure out that they can register these various trademark names only if they have the right to them."

—Vinton Cerf, cofather of the Internet and senior vice president of Internet Architecture and Technology at WorldCom

Solutions, and it wasn't until 1995 that he realized that someone was squatting on his site.

"A guy forged a letter—he didn't even forge my name—he forged the name of someone who really doesn't have anything to do with it," says Kremen of the long battle that still continues. "It was '95 before I realized anything was going on with the name—I was busy running a company—Match.com. They didn't call me, they didn't contact me—they just turned it over. And when I showed up and said, *Give it to me,* they said, *When we see a court order we'll give it back to you.* It took me $3.1M in cash—and I got a $65M judgment out of the guy. And who has $3.1M in discretionary income? But that's why I fought—I knew it was worth it. Network Solutions got out of it [the case he brought against them] because they said, *It isn't property, and we can't be negligent.* An interesting argument, and I think the challenge with that argument is an appeal, and I'm working on that right now. It is property, the judge was wrong. It was in a rare period of time when Net-work Solutions didn't have a contract or a dispute policy, that was the worst of times. But I had sent the registration via reg-istered mail. I served Network Solutions with a court order and they didn't comply with it for 10 days, so I'm actually suing them for 10 days of income, about $150,000."

When I spoke with Kremen via his cell phone I could hear echoes and footfalls on a wooden floor. Curious, I asked him if he was in an empty room. In fact he was, pacing to and fro through room after room in a $4 million mansion he had recently recovered from the $65 million judgment he received. He made a comment about the algae-filled pool he had found and kept on his rounds, evaluating his new acquisition. "Tracking down this guy's stuff is a full-time job, and now he's in Mexico, a fugitive from justice. He's appealed, but there's this interesting rule that says if you're a fugitive you lose your right to appeal."

And this is life in the post dot-com aftermath—even now, perhaps more so, it seems like the Wild West. Only now people fight it out in court. And ICANN is finding itself in the middle of these controversial times; people expecting it to have the authority to do something when is actuality it isn't a part of the government, but rather a non-profit organization.

I attended a small ICANN fact-finding meeting at VeriSign's Silicon Valley headquarters, and found that there were people from many different opinions there. Much of the banter between attendees who were given the podium and members of ICANN was polite, but there were moments when it got downright hostile. I do not envy ICANN's job to standardize the process and make the organization work smoothly. It seems there are so many special-interest camps from so many countries that ICANN surely has a job as for-midable as that faced by the United Nations.

"It's been controversial to do [what ICANN is doing], and it had been done for 25 years by one person, Jon Postel, but he died in 1998," says Vinton Cerf, chairman of ICANN. "Before he died, many of us pressed Jon to institutionalize the function because we didn't think that it should be done on a personal basis anymore, but that it had to be done as a continuing institution. Ultimately, the White House and Ira Magaziner got involved to set the framework for the creation of ICANN. The process has taken place in accordance with a white paper that came out of Magaziners' intervention. It doesn't mean everyone is happy about it, but the system is moving forward pretty well and it's starting to get its funding mechanisms in place, and it's been making policy decisions which essentially are sticking. So, I would say it's in reasonable shape right now but it still has work to do in respect to funding."

"I think we have an overall mission that we have to take very seriously," says M. Stuart Lynn, president and CEO of ICANN. "It's to make sure that the Internet is stable in the areas that we deal with—what's called the 'real estate' of the Internet; the names and numbers and so forth. We need to make sure that the users of the Internet don't encounter strange happenings. So when you send e-mail to someone, you want to make sure it arrives at the right place. The electric utilities provide a nice example for our reasoning; we don't want to become the future power companies of the Internet, where we took it all for granted when it was ample and available, and only woke up and noticed something existed when things went wrong. And so, in some ways, as far as the users are concerned, everything is working perfectly from their perspective. And if they've never heard of us it's okay. Our objective is to make it work reliably, and that's our continuous challenge.

"We want to ensure the full internationalization of ICANN.

ICANN is a very interesting experiment in some people's eyes; some people think of us as an experiment in governance, but I certainly don't see us as a government at all. We do and are responsible for coordinating policy—a grassroots development internationally in the area we're responsible for. We have some work to do before we complete the globalization of ICANN. Today we're wrestling with what's the right governance structure for ICANN, what and how our overall constituency should be represented within ICANN, and how we can be structured to make sure that it reflects the interests of our users. That's a pretty tough one to sort out because everyone feels they are underrepresented and everyone else is overrepresented. That's certainly a challenge."

"ICANN's role is always evolving and changing. We're two-and-a-half-years-old. A good part of the first two years were spent as a startup, where the question was, is ICANN going to exist? Now, I think it's far less the question of can ICANN exist? and more a question of what should ICANN be? And how should we move it forward?"

—M. Stuart Lynn, president and CEO of ICANN

"I think there are some particular issues such as the internationalization of the domain naming system. How will we address the problem of representation in character strings other than the Roman character strings that underlie the English language? And that's of great importance as we talk about internationalization of ICANN and the domain system, and extremely important to communities around the world for whom the English, or Roman scripts are not native. This is an issue that has great bearing of maintaining the root, although we're very pleased by our progress and coping with what could be a very big problem. *We have a lot to do and a lot to work on and I think we're making progress.* When you're trying to bring multiple constituents together who have very different perspectives it's often tough to move things through; and our board is very good at making things happen. We are a transparent organization open to the community; we're not just some closed corporation fashioning strategy in private. Everything we do is public and transparent and we invite anyone who wants to be involved; in fact, we welcome more involvement."

This Internet of ours has certainly created a plethora of issues—some imagined, some not—and as we figure out how to streamline processes, and even, perhaps, how to let go and free-fall and see where it takes us; I think intuition is perhaps our greatest strength in times like these. And since, in the first place, the decision to open Pandora's Box was taken out of our hands, the best thing we might be able to do at this point is to balance the perspective of Bob Young, who believes we should have trust in the original spirit of the Constitution, with the viewpoint of John Perry Barlow, who warns that we should always question authority.

4

Who Will?

After September 11, 2001, everything seems quite insignificant now. What I mean is that our little technology slump seems really unimportant in comparison. We had about a month of mourning, during a time when none of the CEOs I know were really making any strategic plans. Everyone was waiting and watching. And when the smoke cleared and the market seemed to stop hiccupping on an hourly basis, I began getting my calls returned with people's post 9/11 comments that ended up in this version of the book.

We picked ourselves up, counted ourselves among the lucky living, and faced the new challenges. Then, as I checked my e-mails from Dave Farber's list—it's like having some kind of symbiotic intelligence hookup to the rest of the world—I began to see a severe pattern developing. Every day there was word about some piece of legislation to control technology, or a new technology that would aid in ending terrorism—retinal scanners, electronic palm readers, et cetera. Yeah, there was a trend, all right. That was when I decided to change this book (and drive my poor editor, who has the patience of a saint, up a wall with this ever-changing deadline). The world had changed and everything in technology had changed with it. Our attitudes. Everything.

As I look around at my desk, the vestiges of this dead-line—stacks and stacks of microcassette tapes and digital videos of interviews, empty blister packs of Vivarin, half-drank Jolt Colas—nothing in my physical landscape has changed much. Nothing except the computer. Not exactly the computer—rather the connection, the line, the lifeline leading into it.

The Internet had changed as a collective whole after 9/11—we as a world have changed and the collective consciousness of the Web has changed with us. For the first time since I've had the Web, it became integral in finding the opinions of others, of keeping my finger on the pulse. It offered a tremendous value besides my e-mail and a Google search (not that those are insignificant in my life), and the more I began talking to people, the more I found I wasn't the only one. It seemed as though our adolescent toy had experienced a growth spurt.

And as I continued to talk to more and more people about their plans for future products, I not only saw optimism, I saw a determination for them not to become victims of the downturn—and a new challenge to change the world, for the better.

THE PIPELINE

I don't know when I first started doing it, but one of my friends in Los Angeles pointed it out to me in 1995; Trey Nichols asked me to join him for a few days to see a production he had written; shake some of the Silicon Valley stuff off, and have some fun. I regretfully turned him down, saying, "Sorry, sounds like fun, but I just don't have the bandwidth." Trey has had the same AOL account for more than a decade and is a playwright by trade; in other words, he knows nothing about bandwidth. He said, *What?* And that's when I was called on the carpet for integrating techno-speak with *real* language. And I'm not the only one. People are doing this all around me, all the time, diluting the English language with tech talk. It's become the standard here in the Valley. It's become integrated. And as our personal bandwidth—as a description of our free time to be out and about—narrows, we're demanding that the Internet bandwidth—the pipeline coming into our computers and into our PDAs—also expands to take on a more robust role so we can do more with less, so to speak. More bandwidth, less time. And with people traveling less—and the stock of companies that have anything at all to do with video conferencing on the rise—we want our bandwidth to do *everything, and more.*

And it's clear that this 24/7 attitude to be connected to our peripheral devices—as in the things that currently hang on our bodies; PDAs, cell phones, digividcams, etc.—will also bleed over into the next generation of many technologies. But it's all about demand and need, and as Americans, we love to be entertained. So while the rest of the world works out the kinks in copyright, the technologists will build the platforms to bring you movies directly to your handheld. And you'll be able to do live video conferencing from that same tool. Our *Bat Man factor* will go down a bit, and our utility belts won't need to be as sturdy.

Oh yeah, and the method to pay for all this stuff, in a micropayment type of mechanism, will also be part of the puzzle that enables the rest of the technology to flow. Hey, if Napster had spent half their energy trying to work with the copyright owners and enabling a micropayment system instead of fighting for their right to enable the breaking of copyright laws, they would be king. Oh well, lessons learned and all that. . . .

Lawrence Roberts

Cofather of the Internet;
Chairman, Caspian Networks

Lawrence Roberts set up shop just a few miles from Cisco, and you can tell by his intensity that he plans to be a major player in the network space. "I don't think Cisco is our primary competition. Cisco is in this space trying to sell carrier equipment, but Juniper has been a big impact on them already. Anybody who does a good job in the carrier space is going to beat Cisco because it has to concentrate on its corporate space, so carriers usually find that it never meets its deadlines on changes because it's always doing something for someone else."

Roberts comments that the days of acquisitions to purchase companies more agile than your own are probably over with. "I think that strategy is getting tired; Lucent and Nortel totally failed at purchasing companies. Cisco managed to do it more or less, but you can't see the remains of many of their purchases anymore."

Do technologists learn from the past to apply a wiser approach to the present?

"The four of us who won the Draper Prize—Bob [Kahn], Vint [Cerf], Len [Kleinrock], and I—we've been involved for 30 years. Vint was a grad student when we started, but he's in it. We all saw it as a career and we wanted to change the world and make it happen and we stayed with it. For me, given the history, now I see very few people willing to make changes, and it's become more of a religion that you can't change it. It's become more of a religious fervor than not changing it because it's a standard. More that, *It's worked for 30 years and don't touch it.* But really we should. We set up the machines in the core of the Network to be dumb because we wanted to make them work properly, so that if ATT or anyone set up the Network we could explore and experiment from the edge and try different things. We've done that for 30 years and no one has changed a thing. We know now what the problems are, and that it doesn't have any good quality of service, the delay variation is high, the recovery time is slow—the reliability is relatively low, although it's very reliable as a network, but per node it's low.

We know how to improve the utilization of the Network. It [the Network] is running at 40 percent, which is low compared to what it could be—and that's about as high as we can run it the way it's operating. We understand what's wrong with the thing, so why can't we fix it? We tried to do ATM, which was an attempt to try and put some things into another protocol, and that was not the one people were using, and it had a lot of mistakes in it that made it fail in large part. Taking all of that and putting it together, I decided to take that knowledge and design a new switchworks with the current network and protocols, but implementing some of the new concepts that we've learned so that it can handle voice and video, get the cost down and the quality up, and increase stability."

When Larry tells you something, you tend to believe him. He has fire in his belly and a gleam in his eye, and as he told me more he had me so wrapped in his vision that I actually got goosebumps. Yeah, I think he's going to do it; I think he's going to help enable the Internet to go to its next stage.

"What I'm seeing now as we design our product with a number of customers, is that this is the next generation switch for the Internet. No one else has tried to do it, and no one else has the 30 years of experience to understand enough to do it. There are very significant changes in the intelligence of the switch that we've put in to make it work a lot better, a lot faster, and a lot cheaper. People think intelligence will cost money, but it doesn't. Smart people actually work smarter and cheaper. It's the same way with computers as far as I can see. This is such an improvement in the terms of network cost, delay, efficiency, and operation that in order for the Network to shift how it operates people are going to have to copy this. If a carrier puts this in and operates his network at a cost of 10 percent of the cost of his competitors, there's no way his competitors can exist. You really have to switch over at that point. Overall, considering all of their costs, it may only reduce it on a two-to-one or three-to-one basis. That's still a significant enough factor that you'll put everyone else out of business if you continue like that."

Roberts, like most scientists of great curiosity, ponders an issue, does the research, and writes a paper, because that's what it's all still about for these guys, sharing knowledge and creating value for the industry as a whole.

"For the first 30 years, in large part, all we did was increase the number of users and move text," says Roberts of the Internet's slow momentum. "I mean people did other things, but the average volume per person was text and relatively low. From 1999 to now we began increasing the bandwidth per user dramatically. We've pretty much got 50 to 60 percent of the people online in the U.S., and we're not going to double that. So basically the growth per day is now in bandwidth per user. The Network is growing at four times per year as I've recently measured and published a paper on it [www.caspiannetworks.com/tech/whitepapers/index.shtml]. We interviewed all of the T-1 carriers under nondisclosure and found out what was happening. And it's growing even faster at the moment, since people are substituting it for travel. It's been growing very, very fast since the beginning of 2000. That is basically letting us increase it to where everyone is going to have the ability to do voice and video interactively.

We're going to change the Network so it supports that adequately; and people will move many more files across the Net as the bandwidth expands. Today I get tens of megabytes of files every day inside the corporation, and outside the corporation I also receive vast quantities of e-mail with files, or pointers on where to download them. So the industry has basically taken on the Net as the only way to operate; you can't even do your business without it. Today, I know if I'm trying to convince anyone of anything I have to send them an e-mail as opposed to a letter; people hardly look at mail."

"*I recently saw that the program that DARPA started [ARPANET] had a 100,000-to-one return for the U.S. on the money spent—and I doubt if any other program in history has had that kind of return as far as the economic return. That's what ARPANET's goal was—to have a huge impact. What I tried to negotiate in '73 when I left was turning it over to industry, and AT&T said 'No, we're not interested, go away.' They said it wasn't compatible with their network.*"

—Lawrence Roberts, cofather of
the Internet and chairman,
Caspian Networks

"Corporate America has shifted; the rest of the world hasn't yet. I think it'll happen next year or the year after," says Roberts about the rate of acceptance. "We see the growth of the rest of the world at numbers where we were pre-2000. But in the U.S. it's growing very, very fast. So what does this mean for the future? It means that once we introduce equipment that will handle delay effectively, and will support video and voice interactively—once we can do that, and it'll probably be another two years before that's installed throughout the world—I think the growth in bandwidth will have significant possibilities for doing all of our radio and TV over the Net."

Roberts has the future all figured out as far as how people will interact with the Internet and what will be coming out of that pipeline. And, I have to say, he really sold me on this future—it sounds viable.

"People will have one channel in their house and they won't have cable, or satellite, or Internet separately. It will be a single line—a single line that handles everything. And now that I can get my radio and TV and entertainment and everything over the Internet, instead of by other means—then what will I be doing with it? Well, I'll probably be looking at something other than what you will for the same event. I'll probably be using that interactivity to change where I'm looking at it, how I'm looking at it, and when I'm looking at it, and shifting around and doing other things.

"So, when I'm watching a football game, I may be watching a different player than you will; I may be watching from a different place. That technology is available with a little work. My Ph.D. thesis was on taking multiple video views and converting them into a 3-D image, then looking at it from a different viewpoint than any of the cameras; being able to look at it from the side rather than the front or back. Now I can control the camera view of whatever I want and from any point of view. That was easy enough to do with tables and chairs, which is what I did in my thesis, but it hasn't been done fully for people in high motion. It's going to take good computing power and good capabilities, but that's possible. All this means is that I can start thinking about interactive travel, looking around as myself rather than reading a travel log. Interactive meetings where I can be talking to whomever I want, wherever I want; I can be wandering around the halls; I can choose to do what I want to do. If I had a little more capability I would avoid going to meetings. And that's what's happening with air travel being less attractive.

"People are saying that Net meetings are pretty good; I was on a conference call with 200 people on the Web where they were looking at my image, looking at my slides, and hearing my voice over a conference bridge. The voice can't go over the Net right now because the Net isn't good enough yet. All of that can be improved pretty dramatically, so pretty quickly we'll get to the place where the technology is supporting us to use it for video, voice, and ways we've never used it before. That entertainment picture in my mind is what's going to drive the volume in the latter part of the decade. Once we get that online and working you're going to see all of radio and TV shifting over to where they're doing content for you to watch any way you want. What's going to succeed? Nobody can predict that."

What has Roberts seen on an international level as far as trends on the Internet, or using IP? "What we've seen in Korea in the last year or so is that they've put broadband into every house, they're all apartments and high-rises, so it's easy. You can bring fiber to the basement and broadband up to every apartment, and its been a very, very wide penetration of broadband in Korea compared to the U.S. One thing the Koreans are very excited about is multiperson gaming, and so there's a vast amount of that going on. That is not what our society is interested in doing. But they are, and they're doing it and they're finding it very exciting. Just like in Japan, some things go over there that didn't go over here. DoCoMo has huge success with cell phone e-mail; here it was a failure because everybody had much better e-mail and they're not willing to substitute it for a very cheap thing that doesn't have the bandwidth or capacity, or to try and get their e-mail to roll over. I get huge files that I could never get over my cell phone. But, if you don't have anything it's great, and they've had huge success. We may have to move to a much more powerful cell phone here before that happens. I believe the mobile device I'm carrying will have many megabits of bandwidth within a couple of years. That's to new telephone standards and better mobility as well. We've solved some of the radio problems in the last few years. So now you should be able to carry around a device that handles full video, full voice, full everything, and talk to anyone and retrieve anything you want over the Web and have full functionality. How big it is, or what shape it is is something that someone's going to have to figure out. They may like a PDA version, or even bigger; whatever that is it will be a major part of our lives. Another part of it is to get new functionality across it. My guess is that on the cell phone someone is going to do a very good browser that works and has the right resolution and works—and someone else will fail totally. It's a question of how good the engineer is at working out the human engineering and reducing the number of clicks."

So how soon should we all start seeing Roberts' world? "What we're working on is to be able to make all of that feasible is that you have to have tremendous growth of the Network, which is happening, but you have to be able to sustain that growth. The equipment today? What we're seeing is an unfortunate circumstance that starting this year, the demands of the largest nodes in each of the carrier networks is getting larger than Moore's Law would allow the equipment to support. Moore's Law says technology is doubling every 18 months, but soon it [the demand] will have it doubling every six months—so how do you keep up with that with the size of the equipment? If you exceed that capacity you have to put boxes together in a collection interconnected by their own ports. The result is a very inefficient cost—four to 20 times what it would have been if you could have done it right.

"That means you need some kind of switch that can scale to large sizes, what we've seen scale to large sizes is the Internet itself. Our switch is sort of a miniature copy of the Internet, a distributed switch that can be as big as you want without any extra cost—that's virtually a requirement of the future, that you be able to scale to a large size to support the Network.

"Today we have kind of an unfortunate circumstance where if you're the largest carrier in the U.S. who is looking at your cost, then your cost is starting to become more than that of your competitor, who is smaller per bit because you're having to put all these boxes together to do your job. They don't have to because they have a smaller net. There are 20 competitors on the backbone of the Internet, and it's pretty competitive. And if there's no economy of scale, or if there's a dis-economy of scale up at the top, then the equalization moves pretty quickly and the people at the bottom move up. The cost is being reduced by a factor of two every year for Internet service per bit, so the competitor that has the best price and the best service will win quickly; it's a commodity so you can go anywhere you want."

What about copyright? How does Roberts see his picture of the future fitting in with copyright, availability, and micropayment? "If you look at the money spent today on both content and communication, the Department of Commerce figures $60 a month, $20 a month is content—TV and movies. The content is a much lower fee than communications, but it could be incorporated in a single $80 fee to every household. If we went to a flat rate, that would be simple—if

I was looking at a movie I'd be paying the distributor of those rights, and if I was reading someone's book I'd be paying them. Then people would stop complaining about pay per view; it would go to their monthly bill and it would go to whomever you were looking at. I think it'll go that way, I think it'll stay pay per view in a lot of ways. Just like the cell phone, they thought they could get more money, now they're going to more of a flat rate than time.

"To begin with, everything goes to the pay per minute, or pay per book kind of concept. Many authors have said, *If I could just write for the Internet directly and publish it online, and I could charge $1 for my book instead of the publisher selling it for $20 and getting the same money as I would otherwise—and more people would read it.* People like that idea, but it just hasn't been done because of all of the things in the way of making it happen. I think the way things will go is that the big conglomerates will fail and although the content of the past will have been owned by them, the content of the future will be put directly on the Net. As soon as the mechanism is there for me to put my book, or my movie or my whatever on the Net and that I will be paid a reasonable low fee for that use, then I think the conglomerates and corporations will just disappear. There's no way for them to exist. I can put my own thing on the Web and do my own job, so I've destroyed them basically. I think buying them up [entertainment companies] and thinking that it's the future is a mistake—I don't think AOL made the right decision, but who am I to say that to Steve?

"I think that we need copyright laws and digital protection mechanisms—security and payment techniques that allow for things to operate over the Internet and allow you to buy what you need at a reasonable price rather than paying all the middlemen with huge markups—because it's just not effective anymore. You have them cut a big piece of plastic in the store that you're buying—you're just getting the music and the cost is dramatically lower on the Internet, and the content itself is only one quarter of the total economy of the whole system, so if I were just to pay incrementally or in a flat fee for that I will have taken care of the issue. But I have to have the microsystem for it to work.

"Cybercash and all of those people have failed to get that into place quickly and easily—they've done the technology, but there are just things in the way of making it happen easily overnight. I think that we'll have the technology in place after a while to do it. It would help if there was one standard mechanism that somebody backed—if the government would stand up and say, *Let's try this rather then everyone trying 16 different things.* Even without that, something will succeed and become the monopoly standard, like Microsoft did with word documents—that was a huge improvement in the ability to distribute documents, to have a standard of sorts. I remember back in the '70s it was impossible to send someone a word document—I had no way to send it from this computer to that—what word processor are you using? There was no way to transfer it from this one to that one. Eventually it was leaders like Microsoft where there were translation programs that would translate other formats. Eventually that led to 80 percent marketshare for one company. That's fine; it doesn't matter to me whether there is one company, two, or three. As long as there's a standard, then that's great, then I can move stuff quickly around. That's true now of spreadsheets and documents, that's valuable and it has its benefits. But there's nothing like that in the payment system, there's nothing I can use so the average customer has any knowledge of, or has a way to interact with, except credit cards; it is a cumbersome, high payment minimum, with technology geared to $10 or more instead of ten cents.

"I think the overall situation is that we'll get to the point where I can buy your book over the Net and I'll have devices where I'd like to read it. I think I'm getting to the point where reading things on tubes is comfortable, but it's still difficult; you have to have good resolution. When it gets to the point where I can carry around a hand-reader and I can get 10 books or 20 books or 100 books that I've downloaded, and the quality and content is as good as the printed page, I'll find that attractive. That isn't far away. And that's not just for books, it's for video—we could do it if you could just download it over the Net, although we're getting to the point where it's reasonable.

"We've already gotten to the point where downloading music was feasible, and then we got into the copyright problems. Everyone I talked to would have been happy to pay their fair share to the artist, but they're not happy paying $12 or $14 to pay for the mogul. They tried to do it another way, and it ended up changing the industry. I don't condone getting it free when the artists should get their money, but I don't like the fact that there isn't a system in place so I can get it directly. There will be a transition where people will fight to hold on to their artists and say, *You can't go there and make it hard for the artist to move to go direct on the Net*. In 10 years it'll be done and we'll have everything that way—maybe it'll be 20. It took 20 years from when I said voice was going to be on the Net, and I said it was going to be 20 years in 1981. It takes a long time for changes to occur."

Len Kleinrock

Cofather of the Internet; Chairman, Nomadix

The first time I met Len Kleinrock I was immediately struck by his sense of wonder. I could almost watch him take the words that came from my mouth and ponder them texturally, viewing them from all angles, and responding thoughtfully. He is not just a technologist who only speaks, he listens a great deal. And he is willing to learn new things, to see things from different perspectives. The second thing I noticed was his sense of warmth and humor; traits not usually found in a technologist of his stature. So couple those great traits and it won't surprise you to learn that along with being the creator of the packet switching theory, one of the cofathers of the Internet, and the chairman of Nomadix, he is also chairman of a little-known but very cool organization called Technology Transfer Institute Vanguard <www.TTIVanguard.com>. TTIV is a unique forum for the introduction, discussion, and evaluation of emerging and breakthrough information technologies. Through conferences and workshops, experts offer perspectives from managerial, business, scientific, and sociological disciplines. The result is a framework for linking strategic technology planning to business success. And the list of speakers is phenomenal.

"During the conference, using Nomadix technology, the audience can plug their devices into the conference's high-speed Internet access and everyone can be online during the entire conference," says Kleinrock, and I can see that he's quite pleased about being able to so completely enable people to communicate in such a seamless way. "What they should be doing with that connection is looking at our web site with the information about the speaker and related issues, and writing critical e-mails. You shouldn't be playing games—but that's critical in itself because if you're boring the audience, you're going to lose them, big time. So this is a very challenging audience and setup—how can we attract all these great people if they're going to be cut off from their communication? We wouldn't be able to, so we connect them—they're online all the time. That's living and breathing nomadic technology."

It's obvious that, like Roberts, Kleinrock is still in the game, and they are still creating products and ideas of great value; both contributing back to the industry in which they made their careers.

So now Kleinrock has this plug-and-play technology that I suspect will one day be a standard. The name of his company, Nomadix, is based on the root word *nomadic,* which is what he's labeled the industry of any time, anywhere, any device. The enabling technology to be completely nomadic wherever you go and still be perfectly wired to the hilt.

"The user, his device, his IP address and location were all tightly coupled together; that was the right model at the time for deskbound computing," says Kleinrock of the early days. "We have all of the mobile devices now. The architecture had to change—I call that whole domain *nomadic computing.*"

He feels that ubiquity is also part of the equation—the seamless interaction, the ease of use, the invisibility. "Windows is anything but ease of access. I don't want my mother to ever have to boot up Windows. I mean, it's crazy that she would have to do that. I bought her WebTV. The interface issue becomes important and is also an issue in nomadic computing. We want the same GUI—the same appearance—as well as the same interface, no matter where we go or what device we're using, whether it be a palm-top, a wristwatch, a full screen, or a high-resolution display. That's part of making your presence ubiquitous and constant—

your personalized availability to services everywhere you go in the same fashion. That has not happened yet. When I travel, I carry a laptop, a PDA, a two-way e-mail pager cell phone, and a scientific calculator. That means I have five keyboards, five displays, five databases, four different alarm clocks, five different kinds of batteries, and most of them don't talk to each other—it's crazy.

"Nomadix takes the point of view that we want to provide the same set of services to you wherever you go—personalized, customized services, independent of the device you have, in a transparent fashion. And we have attacked a large piece of that, where you can gain access with whatever particular device you have through a plug-and-play capability, and we can identify you through an access control and identification engine that we have. We can authorize your access and also provide the other key piece, which is a billing interface. When you roam out of your area you have global roaming with your cell phone—you should also be able to get global roaming with your IP device, which is now beginning to happen. So if you move into some-one else's IP service area, they have to know that it was you, Sally, who took service from that service provider, get that call record back to them and let them settle the billing behind the scene. Nomadix sits at the edge and notices, *Oh, you're now at this end of the network doing this amount of work,* and that infor-mation goes into the billing system.

"The fourth thing we do, other than the plug-and-play, is the access control and billing. We present and enable these services to you—the same ones that you want wherever you go. It might be access to various ASPs, URL filtering, caching, streaming media—we know your profile because your subscriber database contains that and we use a lot of web-based provisioning and Java pop-ups so wherever you go, once we know you're you, we can present to you what you expect."

One of the things I noticed by this time in our conversation, just as I had noticed with Larry Roberts, is that both men seem to have been living their lives for this exact moment in time where they've been anticipating technology all of these years, working with it, playing with it—and then like well-honed darts, they both hit the target.

"The latest and greatest market we've found is in this new, emerging, exploding domain of public hotspots—the 802.11b wireless public access spots—the hotels, the airports. The piece that's missing in that domain is exactly what we have. Right now they've got the link technology and the applications, but they can't put it together with *you,* the user. We provide that very critical piece of software, so we're very much involved now. The nice thing is the way we've developed the technology—we are link-agnostic, and we don't care what the underlying technology is. It could be copper, fiber, cable, or wireless. It's good that we developed the technology that way because now that the technology has exploded, we're sitting right there, at the right time, and the right moment ready to deliver this immediately. No development time required—*Boom, here we are, take it.*"

When I mention to Kleinrock my observation about timing, being at the right place and time, and not only having developed it from the beginning, but helping it evolve, he says there is a thread that led him directly from where he did his Ph.D. and created packet switching design to now.

"There is a thread there; back in my Ph.D. I used a fundamental principle, that if this system is going to scale to large numbers of anything, it can't have centralized control. It's got to be distributed control. Back then, it manifested itself in the form of distributed routing, and the kind of routing we have now. But, it's true throughout, you have to distribute the capability, the control, and distribution of content among all of the users on all the parts of the system, not in one centralized, all-knowing, all-controlling authority. And that has been the social mantra of the Internet as well."

Does Kleinrock see an end to the technology downturn we're currently in? "Right now we're going through a consolidation, merger acquisition phase, and that'll go on for a little while. It'll be followed by the birth and creation of a lot of technology that will be disruptive, and they'll be able to start new markets, and they'll be rolled up again as they mature. We're in the maturing phase right now. I do believe that there are some giants emerging, and that all of our digital content media will be rolled up into a single kind of service; it'll be an integrated service—we'll get our e-mail, our video, our voice, our fax, our Internet access, streaming data—everything— through one common interface. They'll be new forms of exciting, niche technology stepping forward, be they animated avatars, or technologies based on sound-and-sight interface. Whatever it is, it'll probably come out of small companies that will capture the imagination of the public. It's not like this is the death of the small innovative entrepreneur, but this is just a cycle where they don't have a very strong capability because of the funding issue. There will always be a need for new technology. We've proven that over and over again. I don't see that going away."

Vinton Cerf

Cofather of the Internet; Senior Vice President of
Internet Architecture and Technology, WorldCom

Vinton Cerf has to be one of the most recognizable digerati in the world, just bringing his name to the board of a company or organization brings it respect. Cerf is senior vice president of Internet Architecture and Technology for WorldCom, and codesigner of the TCP/IP protocol. Cerf has been instrumental in many key happenings in Internet history and is currently the director of ICANN.

"In three years time it'll be roughly 2003, and we will probably have six- to seven-hundred million devices on the Net," says Cerf of future connectivity. "My guess is by 2006 we will have somewhere on the order of 2.5 billion devices on the Net; a good 1.5 billion of those will be cell phones that have been Internet-enabled, and the other 900 million devices will be more conventional kinds of personal computers, machines, PDAs, and things like that. In three years' time I expect that a considerable quantity of devices on the Internet will be attached by radio links—they'll be fairly low-power, fairly high-speed radio links. I'm thinking, for example, of Ericsson's Bluetooth technology, which is a very-low distance way of networking things, and that, I expect, will be a very common mode of operation. It will be operating at nearly the same frequency as cellular phones do. There will be a lot of radio-based devices on the Net, some of them longer-distance things like cell phones that reach over miles. Bluetooth is only intended to be a few feet of connectivity; of course this will force us to put in a lot more cryptography so that we can keep radio-based transmissions private. Otherwise, anyone could receive them.

"There will be, probably in three years' time, about a billion-plus users on the Net, and I have a bet right now with Nick Negroponte . . . I think it'll take two or three years to get to a billion users; he thinks it'll take a much shorter time. I think a lot of wireless stuff will be out there and that PDAs will have merged with telephones to some extent, and they'll all be Internet-enabled cell phones, and I expect that most of these wireless devices will wind up doing multiple jobs. For instance, a PDA with a wireless connection to it could control almost any device in the house that's been Internet-enabled by going out through its Internet connections into the mobile house network. A lot of radio-based devices will be online for control purposes, replacing the infrared kinds of controllers that we have now. In fact, you should require fewer such controllers in the end because you can make one single device do a great deal of extra duty when it comes to controlling things, particularly if you allow the interaction to take place through the network, if that makes sense.

"For instance, a refrigerator might have the ability to go online and look for recipes for what can be made with what's in it, or to respond to a query by saying, *Yes, you have milk, but it's three weeks old.* Things like that—and the refrigerator itself will have an LCD display on it so it can be part of the Web and e-mail system; it will augment the message magnets on the refrigerator today. I would expect global positioning to be very important, and probably integrated with a headset into cell phones. And as you walk around, you can ask for directions and get them. In fact, systems that respond to your voice commands will be interpreting speech and interacting with you on a spoken basis. There is a company worth looking at—Nuance—that does software for speech recognition. It's actually quite a powerful technology and I expect to see a great deal more of that as time goes by."

What about the convergence of nano-, bio-, and Internet technology? "In some sense, we're almost there. The best example of this is the cochlear implant, because the way it works is that you interface to it through a transducer that's magnetically connected to your head. The speech processor right now is external, although they're talking about fully implantable devices some day. But the external speech processor has the advantage that it can physically patch to connect to almost anything that is a source of sound: it could be a Sony Walkman, or an armrest on the seat of an airplane that you plug into to listen to the audio, or a telephone system or mobile telephone. All of those things can be plugged into the speech processor. It's powerful enough that if you chose to you could program it to do Internet protocols, or you could add TCIP chips to the chipset, which is what somebody did a few months ago in order to Internet-enable it. So I expect to see a lot of special-purpose chips that will run Internet protocols, and those chips will either be buried inside the device, or sort of attached to the side of it. These devices then become Internet-enabled and therefore controllable through the Network, so people can use third-party applications that may be accessible through the World Wide Web that sends and receives control signals through the Network to an Internet-enabled device on the Net."

"I think the *Next Generation Internet* is a phrase you'll find people using, that's more associated with the government programs and elsewhere, that are intended to invest in R&D to develop new network technology that the Internet can absorb and evolve into using. I guess the best phrase for me is *Next Generation Internet,* and for that it is not a project but a process. An evolution. There are things that will undoubtedly surprise us. For example, the fact that having a large number of devices online by radio link is still not fully understood, or fully appreciated. We may not know, until we reach a significant penetration of wireless devices, what the statistical significance in the behavior of people using it will be.

"The UUNet, which is our [WorldCom's] commercial backbone, is pushing the edge of the envelope in many dimensions. Its scale is larger than most other backbones, so they'll wind up having to confront some pretty serious scaling problems before almost anyone else does. That means handling larger number of packets, and handling them at a much higher speed, so much of our advanced work is happening there. The vBNS network, [www.vBNS.net] is also exploring some very advanced stuff, including the deployment of IP Version 6, which in my view is going to be necessary but very painful to transition to because we're going to run out of address space. There are additional applications including handling voice or interactive games on the Net that are a challenge, and the vBNS will be working on that as well. I have maybe 100 people working in this area in the vBNS section, and there are at least that many, or more, doing advance work for UUNet in Virginia within screaming distance of AOL, that is one of our biggest customers.

"There are millions of people out there, just like millions of ants on an anthill; if you ever watch an anthill—millions of ants go running around and mostly on any given day most of them don't find anything interesting, but there are so darn many ants that every day a few of them find something interesting and they bring it back to the anthill. The Internet is very much like that. There are hundreds of millions of people out there using it and many of them are trying experiments out; they are ISPs, or researchers, and most of them don't have very interesting results. But because there are so many on the Net, every day 3, or 4, or 10 things happen that are significant—important breakthroughs, new applications coming up. As a result, it feels like we are rushing headlong into the future because every day there are all of these new things happening. It's not me, or WorldCom necessarily, although we like to think that we contribute our share to advance work, but it's literally the cumulative effect of everybody trying things out and some of them finding something that makes the Net seem like it's changing so rapidly. I feel like I'm in a privileged position because I've been able to watch this and be involved with it going on 30 years now. I'm having a great time watching it happen; it's hard not to be enthusiastic about something that 300 million people are having fun with."

Bob Kahn

Chairman, CEO, President,
CNRI

Robert Kahn is chairman, CEO, and president of the Corporation for National Research Initiatives (CNRI), which he
founded in 1986 after a 13-year-term at the U.S. Defense
Advanced Research Projects Agency (DARPA). CNRI was
created as a not-for-profit organization to provide leadership
and funding for research and development of the national
information infrastructure.

"More and more people are getting higher and higher
bandwidth over the Internet at a more affordable rate," notes
Kahn. "And voice over the Internet is going to become more
economical, and we'll start to see video. Right now the people in Hollywood are looking to it for the future. If that's the
case, then all of the projections for a Next-Generation Internet program will come to fruition a lot sooner than we expect.
The government may have to keep nurturing it for a while,
though. A lot of the applications that people are thinking of
are the old applications just transported onto a new medium.
I think the real opportunity in the new medium is doing
things that couldn't have been done before.

"There are something between 70 and 80 million homes
right now [in the U.S.] and many are not Internet-ready right
now, and many people don't know how to make them Internet-
ready. They might know how to get a plug into their house, but
they can't afford to have someone come in and engineer it for
them. This is not going to be much of a start unless it all goes
with radio; if it goes with radio there has to be a standard. I
think it will be a while before that plays out, but I think the
potential is there. Wireless is really going to cause the Internet

to proliferate. I think that's quite the sleeper in this business, no one knows quite how that's going to play out.

"There's a notion that a lot more devices can have IP addresses. I'm not sure what you would do with your refrigerator over the Internet, other than use it as a display, and I'm skeptical that that is going to happen any time soon. Will it communicate with services to reorder? Well, maybe the milk is all there, but it went sour, or what happens when someone replaces the milk where it doesn't belong?"

Kahn is readying himself for the future and sits on boards such as QUALCOMM and the advisory board of AT&T. Kind of ironic reflecting on how hard AT&T fought against all of these guys in the beginning and now AT&T has come to the plate supporting the Internet. Then again, ARPANET might never have had the right alchemy to grow had it been under the commercial guise of AT&T, so in retrospect maybe AT&T actually made the Internet possible by *not* swallowing the Internet when it had the opportunity to do so.

"Right now, there's a lot of work in making more effective use of the copper wire that's there; originally it was the ISDN stuff and DSL and even higher speeds, and now there's a lot of effort on cable to get high-speed access, and companies putting fiber into a lot of places, although not necessarily homes. Those are probably going to be the mainstay of the industry, but there is another possibility, which is wireless. Some people have satellite linkups for data inside their homes; it's not very responsive time-wise. There are other options that are enabled with wireless connections, even in the local loop. There was a tremendous amount of money for broadband in the last few years, and if anything there's more of a consolidation going on, but we still haven't solved the local access part of the problem. I think there's kind of a mismatch here that's going to have to be addressed over the next couple of years about that issue."

A thought that has been on all of our minds, including

the cofathers of the Internet, is how will this technology recession affect where we're going in the future and how soon we're going to get there? "To the extent there's been a turndown in the economy, a lot of the industrial activities are slower than they were before, and there is less willingness to get into the longer-term future-oriented stuff. The government funding in R&D has actually increased recently, and the President's Information Technology Advisory Committee, [otherwise known as PITAC], recommended a few years ago that the funding for UIT R&D be increased significantly, and a lot of that money ended up at the National Science Foundation, which has greatly expanded its programs. In the wake of 9/11, we may see more investment on the national security side as well. Perhaps the money going toward national security will go toward trying to ensure that the network we have now is protected against threats and trying to improve its capability so that we can do a lot more things on it than we can now, things involving collaboration among different parties, and video conferencing.

"I think good investments right now would be in broadband, wireless—and anything that makes the Network safer from threats. What I mean by *threats* is something equivalent to flying a 767 into the middle of the Network—anything that could harm the Network. We've done a lot of work on that in the past, but a lot more could be done. Do you remember when the terrorist attack happened in New York? It was hard to get phone calls through, but the Internet was a reliable means of communication for everybody. I'm just happy that no one also decided to attack the Internet. Nobody thought you could bring down the World Trade Towers. If somebody were clever enough to understand exactly how these things work, they could do a lot of damage. Then the question is, *How do you recover from that?* That's what I would do with an extra million dollars.

"The Internet was designed so that it could survive losing key components. It wasn't like the Network had one key place, where if you could knock that out it would bring down the whole thing; it was very resilient on 9/11. It was there, and useable, and anyone who was associated with it was probably pleased with it. I think it provided for a lot of information to be shared, some on the mark, some not. I can't say how it was helpful to whom, because everyone uses it differently. I was able to keep in touch with everyone I wanted to and it kept me up to date on everything from fact to rumor."

> *"The Network is not a single monolithic thing; it is a lot of interlinked capabilities from many different places. I'm sure that every organization involved has done many different things to improve its capabilities and service, and basically that's what we're experiencing today."*
>
> —Bob Kahn, cofather of the Internet and CEO and president of the Corporation for National Research Initiatives

"I'm very optimistic about the future," says Kahn about how tomorrow looks from his perspective. "You have business cycles that come up and down—you have research interests that shift from area to area, but there are certain basic interests that are pretty constant right across the board. I do believe that we'll have a lot more devices connected to the Net and a lot of them are going to be pretty small. I also think the combination of nano-, bio-, and Internet will be for medical purposes initially."

Fred Baker

Technology Innovator and Cisco Fellow

"When a person uses the Internet, people tend to think of their computer in this big cloud and some number of computers somewhere else," explains Fred Baker, Cisco Fellow, where he advises senior management on industry directions and appropriate corporate strategies. He chaired the Internet Engineering Task Force (IETF) from March 1996 to March 2001. In that forum, he contributed to network management, routing, PPP and frame relay, the integrated and differentiated services architectures, and the RSVP signaling protocol. He now serves on the IETF's Internet Architecture Board, and as a technical contributor.

"The structure that's between you and these other computers is not just one network, but a network of networks," says Baker. "We have backbone networks, we have access networks in UCLA, there are research backbones that are used by the Department of Energy, and this that and the other for any number of purposes. Internet2 is yet another research backbone in this network of networks. It's put together by a consortium of mostly universities.

"Cisco is involved in Internet2 just like we're involved with a lot of networks, because there might be something interesting there that Cisco has a chance to learn, maybe get some technology out of it. Maybe a chance to fund some research that is ultimately good for Cisco's future. And hey, at the end of the day we might even make a buck. Certainly Internet2 is not the end of the line, neither is the NGI (Next Generation Internet) program or YesNet. There will be others after them.

Internet2 has discovered that money helps things run, so what they're finding themselves doing is providing sets of what are called *acceptable use policies* the consortium will sell service to a university for the price of membership, and when Internet2 members talk to each other they get one class of service across one set of links, then they'll turn around and sell service to the great unwashed—basically use their excess bandwidth that way and use it to fund the network operations. Networks are kind of shoestring operations; they don't necessarily want to make a whole lot of money. So they'll use their bandwidth in any way they can in order to fund their network.

"Basically, I think the Internet of tomorrow will be very much like the commercial Network of today. In terms of structure there will be some number of backbone networks, and various people in competition with each other providing various services. I think the backbone 10 years from now will be all optical. Backbone speeds have been doubling every year for the last 15 years—and there's no letup in sight.

We're deploying new interesting things like mobility based on Internet on cell phone, and we're providing all sorts of new services. The questions have now become, *Can I run my toaster at home from my office? Can I run the home network from work?* There are lists of new services that are being dumped onto the Internet backbone and that's driving the need for bandwidth up. Certainly, there has to be a point where we don't need any more bandwidth, but I don't know where that is. So I find myself projecting—if it doubles every year, absent of any other knowledge, in 10 years it will be going two to-the-tenth times faster than it is today. So, we're looking at 10-terabit links.

"At this point physics gets really interesting, because the speed of light is an interesting limit," says Baker. "We've been fighting the speed of light since I got into this industry, and that's one of the reasons why we have to keep making chip sets smaller and smaller and more compact. Not only to get more gates on them, and to keep the things cool, but because the distance between one gate and the next is a gating factor at which the speed the chip can go. So at some point we actually get into a problem where taking the message, changing it from light into electricity, and changing it back into light takes too long, so we're starting to think very seriously in research, and we're actually starting to commercially deploy, probably a year from now, a product where people literally make the switching decision in light. This technology is being researched right now."

What about the man/machine continuum? How does Baker see the seamless blending of mind and technology? "One could envision the *Matrix*. I don't. I think reality is at the end of the day, and technology doesn't rule the world—people rule the world. Technology at the end of the day serves people. You don't need a cell phone in a rice paddy; on the other hand, having communication and connectivity brings up a whole lot of interesting capabilities. For example, Cisco's Networking academy was put online to educate people about how to run a network with Cisco equipment. Microsoft has such a thing and there are a number of companies that have this kind of program.

What Cisco has done is put its stuff on the Web so that it now has 2,700 different schools where kids are being taught how to run a network, and doing a lot of their study by going out on the Web and looking at the latest version; what that means is if you can get on the Internet you can get to that material—it's not a matter of, *Can I ship books to the Congo?* All you need is Internet connectivity, and if it isn't all that fast, but you *can* get there, it's maybe good enough. What that means is tremendous to someone who doesn't have a great deal of opportunity. If Vietnam can connect itself to the Malaysian super corridor, which has very good access to the rest of the world, all of a sudden people who couldn't imagine doing any kind of work with electronics have an opportunity to learn."

Kim Polese
Chairman, Marimba

Kim Polese, chairman of Marimba, has never shied away from taking the bull by the horns. She has a great many concerns about the future and is involved in steering legislation to benefit technology. TechNet <www.technet.org/who/>, is one of those organizations. The group consists of a national network of senior executives from the nation's leading technology companies. Its goal is to build bipartisan support for policies that benefit technology and promote growth in that area. This group is forming America's leadership of the New Economy. TechNet is comprised of more than 300 CEOs and senior partners of companies in the fields of information technology, biotechnology, venture capital, investment banking, and law.

"The biggest challenge," say Polese about the future, "certainly from a technology standpoint, is broadband deployment, because it's the biggest thing holding back the Internet from being the primary entertainment source where we tune in to listen to the Internet in our cars, and subscribe to the latest movies. The thing that's preventing all of that from happening, and thus incredible growth from happening from an economy standpoint, is broadband deployment. It's been very slow and right now in a somewhat suspended state. The growth of broadband needs to be spurred, and primarily it's a combination of things. Policy is a very important part of making this happen—it's a complex issue. For example, broadband policy should encourage innovation and competition between different technologies and companies, and we need policy makers exercising regulatory restraint to encourage development of new applications and networks, streamlining laws and regulations, providing incentives for the build-out of broadband—tax incentives for example, and encouraging broadband deployment to underserved communities. Those are all things that involve people focusing on the policy and putting some legislation in place. Broadband is the number one thing because a lot of the investment and economic rewards that the economy will realize and benefit from will happen as a result of broadband build-out.

"Technology will march forward and the innovation will continue to increase, but I think more focus needs to be placed on policy and spurring the rollout of broadband where there's been a standoff between various industry players and segments of the telcos and cable companies—there's a lot of fighting and potential energy being wasted. I think we need to have bipartisan commitment by Congress and the administration to have a national goal of widespread broadband deployment in the next 10 years. That's what we need to do, and it needs to become a real focus. The economic impact of that will be enormous in a positive way. It's going to take energy, focus, and commitment to achieve new policies. There's legislation that's been introduced, it's just a matter of how quickly does it work its way through Congress, and how seriously will Congress take this industry?

"TechNet is making a lot of progress because the communication links have been established and the Internet is no longer a novelty. The initial education process that had to occur has occurred. Whereas five years ago, many of the politicians did not have e-mail addresses or web sites, certainly the opposite is true now. So I think there is an ability right now to roll up our sleeves, get down to the meaty issues, get some action, and accomplish some legislative goals."

James Iuliano
President and CEO, E Ink

Many people say that the only thing stopping the Internet from being useful in content delivery is the method on which it rides and how it is paid for. I'll second that emotion. My Palm XIIx, besides from being rendered completely Internet-useless because of a lack of customer service comprehension, offered little content. I found it useful if I had a minute and wanted to look up stock quotes or send e-mail while I was sitting in traffic, but the interface is horrific and unless you're the end-all, be-all with a stylus, you end up with your calculator or Amazon screen accidentally being triggered—and I can't even convey how useless the bandwidth speed is around here (actually I couldn't even access it from my home in the Silicon Valley foothills). The screen was difficult to read at best (I'm used to doing my nighttime reading by candlelight), and the backlight only served to give me a headache. Basically I purchased a very expensive phone book that went out within its one-year warranty and was replaced by a refurbished one because the returns on the product had been so great. Needless to say, I should have bought a Visor. Or maybe that's the wrong way to think; there are other products on the horizon. Perhaps one needs to look at the way content will be delivered in the near future to understand the evolution from Palm Pilot to reading device. As much as I'd love to skip right ahead to some wonderful nano guy slipping an embedded device under my skin for 24/7 connectivity, other things will need to happen first.

One company that I've been keeping an eye on over the last year is Massachusetts-based E Ink, which spun technology out of the famed MIT Labs. James Iuliano, president and

CEO, has found strategic, heavy-hitting investment, device, and content partners (Gannett, Havas, Hearst Corporation, Lucent Technologies, McClatchy, Motorola, Philips Components, TOPPAN Printing Company Ltd., and Applied Technology Ventures, to name a few). So with many of the players in place, what's all the hubbub about?

E Ink's technology is basically a straightforward fusion of chemistry, physics, and electronics blended to make its product work. The principal components of electronic ink are millions of tiny microcapsules, each about the diameter of a human hair. In its initial form, each microcapsule contains positively charged white particles and negatively charged black particles suspended in a clear fluid. When a negative electric field is applied, the white particles move to the top of the microcapsule, where they become visible to the user. This makes the surface appear white at that spot. At the same time, an opposite electric field pulls the black particles to the bottom of the microcapsule, where they are hidden. By reversing this process, the black particles appear at the top of the capsule, which now makes the surface appear dark at that spot.

The next cool component of this technology is the way the display is delivered: the ink is printed onto a sheet of plastic film that is laminated to a layer of circuitry. The circuitry forms a pattern of pixels that can then be controlled by a display driver. These microcapsules are suspended in a liquid carrier medium, allowing them to be printed using existing screen printing processes onto virtually any surface—thus transforming almost any surface into a display. That is an amazing thing to think about; a display *anywhere*.

"E Ink's position is that there's a lot of content out there and what the world is looking for is a bridge to that content," says Iuliano. "And not necessarily fixed bridges, but mobile bridges, so that we can access that information any time, anywhere, in a format we feel comfortable with. E Ink is positioned to be the eyes of the future handheld devices that will allow us to access that content anywhere and anytime. The exciting thing is that the content exists, but not the distribution of that content—wirelessly. Semiconductor technology is at the point where small devices can act as servers, even. For instance, a phone. So what you have then is that you are carrying around an incredible amount of information that can be beamed to you wirelessly. What you need is a means to read that information, and the ability to read in a way where you don't sacrifice the reading experience that we all get from the first grade on. That's where E Ink fits, we look like and feel like print on paper, we operate exactly like print paper. And yet, we're able to take advantage of all the wonders of digital technology."

The E Ink product has three principal advantages. They are in readability; it reads like print on paper, it has a 180° viewing angle, and the brighter the ambient light, the easier it is to read. The second is low power consumption; once the image is presented on an electronic ink reader, no additional power is required to keep it there, so a battery that lasts you one hour today, will last 100 hours in the future. The third advantage of this product is in its form and composition: it doesn't require glass, and the material used is lightweight, very thin and ultimately conformable—meaning that you can roll it up and put it in your pocket.

"Bluetooth is going to happen and it's going to be a very efficient way to access information over local areas," says Iuliano, whose first text-only product release will be in 2002, with the high-resolution product releasing in the second quarter of 2003.

"Ultimately we'll start off on that road for television quality, but for now we're developing for black and white and then we'll migrate to a full-color, full-motion video. Initially our focus is on what we call reader-centric mobile applications;

applications where you want to dwell and read and immerse yourself in content. Certainly one day we'll have television sets as thin as a piece of paper that you'll carry around with you and that will consume minimal power. We'll be broadcasting to each other and to media centers—real-time images, pictures, thoughts, emotions, and the whole world will be connected wirelessly, and we'll all share the same common pair of eyes in electronic ink displays. Our approach is that we'll make our sheets of ink available in an open source standpoint, so if there is a visionary who has an idea for a device, whether it's a wearable device or clothing, or eyeglasses or architectural—it may be the walls of buildings—we will provide the sheets of ink to such visionaries for them to include in products. We want to enable that kind of creativity, we're not necessarily going to develop those kinds of products."

Joe Chouinard

Vice President, Visa's New E-Commerce Channel

The big thing needed to tie together all of the cool new technologies mentioned in this and the other chapters is a widely accepted micropayment standard and a 24/7 anywhere/anytime wireless solution. In our FutureNet world of the future, Internet users will be able to purchase Internet content (including bandwidth, content, music, video and services) via an easy to use, secure micropayment system directly accessible via a quality device with easy user interface. Of course, who else would be leading the charge except Visa—the company that has learned the seamless art of ubiquity from its decades of experience with credit cards and online services.

Joe Chouinard, vice president of Visa's new e-commerce channel, has been with Visa for 12 years and experienced its early efforts with the Visa Cash program. Now he's gearing up to move it to the next level. After all, until we get a payment system in place that's easy to use, we won't be able to pay the artists for their work, or even use micropayment services. As you may or may not have noticed, pornography has figured out that micropayment systems work quite well for it, and the adult industry is weathering this recession just fine. It has done this, for the most part, by club conglomerates, so you can purchase in advance from a number of services and have an account with your online money account. We may want to take a lesson from that market (it has always led technology and business models) and apply it to the mainstream market. There's a pony in there somewhere, and I have a feeling it's not going to be just a pony, it's going to be Seattle Slew.

"Regardless of the value of the payment, moving money costs money," explains Chouinard about Visa's biggest challenge in the micropayment business. "At some point you run out of economies, you reach a minimum amount below which it's very difficult to push the cost of moving money at a lower rate, so when you start talking about micropayment mechanisms of extremely low value for purchasing, for example, a page of content. At some point there are no more economies of scale and the Internet can't provide any more lubrication to that system to remove some of the inefficiencies, and on a percentage basis it becomes prohibitively expensive to try to process those kinds of transactions. So what we've seen is a tremendous amount of infrastructure is required to process payments and it's primarily based around critical mass. At this point in time the roadside is littered with the bodies of micropayment systems that have come and gone. What we've found is that people like the tried-and-true methods in place, and we came along at a very fortunate time in the evolution of commerce and have successfully grown around the world with more than a billion pieces of plastic with Visa brands on them; more than 20 million merchants and 20,000 member banks issue them—we've become the medium of exchange.

"Cash or checks don't work well on the Internet, or on any Internet channel. We are the preferred method of exchange for Internet transactions to the point where 93 percent of the transactions are completed utilizing a payment card of one or another, and 50 percent of all transactions over the Internet are done with Visa credit cards. What we're trying to do is extend the use of those cards in a safe, secure, simple manner into other channels, including mobile telephony in its various forms, interactive digital television, and other channels that will develop along the way. We've been developing to be on par with content providers such as a publisher and payment providers such as financial institutions that will be able to count on us for certain pieces of functionality being there within the infrastructure so they can deploy their products or services in a way that can be interacted with in a common look and feel manner across different channels."

Visa means to seriously enter this field and has joined with MasterCard, American Express, and JCB to begin looking closely at the issues via a newly formed consortium specifically on the mobile payment industry. The consortium, involving mobile, technology and financial industry leaders, will aim to address current market issues and expand the global potential for mobile commerce growth.

Jaap Haartsen
Chief Scientist, Bluetooth

One of the things you can't avoid hearing in conversations about the future is the company named Bluetooth. Jaap Haartsen, one of the creators of Bluetooth wireless technology, joined Ericsson in 1991 and has since worked at sites in RTP (United States), Lund (Sweden), and Emmen (the Netherlands) in the area of wireless technology. In Sweden he laid the foundations for the Bluetooth radio concept. He also played an active role in the creation of the Bluetooth Special Interest Group and served as chair for the SIG air protocol specification group from 1998 to 2000. In April 2001, he became chief scientist of Ericsson Technology Licensing AB, an Ericsson company fully dedicated to Bluetooth IP. Currently, he is located in Emmen.

"My vision for the next 10 years relates to *embedded connectivity*," says Haartsen. "In the last decades, we have seen our world changing by the advent of the microprocessor. This has led to *embedded computing*—any device equipped with a microprocessor, thus providing this device with some sort of intelligence—processing power. This has made our devices more powerful and versatile and has led to great progress in automation. The next step I see is *embedded connectivity:* any device is equipped with a small, cheap, low-cost radio. This radio provides a wireless interface to the inside—the intelligence—of the device. By connecting devices and exchanging information among them, completely new applications appear. Devices that are coming into each other's radio range, automatically detect each other and establish connections in small networks. It is like the Internet on a micro scale. These micro networks form personal networks that can be linked to the real Internet via fixed or mobile access points. The latter can for example be a mobile phone, which is the bridge between the personal network and the mobile Internet."

So where does Bluetooth see its future market? "Back in 1994 and 1995, Ericsson launched a study on a radio-based cable replacement technology," says Haartsen of the method used to define its future. "The first application was a wireless headset to the mobile phone. However, it was soon realized that it could be applied for replacing the cables between the mobile phone and any of its accessories—hands-free, PC connection et cetera. It was envisioned that mobile phones would be a focal point, your communicating device and a mobile access point to a WAN. To allow wireless and peer-to-peer communication to and from the mobile phone, a new RF technology was needed.

"Quite hard restrictions were specified in the requirement specification. It should be very power conservative, have minimum physical size, and be cheap—designed for a single-chip solution—and be allowed to operate worldwide. Therefore, it should operate in a license-free band and be robust to interference. Designing a radio interface enabling a single-chip solution was quite a challenge for the engineers at Ericsson in Lund, Sweden. The work started out as a research project on single-chip radios, where the air interface was merely the vehicle for this project. After a few years, project MC Link [Multi Communicator Link] was evaluated. It was a master-slave concept with seven slaves. Further design and development was made and the solution turned out to be quite unique.

"To gain market acceptance for a technology, it needs to be open, free, and widely used," says Haartsen. "Ericsson decided to seek partners and the SIG was eventually formed. The name Bluetooth was chosen as the project name at the official launch in May 1998."

Did the technology downswing have an impact on Bluetooth, or did a marketing shift take place because of it?

"Initially, the goal was to replace cables and to make it possible to synchronize and exchange data between various handheld mobile devices. However, it turned out that even more applications and devices could benefit from using a low-power, cheap, and small RF implementation like Bluetooth. For Ericsson, the scope of Bluetooth was not really changed—we still position Bluetooth for *mobile wireless connections on the go*. Stationary devices can also benefit using Bluetooth. Various industry segments are now also involved in the development and design of Bluetooth products, such as the health care, automotive, and process automation industries.

"The turndown in the economy has not had any impact on the technology development as such, but the willingness to invest in a new technology is likely to have declined during the last year or so. However, looking at the market today, where 1.5 million products are being *Bluetooth qualified* each day, it's hard to see a decline in the development, launch, and deployment of Bluetooth products. The feeling today is more full-steam-ahead enthusiasm."

So why is it that the market is so hungry for Bluetooth technology? "Cables have always been a nightmare," says Haartsen. "From a failure point of view, and also from a convenience point of view. Bluetooth will be replacing the cables that connect various devices together. In addition to just replacing the cable, we will see new communication scenarios between devices that we never thought could be possible. For example, mobile phones and cameras, mobile phones and TVs—remote control using WAP over Bluetooth. This will make life easier because we can combine devices together in a very flexible way, hence using the devices for what they are aimed at, and using Bluetooth to connect them together, rather than trying to build everything into one single device."

How do these strategies leverage the Internet? "Bluetooth will be the technology bringing the Internet to mobile devices while on the go; either using the mobile phone as a mobile access point that connects your PDA to the Internet, or accessing the net over a fixed access point located in hotspots. It's likely that Bluetooth will move into home appliances once a critical mass has been reached and the price for the implementation is reduced. This will open up for the intelligent home, where many devices—TVs, VCRs, CD players, fridges, and lamp switches—could be Bluetooth-enabled and accessed using a Bluetooth-enabled remote control, mobile phone, or PDA. I don't think we have seen or can foresee the whole evolution or revolution of Bluetooth in the home yet. But it will move into the homes for sure!

"We at Ericsson are very committed to Bluetooth and will make sure it gets out on the market and designed into various devices. Communication between devices will most likely be of more importance in the future than today, simply because we will have more and more gadgets for various things. I don't think we can imagine today what kind of devices these could be, but taking into account the unique advantages of Bluetooth, we believe there will be products based on the technology from a starting point, rather than enabling already existing products. After all, a mobile phone is still a mobile phone, with or without Bluetooth. The same thing with a laptop—it is still a laptop, with or without Bluetooth. But the opportunities for these devices increases thanks to Bluetooth. New devices and appliances might be designed with the ambition of using the wireless technology primarily. For example, the functionality of such a device wouldn't work unless a suitable wireless technology was in place. The Bluetooth future is bright; we are now in the beginning of a new gear in the mobile revolution."

Hossein Eslambolchi
CTO, AT&T, President, AT&T Labs

Although many in this book have mixed feelings about AT&T's early involvement, or lack thereof, with ARPANET, it's clear that it's not going away anytime soon, and that it is not planning on missing any further opportunities with future technology.

"First of all, IP will eat everything," says Hossein Eslambolchi, who is CTO of AT&T and president of AT&T Labs, about the future of the Internet. "Second, broadband will be common. Third, most everything will ride over optics. Today we have IP riding over SONET [Synchronous Optical Network] and DWDM [Dense Wave Division Multiplexing]. I believe that SONET will be eliminated and that IP will ride over optics. Also, networks are getting smarter, with more intelligence at the core of the network.

Further, I believe data will move more into Internet services, which will improve in terms of reliability and scalability. That may take shape as private line services. Home LANs will proliferate. A lot of effort is being put into wireless standards such as 802.11b, which someday will let residential users through set-top boxes get Internet downloads such as DVDs to a television or stereo. We'll see the rise of the wireless Internet—we've seen the second generation of wireless and 2.5G. Now we will see 3G and 4G."

So what does all this mean for AT&T? "It means we have to move faster to extract value from AT&T Labs in the form of a new generation of data and IP services. We have to extend our lead in managed services, in LAN and WAN connectivity solutions, in streaming media and content delivery, in MPLS . . . you name it. It means we have to put technology to work to integrate our operations systems, e-enable our customer connections, and leverage the intelligence and reliability of our network with new, edge-based capabilities that make customers' lives easier and their businesses more productive."

CHAPTER 5

FutureScope

So many times we are destined to relive our past if we don't learn our lessons from it. It's a torturous thing we must go through as a society—the lessons have to apply on all levels for us to learn collectively. So much like that Pearl Harbor/ World Trade Center example in the first chapter.

When I was a kid I was brought up on a naval base on Oahu. It was 1975 when I moved back to the mainland where I had been born (at Stanford Hospital in the heart of Silicon Valley). At the time of my return I was 10 years old.

Growing up in Hawaii, I was used to the constant air raid drills at school that would either have us assembling on the blacktop or cowering under our desks; this was a normal thing. One of the first field trips we went on was to Pearl Harbor, where we were shown footage of the bombings, and where the docent pointed over the edge of the ocean-based memorial into the shimmering blue tropical water and said, "This is where many of the men who died ended up—dead in the water. Trapped in the battleships that were blown up, sealed in compartments that still can't be forced open for fear of them blowing up." A pretty heavy field trip for an eight-year-old. Well, this girl—me—whose father has always been her hero, could not understand why he couldn't engineer some way to get them out. I finally understood during one of his deployments back from Vietnam, when he explained that they still would be dead, and that some things have to remain in the past as markers for the future. It was a memorial, and we must remember.

So when I was 10-years-old, we were stationed back on the mainland. I couldn't understand two things: (A) why I had to wear shoes to school, and (B) why there were no air raid drills. Were we not supposed to remember what happened all those years ago and those guys who were still sealed up like sardines under the tropical, shimmering blue water? I broached the subject with schoolmates and got blank looks. My new teachers didn't grasp the whole thing about air raid drills. I got into the new mode of things, and I forgot. I forgot until I saw that live footage on 9/11. And I immediately thought, this is just like Pearl Harbor; why hadn't we been doing our air raid drills?

I thought about that lesson, because it stays close at hand now. But there is always a time when you want to let your imagination soar without being too cautiously optimistic; where some people see warnings, others see challenges to be met, hurdles to clear without looking back. We all have our versions of the future.

Visionaries are not easy to find; as a matter of fact they're downright difficult to locate. There are many who are self-proclaimed, who pronounce shocking future bits from every media soapbox you pass. Certainly with this much *future* going around, someone must have a bead on it.

Being here—in Silicon Valley—and, metaphorically (and sometimes physically) walking among giants every day, I am excited to get up in the morning; thrilled to have meetings and take calls with people who are doing things in their work to bring technology a little further along. It seems that every

> *"I think it's unforeseeable—the future of technology—there is just no way to know. . . . That's what makes each one of these revolutions so exciting . . . it's because all the prognostications are always wrong. I mean, at the moment of their inceptions no one really understands what these technologies are going to do for us. Therefore, it is impossible to foresee how they are going to be used. How they are used is a sign of maturation, How they are going to change the world? I'll have to get back to you on that one."*
>
> —Dave Winer, chairman & CEO,
> UserLand, Inc.

day now someone is calling to tell me about the glimmering of a new technology. I attend the World Internet Center <www.WorldInternetCenter.com> pub nights every Thursday to hook up with some of the most brilliant people in the world and talk with them about the future. Sure, we were hit for a while; you never really get over mourning for the loss of thousands of lives taken from us via a live television feed—no, you move on, as Bob Dylan says, *You keep on keepin' on.* And that's what I've seen. Not the loss of the WTC, or the fear of having a Bay Area bridge blown up from under your car wheels on the way to a meeting, or even the pounding news of more layoffs are going to keep anyone down, not here, not now. Not ever.

People are still creating a future with technology that will enable us to do anything we wish, anything we can possibly

"*I* was at the [MIT] media lab in '86 and really trying to figure out what it was all about. What summed it up for me was someone who was writing software: he said, 'What we're trying to do is connect our nervous systems to the computer. One thing we'll have to think about is not only do we have to debug our damn computers, which you'll have to do decade after decade—but now that it's all hooked up to our bodies, we'll have to debug our bodies. One day you're computing away and suddenly you can't stop stuttering— how do you undo that?*"

—Stewart Brand, cofounder of The Well

dream. With this empowerment also comes the ethical, moral, and legal dilemmas for which we, as a global society, will have to provide insights and solutions as we struggle to solve our present and future technology issues. We should learn from the past and brace for the future.

Paul Saffo

Director, Institute of the Future

Paul Saffo isn't the kind of guy who pussyfoots around his opinion—and if he has one, you immediately know about it without any mincing of words. He is known for being outspoken in the field of technology. And when he talks about trends, even the heads of Fortune 50 companies lean in to listen. He currently is the director of the Institute for the Future <www.IFTF.org/>, a Silicon Valley–based, 30-year-old nonprofit research firm that forecasts technological, demographic, and business trends to help its clients—which include AT&T Research Laboratories, Bristol-Myers Squibb, Cisco, Eastman Kodak Company, Sun, and GM. The group specializes in long-term forecasting, alternative future scenarios, and the impacts of new products and next-generation technologies on society and business.

"The Internet is still synonymous with people talking to other people, but we're seeing a fundamental shift," says Saffo of what the future holds for the Net. "The biggest growth in the Internet is not in people-to-people, but in machine-to-machine. So what we're going to see in the next 10 years is that human-to-human communication is going to become an increasingly smaller proportion of the total Internet traffic. That's a big fundamental shift. The 1980s were about people talking to people and using e-mail; the '90s were about people accessing information. The '80s were shaped by the microprocessor in the processing revolution; our computers were defined by what the process was—words, figures, charts. The '90s were an access revolution triggered by the advent of cheap lasers which gave us all those communication conduits we use, and the decade was symbolized by the Web. This new decade is being shaped by the advent of cheap sensors. We're basically in the process of hanging eyes and ears and sensory organs on our computers and networks and asking them to observe the world on our behalf, and manipulate that information on our behalf."

"This is a world where we'll have home alarm systems where everything is wireless talking over 802.11 networks to each other using the IP protocol, and then communicating upwards to a security company."

—Paul Saffo, director of the Institute
of the Future

Saffo believes that no matter what the technology, it will have different facets of problem and solution sets that will continue to be a challenge for tech industries to solve and move forward. "Everything new always comes with a hidden curse and new technologies are always a mixed bag—they solve old problems, they create new opportunities, and then, in the process, they create new problems we didn't anticipate. The Internet is no different than any other technology in this regard. The only difference is that with all the other technology that has happened in the past we knew how the story would turn out—in this case we don't know how the story will turn out. With the Internet there's a lot more suspense and uncertainty. And frankly, this is a moment in time— thanks to 9/11—where everybody is in so much of a dis-Utopian mood about technology, but the advantage of technology is that it's pretty unstoppable. We're going to aggressively use technology to get us out of the jam we're in with the terrorists. For example, in the Gulf War, the star technologies were surveillance satellites and smart bombs. In this war, this has really become a sensory war, with unmanned vehicles and sensors on the ground. The first casualty of this war was a UAV [Unmanned Aerial Vehicle] called a NAT, it was flown by the CIA, and our first attempt to kill Mullar Muhammad Omar was not done with a fighter jock and a jet, but with a Predator UAV with two Hellfire missiles under its wings."

Does history repeat itself in Saffo's eyes? "World War II and Pearl Harbor gave a huge spurt to a whole set of technologies—the antiterrorist conflict is doing the same. It's giving a big push to sensor information technology, and also biophysics and biotechnology. This is a government mobilization around foundational and applied technologies that may eventually approach the scale of what we did because of WWII. And if you look at WWII, the most important invention was systems-thinking and the industrialization of research and development—the modern R&D think tank—which was typified by the Manhattan Project and institutionalized with the creation of RAND just after the end of the war."

What about looking farther into the future? Saffo feels that human embedded technology devices aren't going to happen. "We're not going to put subcutaneous phones on our person for a couple of simple reasons: the technology changes so fast that you'd have to be splitting your skin open every six months—upgrades would become a real problem; ask anyone who had product recall on a hip replacement or a pacemaker. We will explore—not anytime soon—direct neural interfaces, the stuff of science fiction that Bill Gibson wrote about in *Neuromancer.* But that's a ways off, and it's still very much science fiction, and we're still trying to figure out how to do direct retinal scan images with lasers—Scott Foster and his

team up at Human Interface Technology [HIT] lab <www
.hitl.washington.edu> is working on that. We're moving from
man/machine interface to man/machine symbiosis, where there
is an even deeper interdependence between humans and their
artifacts. That is very much the theme that's afoot, but it's going
to be a more supple process than people sticking computers
under their skin."

So where are we going as technologies emerge and converge into something that will have an even more profound
effect on us than it already has? What does our future look like?

"What I am as a forecaster is really a historian of technology who spends most of my time looking at technologies that
don't exist yet, and I can tell you that every wave of new technology has had books with last chapters asking those questions. We tend to invest our fondest hopes and our deepest
fears in new technology, and in fact it turns out that neither our
hopes nor our fears are realized. We muddle through somewhere in the middle. And even as we speak there's plenty of
growth and change and excitement in the Internet. But the
center of gravity is moving away from information technology.
The real revolutions that will change our lives in fundamental
ways are all in biology and biotechnology. Information technology will play an important supporting role, but while the
last 50 years have been about information technology, the next
50 years will be about biology."

Dave Farber

Technologist; Activist; Former Chief Scientist for the Federal Communications Commission

Dave Farber, recently the chief technologist for the FCC, and one of the visionaries who built the Internet, has a great point about technology and the way it works from a human acceptance standpoint.

"If you go back to the '50s, people were saying that in about 25 to 50 years computers will be implanted in you and you'll be wearing goggles. . . . To change the process—to change the way people behave—you have to give them something that will really make a difference. And that comes very, very rarely; when you actually have something that has a profound impact on the way people operate. People make small changes, but the majority of people don't want to make any changes," says Farber about the rate of change he's seen through technology cycles.

"I don't see that happening as much as satisfying natural needs to be in communities. You'll have some people with communications coming into their nervous system, but probably not as much as you'd predict right now. I think if I had to predict anything, we'll be closer to *Snow Crash* [by Neal Stephenson], an interesting science fiction story set in the relatively near future—Metaversus and virtual reality. I have a simple metric—put yourself in 1952 and ask yourself what has really changed? The highway system made a profound change from a social aspect. Jets got faster, they dramatically changed things for a small part of the population, but not for most people. Computers—yes, they have changed us. There were predictions that they were going to be implanted by now, but things are still not integrated.

"Back then, people would have told you on a stack of bibles that we'd be able to simulate a human being's thinking process—we're nowhere closer to that now than we were then. Everything is subject to serendipity; all it takes is one smart guy to say, *Here's a good idea,* and you could have dramatic changes."

Douglas Engelbart

Cofather of the Internet;
Founder, Bootstrap Institute

Douglas Engelbart is one of technology's unsung heroes. If you're reading this book online, take note: that thing in your hand, otherwise known as a *mouse,* well, that is one of Engelbart's many legacies.

Engelbart was drafted and serving time in the Navy on a jungle island in the Philippines when he looked up and saw a kampong (hut on stilts) with a sign that read *Red Cross Library.* Of the small selection of reading material, he honed right in on the magazine that had printed Vannevar Bush's vision of the future. Bush, the guy who actually managed the 6,000 scientists who built the atomic bomb, was the nation's chief scientist—and man, was he a dreamer (see Chapter 1 for details). Bush felt that the answer to humans evolving and becoming more intelligent was to feed them massive amounts of information through 24/7 anything/anyone libraries that were easy to manage. Well, here was a younger and naive Douglas Engelbart, 20 feet up in this kampong, with humid tropical air sucking at his clothes, and the always present sound of a chorus of cicadas filling the air. And there was Vannevar Bush's statement about the future. It had quite an effect, as it still does.

When I visited Engelbart at his Silicon Valley home, he showed a deep concern for the ecology as well as the humans of the earth. He pointed out some basic information that made me view things in a different way. Many environments are evolving when science comes along and gets involved; such as a case where there is a mosquito-infested area in a third-world country due to a body of stagnant water;

engineers and scientists come in and drain the lake, killing the mosquitoes that carried the malaria. The area is soon flourishing, and the population in that area goes up exponentially— thereby causing new problems. What then? What other problems has this solution created? Engelbart sees the world solving so many problems by virtue of its technology and science, but then it's a case of be careful of what you ask for.

"I saw the problem as the world getting more and more complex at a higher and higher rate because there's so much technology coming around that solves more complex problems, but they have to be dealt with collectively," says Engelbart. "Our ability to cope with complex problems hasn't grown nearly as fast as the complexity and urgency of those problems. Mankind may very well be doomed if we don't learn how to keep up with the problems. Back then, I thought, *Why don't I commit to a career of seeing how much I can improve our ability to handle urgent, complex problems?* And that's what's been motivating me. The emergence of the Internet just made it possible to take collective action on a wide scale."

What Engelbart is deeply concerned about is our rate of knowledge of the population in comparison to the technology that is coming about, and its sustainability.

"I am concerned about the educational system—sure it's falling short today, but think of what it will look like tomorrow. A friend of mine who is a university president commented about a statistic about the way the world's knowledge doubles. He said someone had done some study and looked at the world in the 1100s and asked how long it took for the world's knowledge to double. He said it took something like 600 years, then it took another 400 years to double, and it kept taking shorter and shorter time periods until we come to today, when it takes something like 20 years. And how long will it take 20 years from now? Perhaps it'll take three months.

So what will the schools be like then? And where do you find anyone trying to get ready for that rate of evolution?"

Engelbart has his fingers on the pulse of the knowledge and technology growth, and in 1989 he founded the Bootstrap Institute <www.bootstrap.org>. Engelbart felt there was a great need to pursue the research and development of enabling technologies as well as the best practices and strategies to develop and deploy them. He works with members of government, industry, and society.

> *"The actual transmission capability of the Internet is just in its juvenile state right now. We'll have very wideband wireless things very cheap. What you call your workstation won't need a physical connection. Pretty soon you won't have a cell phone, it'll be a watch, or your glasses, so that you'll be able to see what anybody sees if you wish. The Internet of the future will be just a universal transmission system with very wideband capabilities, and very cheap. What will people do with it? Nanotechnology is bound to be a part of it, the ultra wideband is already providing device potentials."*
>
> —Douglas Engelbart, cofather of the Internet and founder of the Bootstrap Institute

Engelbart has always remembered what Vannevar Bush wrote about online knowledge volumes, and believes that one day some sort of online books will be key to our learning process. Even as little as eight years ago, ebooks were still hype and pie in the sky. Nothing had come even close to passing the hammock test (where you could comfortably read a book on your back sipping a margarita and sitting in direct sunlight). Very few people at that time thought there was a future for digital books. As a matter of fact, in 1994 (about the same time Amazon had come up on the radar), I built a prototype web site for the sale of books online where publishers and authors could offer their books directly to the public. The business model I proposed had three revenue models that brought the trilogy of the reader, writer, and publisher together to form a solid business.

The model I had devised would have probably proven more stable than Amazon, but first to market was important back then. Meanwhile, I took my laptop to many of the top publishers in New York to meet with the publishers, their marketing people, and their editors. Everyone looked at me like I was crazy—they all thought the same thing, books won't sell online, although Warner had begun making progress by that time.

I even met with one associate publisher, who had been with mainstream publisher St. Martin's Press for many years and who did not even have a computer. It would take a few years, but all those publishers now have their own bookstores online but have failed the hurdle of building a community within their meager marketing budgets; basically their web sites are a loss leader. So, I know firsthand what prejudices Engelbart faced at that time, and the obstacles in this archaic industry when one day he spoke to a group of librarians who were very much in favor of keeping technology out of their libraries.

"I was a keynote speaker at a national librarian conference event about eight years ago and I said that it was inevitable that all publications would become digital and there'd be no more hard copy; I wasn't expecting the chill that came over the room," says Engelbart of the reception he received. "People told me that there's so much about a book that makes it difficult to replace, and I say what is *it* about a book? They say, *It's a solid kind of thing, something you can hold in your hands. And I ask, Don't you think technology will be able to replicate weight and make the pages look however you want? Don't you want to crank up or down the font size?* One day you'll be able to read your detective novel, your newspaper, anything you want from this same device. In a few years the display will be just the glasses you wear. I mean, why would you want to have books, when there's so much more flexibility you can have with something else? One day they'll be an offering so that you have a way to look at the content and it will parse the sentences so you have a way to automatically go through it and different parts of the text will have colors or brightness and your sensory perception will be able to move much more quickly," says Engelbart who was very much a part of the human factors development of the computer/Internet technology being integrated into the products we currently use. "People look at me strangely, but I think that's all absolutely inevitable—and the sooner the better because it will help us harness our knowledge."

Kim Polese
Chairman of Marimba

Kim Polese was there at the birth of Java and continues to be an innovative part of today's Internet as chairman of Marimba <www.Marimba.com>. She also is very active in setting the pace for government legislation that oversees technology.

> "*Thinking of future investments, I would invest in public education, because the success of our industry and our economy of the future rests so heavily on our ability to have an educated workforce that can be productive and able to innovate in the new way that we will have to remain competitive as a nation. There is no better place we can put that money.*"
>
> —Kim Polese, chairman of Marimba

"There's no question in my mind that we are rapidly heading toward a merging of digital and biological technologies that will enable incredibly powerful applications that could range from diagnostics to the ability to create microcomputers out of electrons and have them perform tasks. It's an almost limitless future where you have the ability to embed powerful computers that today are on our desktops, but will eventually be smaller than a grain of sand. This is all far-fetched, future science fiction kind of stuff, but it's not really because over time we will be able to increasingly use technology in the form of atoms and biological matter to actually perform the functions that today need memory and standard computer hardware.

"I wonder about it all the time, and I can't really envision that world because I know that it is so far removed from the world we live in today, which is largely analog and physical, that no one can conceive of what life will be like in 50 years because we have no context for that future. That's how daunting and dramatic the changes will be in the next 50 years."

Leonard Kleinrock

Cofather of the Internet; Chairman of Nomadix;
Chairman and CEO of TTIV Vanguard

Len Kleinrock, professor of computer science at UCLA, chairman and CEO of TTI/Vanguard <www.TTIVanguard .com>, and chairman of Nomadix <www.Nomadix.com>, was there from the beginning. He had the wherewithal and vision to design what would become the core technology in Internet technology—packet switching. So what does he think now as we hit the 30-year mark of this industry? What will the Internet become?

> *"There's another move afoot: it's not a sinister move, but what's happening is the traffic on the Internet now is going to be generated by smart devices—embedded technology that sits in the environment and measures things and does things, and software agents that act on your behalf."*
>
> —Leonard Kleinrock, cofather of the Internet, chairman of Nomadix, and chairman and CEO of TTI/Vanguard

"It will be invisible," says Kleinrock. "It will literally become part of the environment and users won't even think of it. I think it will be part of our biology—embedded. The first move will be automatic drug dispensers, automatic monitors, then the next move—the genetic thing; which is a whole other topic I won't even touch. But, I think there will be embedded technologies that will serve us in interesting ways—of course, people shouldn't be subject to that without their consent. For instance, if something about my medical history is always with me, that's not necessarily a bad thing."

Kleinrock believes that our future will be filled with what he calls software *agents* that will do our bidding and make life more efficient for us on many levels.

"They will basically be watching the economy, doing the stock transactions, running businesses, etc. Where you might feel that the biological transfer is a dangerous thing—I don't know if you'd really call them dangerous, but these other things are kind of taken out of our hands. Things are going to happen to certain extent; and these things are going to happen at light speed. An event will occur one place—and these agents will know immediately about a political, or financial event and all of these agents will work on the data and act on it far faster than a human can absorb. But things will be happening at light speed in a pervasive way in a highly sophisticated fashion, which means we will no longer have control. Right now we can't turn the Internet off, and as we give more and more responsibility to function to these agents, we will be losing control of our own commerce, and business. There's going to be a powerful force in the background on all of the time.

"I don't think that machines will ever spring into consciousness. I think machines won't exhibit creative aspects directly, but they will have lots and lots of control over what goes on in our lives. We shouldn't think that artificial intelligence will behave like human intelligence. That's the wrong view. Artificially intelligent things will do things that humans don't necessarily do well at all. They'll follow rules to some extent; and those rules may sometimes take us into directions we didn't intend, and into the unintended consequences. These agents will discover things, find new ways of looking at things, they'll process data. There's a world out there that's happening and is very hard to fathom at this point, and we really don't know which way it's going to go. But there'll be a lot of unseen activity that grows and takes place on the Internet. It's kind of another culture that's developing, and it's going to be hard for us to maintain control of it, just as we don't control it today."

Bob Young

Chairman, Red Hat; Founder, The Center for the Public Domain

Go into any tech company lunchroom around the world and mention Bob Young's name, and you'll get a mixed bag of responses. If you're talking to Microsoft programmers, they'll probably roll their eyes and say something about a bleeding heart liberal. If you walk into a room of open source guys, for the most part, you'd probably find that there is a sense of respect for this Canadian who founded a little company called Red Hat. Why the mix of emotions—the either you love him or hate him approach to this man? Because no matter what Young is talking about, he is passionate. The cofounder and chairman of Red Hat feels very strongly about patent and copyright issues—and is honestly more learned on the Founding Fathers and the history of the U.S. Constitution than any American I have ever spoken to—that he recently founded (and is the chairman of) The Center for the Public Domain <www.centerforthepublicdomain.org>.

"I view predicting progress something like forecasting weather," says Young, who has seen good and bad predictions about technology come and go. "If you look at the day before the prediction, and predict that it will be the same today, you'll probably be right 75 percent of the time. We talk about ASP models and delivering data processing through a network, and I say, *That sure sounds like computer timesharing in the 1970s.* This is the problem with all of these patents and copyrights; a lot of these concepts need to be recycled. The guys who are building the next generation of technology need to get their hands on it—or be allowed to use, or to build on that technology—on what went before them.

"I tend to look at whatever is on the Internet and say, *it's bound to be better, cheaper, faster,*" says Young of the obvious changes he's expecting. But what of the technologies such as wireless that have tried before and failed, but are just now starting to get a foothold? "One of the things that is happening even faster than I predicted is wireless. Wireless went through that boom-and-bust phase that no one is talking much about these days. I'm actually connected wirelessly in three different ways. I thought about this the other day, and I can remember a couple of years ago when I heard all of this hype about wireless and I said, *This is so much hype and either it won't happen, or it won't happen as quickly as all these guys are predicting.* I remember thinking, *Industry is in for a huge bust.*

"Then the industry went into a huge bust, and here I was patting myself on the back and thinking it was all hype—except that I'm using a Macintosh here at my home that is connected wirelessly to a hub in my basement. I have a Handspring device that has my telephone, which is a wireless telephone that connects me to the worldwide telephone network, so I can reach anyone by voice that I want to. And I can look at stock quotes wirelessly by this device. I'm thinking, *This is great; at the rate this is going I may never have to plug things into the wall ever again.* That's the kind of progression I saw. You can take a trend like that and start extrapolating it and saying wireless is going to take over the world and you will not plug your computer into a wall anymore. Convergence is another big buzzword, but it's happening. My Handspring, for instance—I used to carry two devices in my pocket; now I only carry one. I still carry a paper notebook with me, but if I could merge my Handspring into my phone into my paper notepad and make that my laptop computer . . . you see where I'm going?"

"*Certainly a convergence of my devices make my life easier. There are human limitations to things, which will keep the future looking a lot like the past. Some of the more far-fetched things will not happen because we as human beings will not take to them.*"

—Bob Young, chairman of Red Hat
and founder of the Center for the Public
Domain

Although Young sees tons of practical uses for future technology, he has his doubts when it comes to technology that may give you far too much information. I see his point but feel, as always, that technology that keeps users happy with *too* much information—such as the ability to see someone naked 24/7 on a mobile device—will find a market that will probably be developed by the wildly successful online pornography industry. Young feels that for the mainstream market, too much information will be an issue.

"Videophones are the best single example of a technology that has not been embraced in the mainstream; it has failed in three attempts. And the reason it has is because, interestingly enough, people don't want to have other people looking at them while they're talking on the phone. Without a videophone, I can be sitting here in my underwear, picking my nose, and you still think of me as a bright, competent human. The last thing I want to happen is to have you distracted.

"If we were given the technology to read each other's minds with embedded/wireless technology, behaviorally none of us given the power would use it. That's probably for the same reason that I don't want you seeing me while I'm chatting on the phone. By not allowing me to be seen by a video phone, it also allows me to multitask while I'm talking on the phone. For those same reasons I need to be able to fully form my thoughts before you know what they are; I need the discretion of keeping private what I am about to communicate. Whereas if people read my mind as I process my thoughts, as opposed to after I've thought them through. . . . What I mean is that human behavioral preferences will allow the future to look an awful lot like the past. Humans are not changing; it's our attitudes that will change. Whether I think a woman would make a good president of the United States—that attitude is changeable. You can be certain my father would not have thought so—actually, my mother would have thought that that was the stupidest idea. Whereas it's an idea I'm comfortable with, and my children would think it would be Neanderthal to think anything else.

"It's human behavior and instinct that will limit the more wild and crazy visions of where technology is going and it will cause technology to typically be more of the same. Looking 50 years out . . . hopefully diagnostic tools will be able to detect more things. There's no question that the tools that the doctor uses will be dramatically improved for diagnosing and prescribing cures than we have today.

"Our visions where we will be always tied to a monitoring device won't have a chance because, think about it, we're all hypochondriacs under the skin; it's just a question of the degree. If you have a monitoring device telling you what is wrong with you at any given time—*your vitamin C level is slightly reduced, your blood level of copper is slightly enhanced*—if you have an embedded monitoring device it will let you know all of these things. Of course it will have a little warning that the government will legislate every time it finds one—*too much copper will cause X in alcoholic women over a certain age*. . . . I don't know about you, but I don't need a machine telling me what's wrong every morning, because I know it will make me sicker. Do I need a machine telling me when I'm hung over? I already know that I'm hung over—I'd rather forget about that fact. People will reject that."

Judy Estrin

President and CEO, Packet Design

Judy Estrin, former CTO of Cisco Systems, has seen technology rise and fall and feels that there are very practical here-and-now aspects to technology that she sees continuing as trends. Having had Vint Cerf as an advisor while attending UCLA, and being the daughter of Gerald and Thelma Estrin, both prominent technology professors at UCLA, Judy Estrin embraced technology at a young age and has seen the seamlessness of the Internet occur, and its practical applications blossom.

"I was talking to a parent at my son's school and she said, 'I have to take my kid to the library.' I thought about that, and it had never occurred to me to take my child to the library. And then I thought, *Does my son know how to do this?* And I thought, *No, he knows how to find things on the Internet.* He sees the Internet as a tool in the same way that we think of calling information for a phone number. I think that today the Internet is a critical capability for everything we do, whether it's doing e-errands online, finding a community, or receiving medical support. I take it for granted at this point, but I worry about the people who understand technology and have access to it becoming more literate than the people who don't have access to it who are being left behind. Our own future of feudalism; I get concerned about that and that we'll end up with an information-elite class."

Estrin is a mentor for women all over the world. She understands technology, she has helped direct the technology at several top-level companies, she is a risk-taker, and a humanist. The industry recognizes her genius and she is on the boards of such companies as Sun, Disney, and FedEx. As a woman technologist, she has seen the industry's prejudice from ground level and wants to prevent its pervasiveness in the future.

"We need to make sure that girls and women don't end up disadvantaged in an age where technology plays a role; not just in technology careers, but any career. The statistics show that girls' interest in science and math drops off when they hit the fourth grade; until then girls do just as well in math and science as boys, and then there's a very clear drop-off. So I think some of the issues we have as women in the workforce have to be looked at back in the elementary and middle schools. How do we teach so we make sure that girls embrace technology the same way boys do? We need to think about this now so that we have these mechanisms worked in, and we don't end up in the workplace and in life with some inequality no one thought about."

Brewster Kahle

President of Alexa Internet;
Cofounder of The Internet Archive

As we build millions of web pages every day and then take them down the next, who is there to document these changes? Some of them are important in chronicling our history. I mean, it may not seem that we are living in times where anything is going unnoticed, but we are. Vannevar Bush would be rolling over in his grave if he knew that his dream of having a storehouse of collective knowledge and the tools to access it were almost within our grasp, but how can we now recapture all of those sites that are gone? For instance, how could we even possibly explain to our children's children about the bubble without actually showing them the preposterous web sites that got funding—I mean, *actually* show them? Brewster Kahle, president of Alexa Internet and director of The Internet Archive <www.alexa.org>, found a way to do so.

And that was the beginning of the all-out effort to chronicle our digital heritage. "Alexa is short for the library of Alexandria," says Kahle of the root of the concept for the Internet Archive. "The idea was to see if we could organize and catalog the full Web so that people can find their way through it. We didn't think that search engines would scale to absorb all of the web sites. How are you going to find your soccer team schedule when those words are just not unique across the globe? So, Alexa's concept is that it would archive the full Web and produce a catalog leveraging the usage trail of hundreds of thousands of web servers. So it was the mechanism of building an automatic Web catalog, and that's what the core of the Alexa service is. Along the way we built a full

"*A friend of mine in college said, 'You're an idealist and a technologist—paint a picture of the future that's better because of your technology.' It's very easy to piss and moan about everyone else's stuff—back then it was nuclear war and all sorts of things like that. It's harder to say, 'What's a positive thing we can do with this?' I could only come up with two things: one was encryption to help people remain private, and the other was building a digital library. I thought building a digital library was just too obvious. The stuff I went on to create didn't really change the world, so I went back to the drawing board. I went to librarian school for a while to find out what libraries do—how do people use them?*"

—Brewster Kahle president of Alexa Internet and cofounder of The Internet Archive

archive of the Web—again trying to build the essence of a library; a large collection of information of past versions of the Web. Basically it's the ability to have a *wayback machine*—to actually surf as if it's a different time. There's this question—can we trust the publishers to have the only copy of the past? I think we've demonstrated over the centuries that that isn't a good idea. Having libraries really take up their role in the digital world of keeping copies, making free access to researchers, allowing access to the material in ways that are different from how the original publisher intended. Newspapers are thought of as things that were going to be read that day, and it's very helpful looking back in time."

In actuality, if you go to the *wayback machine* on The Internet Archive's site, you can relive the past. Having recently felt nostalgic because of losing my eBay bid for a mint-condition webvan annual report, I looked up webvan. And there it was in all of its glory and incantations. The Archive began taking snapshots since 1999, so you could physically see the hope and enthusiasm go up and up—and then see it cut back, and finally die. It was a digital documentary of the highs and the lows. And it had been captured, documented, and archived so that other generations after us will also be able to view that period in time.

"The first and last time that someone tried to collect all knowledge in one place was at the Library of Alexandria—they had their charter of getting a copy of every book from all of the peoples of the world. And you know, I think they came pretty close. They had on the order of something like 500,000 scrolls—and it's really because they had a new technology called *papyrus*. The Syrian Library, which was about four centuries before Alexandria, was a phenomenal library and had about 70,000 clay tablets stored in it; and the library of Alexandria just blew them away because they had this new technology. But it wasn't universal access. It was maybe the cultural heritage of many different peoples of the world all in one place so they had the key writings of the Greeks, the Egyptians, the Hittites, the Hebrews, the Romans—all in one place. And I'm making this up, but it has to be true, I think the people who had access to this library began to have an understanding of human nature in a transcendent way that got them outside of their cultural context and allowed them to see the bigger picture. That must be what you get when you have a collection that's manipulatable. It finally burned to the ground and was dispersed."

Does Kahle think this technology will make all of us wired human beings more intelligent? "I don't know exactly how we're going to blend this in with our everyday life; I certainly have a cell phone in my pocket at all times, but do I really want that implanted into my head? Gosh, I don't know. I think that the Net and these tools are already an extension of our memory. When I talk to people on the phone, they're usually looking things up on the Internet at the same time; they are kind of a cyborg already. People prefer to talk on the phone so they can do that—because they're using the computer, the Net, their own e-mail history—their *history*. So I think we're already becoming dependent on these tools and it's our job to make them really, really good. The tools today are pretty pathetic and barely useable, but people are finding such value in them that they're turning off their televisions. They're tuning into what they're interested in, not what someone else wants them to see.

"It's not just 500,000 channels of nothing on the Web. People are very particular and very peculiar in their Web searches; we know what people are using and we know how people are using it. We don't know who is who, but we do know where people surf and it's not true that we're couch potatoes, which is kind of the 1970s/1980s cynical view of humanity that people are stupid—*not you and me, but most people are really stupid and they want to sit there and become Homer Simpson*—it's just not true. Surfers are very different from each other. There are a few things that people want that's the same—news, sports, weather, but if you get out of the very small core, then people visit a very wide range of sites and a constantly changing set of information resources. Given the opportunity, people will be very particular and very peculiar. I find this a very optimistic, healthy, and wonderful conclusion. If we all really were just the bunch of couch potatoes that a lot of people in the media business try and make us think we are, then that would never have appeared. AOL would have been plenty for people—*we give you 10 channels, they're right there in front, what else do you need?*"

Given that the Web is expanding so quickly, how big will the Internet Archive's capacity need to be? "Every snapshot we take of the Web is about 15 terabytes. Our total Web collection is over 100 terabytes. How big is a terabyte? If you look at a book with illustrations, it's about a megabyte, so a million books is about a terabyte. The Library of Congress has about 20 million books; so on the very top end, the books in the Library of Congress are about 20 terabytes. We have five times that, so the Web is getting very interesting—it is the library; you can have universal access to our comprehensive cultural history. What if every book that has ever been made public could be revitalized, and we could make that knowledge part of the human consciousness? What will come out of that? I don't know, but I want to live in that future and I want to give that future to my children."

Bob Glass

Futurist

Bob Glass came up through the ranks of technology companies like many of the greatest technologists, via his psychology background and combining it with human factors. Once the human interface manager for engineering at Apple, and then on to Sun with his team in tow, Glass saw that you have a choice: make your technology a bad user experience and people won't use it; make it a flawless experience and it will become a standard. He was at Sun, heading up a team of technologists who were anticipating the way that technology was heading, when they came up with the following user scenario.

"You first pick up a sheet of paper with an active surface," says Glass. "When you pick it up it authenticates you, it makes sure you're a subscriber and that you've paid your dues. Now, imagine if the active surface is also watching where you're looking. Maybe every other pixel is a camera. You pause on a paragraph, it turns red in our little scenario, it goes out to the Internet and pulls in the background material and maybe some video, and it becomes an interactive device. In this case, in our original story, the story was about a flood in Holland wrecking the tulips, and the CEO of the company was about to get on the Internet to make a speech.

"So, we thought okay, we know what chat rooms are like today, but how are we going to use them in the future? From glancing at that paragraph and the sheet knowing that I'm looking at it, it brings in other stuff and says that the press conference is going to happen and it channels me in to the conference. The thing is, I don't want to just *watch* it. Have you ever *really* thought about the Internet? When you're in a busy city there are thousands of people around you. When you're on the Internet there are also thousands of people around you, you just don't know it. Maybe in a chat room you may see a little of it. And we said, somehow we've got to get this sense of society . . . of community. We'll take an example, the chat room. So now I'm watching this video-conference, but separately I'm chatting. But I'm visually chatting—not like typing on a keyboard. And this person is a trusted person whom I know very well, this other one I don't know very well, so her head is smaller . . . building in these little vision cues.

"So while this press conference is going on I could have private conversations in a chat room. I finish and I get a call from you saying that there's a ball game on, so it now turns into a video broadcast system of the ball game. Let's say that you and I would normally go to the game, but I can't go, so your head is big on the screen because I trust you, and now we can talk about the game while it's happening."

Glass made a 90-second video out of this scenario for Sun; not long after that his team was disbanded while Sun concentrated on other technologies within the company. "We made it into this 90-second animation and everyone was saying, *This is stupid, no one is going to have technology like that.* Lo and behold, I started looking back through some military stuff and there was a company that had recently released some continuous thin film technology for the military that was in fact going to enable this stuff. For this particular project—looking at the paper and pausing, going to the Internet, holding the paper and tilting it, having objects work and not work—we received 13 patents. I believe once this technology really happens, Sun is sitting on a real gold mine; they just don't know it. They'll probably trade it off because you know how patent portfolios get traded."

Although Sun chose to not pursue the technology at the time, there are many other companies that are.

Glass has always been ahead of his time with the projects he's worked on. "I think 10 or 20 years from now it won't be anything like what we have today. I think we'll have some kind of technology aura with our personal information that will somehow be hooked up to every other aura. I think the Internet becomes the backbone of what will become nano-technology. With this technology, if I'm out on the street my aura will read yours and yours will read mine, and it'll give us some information about each other. It would tell you something like that we both have parrots, and that I should get to know you because you have an Eclectus bird.

"For me, right now, the Internet is frustrating and not at all what I want. The fundamental differences are that I'm sensory psychologist and right now I can only see and hear, so I'll keep waiting for the technology to evolve, but it will get there. I believe in 10 to 20 years we'll have smell, we'll have touch—we have this today, but it's not widespread. Taste—who knows? But the important thing is that I think the idea of using a computer will just go away and become part of us."

Alan Cooper

Chairman, Cooper Interaction

Alan Cooper is the outspoken author of *The Inmates Are Running the Asylum: Why High Tech Products Drive Us Crazy and How To Restore The Sanity,* and the father of Visual Basic. He currently serves as chairman of Cooper Interaction <www.CooperInteraction.com>, a company that works with developers to create positive human/machine user interaction—one of the biggest challenges developers of hardware and software have faced since the beginning of the industry, and an issue that becomes more complex every day as technologists strive for that ever-illusive ubiquity, and something I like to call Nirvana *(nerve-on-ahhh,* yes, say it out loud, this is a pun. Nanotech will meld technology and your nerves, so the Internet will, conceivably one day be able to stimulate your nerves. *Nerve-on-ahhh.).*

Cooper looks toward an era when computers will be part of our bio system, our nervous system, able to react to the slightest change and need in our sensory perception. *Nerve-on-ahhh*—a time when technology will enable us to fully indulge in work and play, and we'll hardly have to leave our heads to do so.

Cooper Interaction is working toward flawless interaction of the user with the computer, and although this industry is still in its infancy, Cooper believes that technologists are just now starting to see what the future holds.

"In the future, our present concepts of privacy will be over," says Cooper about one of the things that we'll need to give up holding onto if we're going to take full advantage of the future. "The Internet means that every computer will be connected, and Moore's law tells us that in just a few years it will be cheaper to put a computer into something than it will be to paint it. So all manufactured objects will have computers in them. And because they have computers, they'll have software, and because they have software they'll have behavior. Which means it's a permanent employment contract for guys like me who make behavior goods, as opposed to making it technically competent. It means that everything is going to see, and everything is going to hear. There was no Internet 10 years ago. I mean there was, but it was this tiny balkanized thing buried in a few thousand universities. We've seen radical changes in 10 years, and we're going to see more radical changes in the next 10 years.

"There's a theater in San Carlos, California, that was torn down—the Circle Star Theater. It was there for about 30 or 40 years. They tore it down and built a new office building there [Liberate], and between the building and the 101 Freeway they erected an electronic billboard—an LED matrix that has a high-resolution picture about 20 feet across. I'm sure it cost them a lot of money to do that, but Moore's law says that in 10 years, for the cost of a new Buick, you'll be able to have all of the outside walls of that office building coated in the same stuff. So what's to stop companies from doing that?

"Ten years ago buses had advertising cards on the inside and on the outside. Now you get buses that are wrapped in printed plastic to make the entire thing like a billboard. What's to keep buses from having completely digital, changeable surfaces as they drive around town? The point of all this? It's that the Internet allows every computer to talk to every other computer. So the skin of your bus is a computer and the east and west walls of your office building are a computer; they're all going to be talking to each other. It means when I go into GAP and buy a pair of khakis, they're going to have a chip sewn into them so it automatically handles billing, antitheft, and inventory. When I take those home and I walk into the house with them, those jeans get automatically

entered into my home inventory and my home security system. Then when I put on my plaid pants and my striped shirt
they will automatically talk to each other and say, *This is bad,*
and they'll warn me."

> *"I think that our business community hasn't
> figured out how to create software—and the
> Internet is software—and all products are going
> to have software, even your pants from Gap.
> What it means is that every product in the world
> is going to be a digital product, and one of the
> key elements of those products is behavior. Our
> business world doesn't know how to create
> behavior that satisfies and allows us to
> understand how to control it."*
>
> —Alan Cooper, chairman of
> Cooper Interaction

Cooper believes that our future will look very different
because materials that are rare and valuable now will be easily
manufactured with future nanoalchemy, and we'll have to figure out how to apply value to our ever-changing currency.

"In the future, I do believe that there's going to be a resur-
gence of the craft movement; I think we're going to see that
things made out of wood and stone and labored over by crafts-
people will be highly valued and prized in commercial circles.
When you start thinking about miniaturization you rapidly
come to nanotechnology—[Eric] Drexler has this approach
about an appliance that's about the same shape and size as a

microwave oven, except that you punch the button on the outside and you open the door and there's this brick of gold that was just self-assembled by nanobots; they destroyed themselves in doing so. Writing a program to create a nanobot to build an atom of gold and having it build another robot to do the same because the atom of gold is fairly uniform. The idea you can punch a button on the machine and get a brick of gold also means that all the currencies in the world will be thrown into chaos. But, programming a nanobot to build a brick of gold will be fairly simple, but how do you get a nanobot to build you a ham sandwich? That's a very complex thing.

"It's not at all clear to me that you can create a nanobot to create a ham sandwich, because it's software that will create a ham sandwich and I don't think we'll be able to achieve that level of perfection, although I think that writing software to create gold and rubies and diamonds and impervious hard steel will be easy. At a certain point—30 years out—you are looking at self-replicating nanobots, but at that point I think you'll see that all the things that we hold dear in this world—machined objects, gems, steel, will become dirt cheap.

"*Right now the physical infrastructure of the Internet is a very expensive, complex thing. You have to have big corporations with big trucks with big burly men to physically stick poles up and stretch copper and fiber optics down the middle of the streets and it's not really a Web so much as a hierarchy.*"

—Alan Cooper, chairman of
Cooper Interaction

"I think the Internet will eventually become this great democratizing of intelligence—everyone becomes as smart as everyone else because they have access to the information that everyone else does. I don't think that'll apply at a personal level, but it will apply on a community level—that means some farming town in Germany is going to have the same access to intelligence as a building in New York City. What do you choose to do with it? Then there's the other extreme—the people in the rocky high desert in Afghanistan—what do they choose to do with it?"

Charles Ostman

Senior Fellow at the Institute
for Global Futures; Futurist

The Institute for Global Futures (TIGF) is where you'll find Senior Fellow Charles Ostman doing his best to push the envelope a bit farther. Ostman, no stranger to future technologies, has 25 years under his belt in the fields of electronics, physics, computers, artificial intelligence, and, most recently, various aspects of applied and theoretical nanotechnology.

The Institute for Global Futures is a consulting group that provides strategic research, analysis, and business development services to startups and institutions worldwide, including Fortune 500 companies such as Compaq, Fujitsu, General Motors, Kemper Funds, IBM, Nortel, AT&T, Sony, Lockheed Martin, GTE, General Electric, MCI, and Lucent. The focus toward of TIGF is examining the synergistic relationships between emergent advanced technologies and the economic environments in which they may be fostered.

The institute also works with various government agencies engaged in technology development, including participating in the formation of the National Nanotechnology Initiative, a $500M fund recently signed into law.

"When I think of the Internet, I don't think at all about web pages, blinking sales banners, chat rooms, or anything even remotely related to that realm of pedestrian Web traffic. In my frame of reference, the whole dot-com veneer is just that, a surface that many people seemed to fixate on, almost as if it had evolved as a form of an electronic cult phenomena," says Ostman of his view of *The Boom* and *The Crash*. "The Internet is vastly more important, more crucial—mission-critical to our current and future ways of life and being than providing a way to buy widgets online, or looking at someone's pictures. What many people don't see is the potential for the underlying infrastructure that may one day provide the answer to getting what we need, what we want. A vehicle for the delivery of software processes that facilitates the creation and manufacturing of everyday items.

"What will this mean as an industry? How will this change our lives? Think of what Gutenberg's press meant at the beginning of the Renaissance of Europe; it changed the world, it evolutionized the world. Suddenly new knowledge was available, and publishing began to spread and evolve on its own accord. Now, all of these years later, we have the equivalent of a Gutenberg press, except now it's real-time, globally connected, and soon we'll be able to send information—processes—over this platform. What the Internet's future could now represent is a delivery system for manufacturing instructions to self-organizing nanobots. Specific instructions for materializing commerce at the end point where they are sent."

So does this mean the Internet will be used as a super-information highway to deliver the process for a Versace suit—tailored specifically for your body at a small boutique where a technician, for lack of a better word, will oversee the downloading of the process to the awaiting nanobot that will create your suit? Then, one only needs to wrap it up and have it delivered (no need to sign for it because your Internet payment account has already been mechanized to do so)? Ostman feels this is possible in our future world.

"The emergent industries of biotechnology, nanotechnology, and infotechnology are converging into an industrial and cultural realm. I refer to such as the *info/bio/nano trichotomy* of the future. We are crossing into a realm where the very definition of what a lifeform is, or even might become is becoming something of an arbitrary reference. The *Bladerunner* model is not that far off. In fact, the beginning edge of that realm is already here.

"The tools by which life can be *reorganized* at the molecular level is no longer a frontier science, but rather a very rapidly emerging industrial revolution. But what does this have to do with the Internet? Almost parallel with the biotech industry is the quickly emerging nanotechnology industry. Over the past decade, the science of nanotechnology has evolved from what had been a somewhat mythical, and not very well understood area of science by the general world, and is now very quickly being looked upon as a serious solution to an otherwise unsolvable collection of problems. The key to understanding what nanotechnology really is about is to think of it as a manufacturing process at the molecular scale. All living things, for instance, are *biological nanofoundries* in that within the living cells molecules are connected and reconnected as an assembly process. Nanotechnology is the *manmade* version of this process, extended to many different types of materials which can be instigated to self-assemble and organize into complex structures. And what do you think is at the very core of enabling this next evolutionary transitional threshold, this rapidly approaching horizon that we are about to be confronted with? Answer—the Internet."

Ostman also feels that relatively soon the basis of the Internet infrastructure will also feel a huge turn of the tides; those who are ready, flexible, and willing will survive—those who are too stiff in their technology will become dinosaurs.

"Currently, chips are created by growing large cylindrical crystals of silicon, which are then sliced into wafers, and then those wafers need to have their surfaces milled and etched with microscopic features. This is an extremely complex process. Chips of the future won't be milled and etched; they'll be grown directly, quite literally. Process management, in this context, is not meant to be the narrowly defined reference to, say, integrated circuit manufacturing production lines. In fact, speaking of integrated circuits and such, there won't be chips. The process in which chips are created, as in other manufacturing of the future, will be more in the arena of complex molecular systems, grown for a particular purpose, and embedded in virtually everything. In the future, the whole concept of enormous, highly centralized—and also highly toxic—multi-billion-dollar chip foundries will have long since died a somewhat unpleasant economic death due to the realities of rendering such endeavors as being hopelessly irrelevant. In this future environment, process management becomes the key skill, the primary dividing line between those who thrive and those who, metaphorically, perish.

"By this time, the Internet will also develop into something that is living and evolving. The Internet is a spectacularly complex *tissue system* at this point, that will itself not be run and organized with the current, already overburdened, often close to failure mode of traditional routing engines, which themselves are in essence huge switch systems run by clusters of computers executing tens of millions of lines of mostly hand-generated code.

Think of the Internet as an organization of future routing engines—if that term still applies—in which the computers themselves are self-evolving, self-correcting platforms utilizing evolutionary computing and other forms of biologically inspired processes to contiguously optimize their own existence, as a, if I dare say, *living system*."

Where is Ostman going with this theory of a *living* Internet? "Knowledge itself, as it evolves in the future, will become something akin to a living thing which itself is physically constructed from nanotechnology-enabled self-evolving hardware and software. Our knowledge realm will have expanded far beyond anything that one might currently refer to in terms of a data base, or an online library. It will have become, in essence a form of self-organizing collections of experience domains created on a massively ever-growing scale. The autonomous agents and related self-motivating software components of today will have also evolved by this time into something much more robust, as a form of synthetic sentience, to which we, the human species, will become evermore synergistically dependant—a form of human/Internet symbiosis."

Lakshmi Pratury

Volunteer Director, South Asia Region
of Schools Online

What is it that's causing the digital divide to grow wider? Obviously it's a case of the accessibility, or lack thereof, of computers to people, especially children. As I see my niece, who is going on 14, using her e-mail to communicate with me more so than the phone and exercising her ability to grasp high-level user concepts as we talk about technology, I know that she'll do just fine in tomorrow's world.

My father, who turned us both on to using computers— she as soon as she could reach the keyboard from his lap, and me when I was about 10 (in the mid-1970s)—always made sure that we were never intimidated by technology. My dad even went as far as teaching me how to rebuild my Mustang's engine by the time I was 16, and initiating me into the joys of solo air flight as well. Not all kids, let alone girls, are that lucky. In this fragile world economy, some parents don't have the wherewithal to obtain computers, or even keep a roof over their heads and their families fed.

Now that technology is the driver of education and it's increasing at a very high rate, the issue of the digital divide has become even more urgent. In my own travel and contacts with parents and teachers in urban and rural areas, I've noticed that as you get farther away from the technology pockets in the United States, the focus of computers as a tool of supplemental intelligence becomes less important. As a matter of fact, I have run into educators who believe that at this point the Internet is basically porn and shopping— nothing to leave children to their own devices with. So instead of educating children about appropriate use, they abolish computers from their teaching programs. That's scary. When you leave the United States, the importance of computers in society shifts in and out of focus, from crystal clear to completely blurred. It's not unusual to find extreme opinions from culture to culture about how parents feel a computer should relate to their child and that child's future.

One thing I realized early on while traveling to Southeast Asia beginning about a decade ago, was that no matter how deep in the jungles I trekked, I could always find someone with a cell phone. But I could go into village after village and not find a computer, or even someone who knew how to use a computer. Today, however, there are cell phones that give people who never had a computer the ability to send e-mail and even surf the Web. What I'm saying is that wireless and Internet technology has permeated even the deepest of jungles, and reached out to people who have never used Windows or even booted up. What does this mean? It means the future is here—and if we don't train our children to relate, to interact, and to revel in it, this future world will leave our kids behind.

Lakshmi Pratury, Silicon Valley technology venture capitalist, saw the digital divide happening in her home country of India and knew that something radical had to happen to change that country's future. Now she is involved at the ground level as the volunteer director of South Asia Region of Schools Online <www.schoolsonline.org>, an organization whose mission is to help ensure that schools all over the world have effective access to the communication and information resources of the Internet. Since 1996, Schools Online has provided its resources to more than 5,600 schools in the United States and to more than 200 schools in 19 other countries.

"In India, most parents will do anything to ensure a good education for their children, and they see computer technology as an opportunity for their child to progress," says Pratury. "There are even stories of cab drivers and rickshaw pullers who save every penny to buy a computer for their children because they believe that it would ascertain a better life for him/her, providing opportunities that could rid them of the cyclical poverty patterns they have lived with for generations.

"At a national level, India is also encouraging the integration of computers and education because they want to retain their position as the most successful exporter of software skills. Indians, in general, have learned to leverage their abilities to excel in science, math, and computer skills and apply it with their knowledge of English—all skills in demand worldwide as white collar programming talent. The government wants to assure this knowledge continues to be imparted to children from a young age. To that end, the high school curriculum has computer education as a mandatory subject, where children learn the anatomy of a computer—how it works, read books on C++, Visual Basic skills, et cetera.

"In many cases, children read the theory, but may never have had the opportunity to see a computer, let alone work on one. I went to one such school last year, where we had a question and answer session with the children. When we asked how many of them have seen a computer, only 5 to 10 percent raised their hands. When it was their turn to ask questions, some of the questions asked were, *What is the difference between RAM and ROM?* and, *Is studying hardware better than studying software?* They also had other more high-level technology questions. Basically, this session showed us that most of the students had theoretical knowledge but no practical knowledge."

Pratury believes that this type of learning poses two problems. First, a large percentage of the children will know the full capability of a computer; they will know how to program it, theoretically, but will have no practical experience, or know how to use the ever-evolving Internet. The other issue Pratury brings up is that the computer is being taught as an end itself: Learn computer skills and you will have a good job. What about the kids who want to choose a different career path? How will they learn to use the computer in that capacity? How will they learn that it's not the mastery of the design, programming, or maintaining the computer system (engineering, programming, systems administration), but the computer's practical application of the human, that is what the future of technology is all about?

"The problem is that computers are seen as machines that need to be understood and managed," says Pratury of her biggest challenge in India. "Most of the courses are in computer assembly, learning SQL, C++, Visual Basic, networking, systems administration, et cetera. There is limited emphasis on teaching and giving exposure to a child to navigate the Internet, where the computer becomes a vehicle that can bring back information that can add new dimensions to one's learning process.

"In teaching the importance of the Internet, I often give the analogy of cell phones. I ask the children how many of them know how to use the cell phone, and about 80 to 90 percent of the hands go up. Then I ask them if they know how the phone works—what kind of chips are used in manufacturing them, what kind of software is used, what kind of transporters are used. Basically, details on how the technology actually works. Barely any of them raise their hands. Then, I tell them that computers are the same way. For those who want to understand how they work, they can learn the languages, designing and become engineers, but the rest of them should be able to use computers the way one uses cell phones. Then I talk to them about the Internet and how you can surf the Web, get information about anything that you want to know, and that it holds the magic key that can open the door to the world of knowledge."

Pratury attributes the success of the program in India to using teachers who are not computer experts, but rather people who know their way around a computer and the Internet. Another important attribute is the time spent in choosing schools where the principal is committed to making the program successful and undergoes basic computer training with the teachers. "We also choose people who really believe in the power of communication. When we had the first meeting in Mumbai, one of the school principals told me that their school had no resources to buy computers. This was a missionary school, an orphanage that also provided shelter for children with HIV. The principal of the school really wanted to make sure that these children also have the same opportunity as wealthy and healthy kids whose parents could afford computers. With all their savings, she built a room for a computer center, not knowing where the computers were going to come from. She told me that the day she finished the center, our volunteer in Mumbai walked in and asked her if the school would be interested in signing up to have an Internet learning center. She had tears in her eyes as she was telling me this story, and told me that our program has provided her with something she thought was only possible in her dreams.

"Our volunteer told me that when we did the two-day training for the school principals, they all came on time, and stayed way beyond class hours wanting to learn more. At the end of the classes they all wanted to share their feelings. Most government-run or aided schools are so busy struggling just to make the teacher payroll and keeping their children in classes that no one sees the principals or teachers as a resource that needs to be continually trained. This was the first time someone was taking the time to teach them something new."

"We had a teacher training volunteers and teachers in another country; she wanted to show them what the benefit of the computer was so they would first learn that it was a tool they could use to make their lives more efficient. Instead of starting the session by explaining how the computer worked, the teacher said that she had forgotten to bring her teaching notes. But . . . no problem! Because she could log online, go to the web site where she had originally downloaded the information from, open a Word file, and prepare the lesson right in front of their eyes. Now, suddenly, the training was about how to teach their classes more efficiently using the Internet, and not about how to use the Internet. Bottom line? Show them the benefit and the application and not the features and technology."

—Lakshmi Pratury, volunteer director of
South Asia Region of Schools Online

One of the ways that Schools Online has been able to create a successful base of millions of dollars in donations and cash to build its program is to bring personal awareness to the issues that face the organization. They did this, and recommend this to anyone wishing to create a nonprofit that bridges the digital divide by having personal stories, especially on video, to give to philanthropy departments in corporations and news organizations. The organization is currently recording the personal stories of adults and students before and after they were given the Internet resources. Schools Online intends to make the footage into a full documentary to spread the word that proper implementation of Internet technology can make a difference in how the world learns.

> *"I think when it's a choice of including the global reach or not, I'd say go for the global, even though it's probably problematic because you start getting into all kinds of language and culture clashes, and all that good stuff. I think the Web is a global context, and it's probably worth making some effort to make sure that happens. It could be translation software, or translation services—one thing about a-synchronistic communications is that it should make translation very easy. So if I am somebody in Japan who doesn't speak English, and if you don't speak Japanese, we should be able to have a perfectly decent e-mail exchange through an intermediary who speaks both English and Japanese. That should be easy to do on the Net, and it's still relatively difficult."*
>
> —Stewart Brand, cofounder of The Well

"In India, my father's generation fought the British and went to jail, and sacrificed their personal lives to give us freedom," says Pratury. "Their point of contention was that our country was divided into India and Pakistan, and subsequently

Pakistan into Pakistan and Bangladesh. Those who fought for freedom saw the fruits of their labor turned sour by religious riots. As years passed, we became even more separated from our neighbors, and now there is the very real threat of a nuclear bombs looming in everyone's thoughts. If we cannot make peace with our own neighbors, how can we have a prayer to make peace with the world?

"My hope is that if the children from the region start communicating with one another, if they understand that the children from the other country have the same hopes, aspirations, fears, and doubts that they themselves have, maybe, just maybe there is a chance that they will think twice before wishing death upon an imagined enemy. My belief is that it's not what we know that makes us believe that we have enemies, but rather what we do not know that makes us create an enemy. My dream is that one of these children who takes the time and has been given the opportunity to know their neighbors will grow up to lead their country. Then, he or she may be willing to remove the smoke of gunfire that distorts clear vision and walk across the borders to hold their long-lost sibling in a tight embrace. Once we befriend our neighbor, we are able to lift our heads and see that the whole world can be encircled in that embrace. Then the freedom of Cyberspace will truly be instrumental in creating a global village."

Jerome Glenn

Futurist; Director, the Millennium Project

Before 9/11 we thought of a terrorist attack as a physical thing. Now, in its aftermath, we see things in a different light. On what seems a daily basis, we hear of anthrax deliveries in the mail spreading biotech madness . . . and of biological warfare on a larger scale. There are now a plethora of ways to look at the possibilities of the end of the world as we know it. As you go through your everyday life, most of you are probably surprised that there are those among us, and in other nations, whose mission it is to spread peace, to walk through the possible scenarios and work through them . . . to talk with others who are doing the same thing and find solutions to the growing number of ways the world could end up in a tough situation.

Jerome "Jerry" Glenn, director of the Millennium Project at the American Council for the United Nations University <www.acunu.org> is working extremely hard to spread the word about technology and the potential for tragedy; and also to tell of the wonders of change it has, and is, creating.

Back in 1973, Glenn took part in the early NSF-funded experiments with computer media and communication. While partaking in that program, Glenn managed to hook up 26 developing countries to a type of *Internet* communications system called CARINET, which turned out to be the first world computer network.

"We'd take a phone, hook it into a dedicated data line at Cable & Wireless—they didn't have public dial-up then with packet switching. And we'd connect it to the switchboard so I could call in from another country to Cable & Wireless and say, *Give me extension 255,* or whatever it was, then I'd hear a ring and the modem and then put the phone into an acoustic coupler, wrap it up with a hotel towel, and then make the connection. That's the stuff I was involved with to help countries make up their minds to get public dial-up packet switching. So they could eventually play in the bigger game."

The project went into the 1980s, as did its success. The whole point of the project was to broaden the commercial markets for poor nations, that would benefit from both information give-and-take and the posting of their goods for sale.

"I generally would cast it as a less costly telex and the idea that, unlike a telex, the network wouldn't necessarily need to know who your request was going to, whereas with your telex you had a number. With a network, if you had a number of different agencies you could say, *I want to build a hand-built electric insulator out of this—what's the mix, what's the temperature, and what are the specifications?* You send it out to a net, and up comes VITA [Volunteers in Technical Assistance], an organization that knows how to do it, sends out the specifications, the guy builds it, and starts exporting his new electric insulators. When I told VITA that their ham radios could be hooked up to satellites through modems they said I was crazy. They checked it out and now VITA has VITASAT, which is a ham radio computer e-mail worldwide system. It was 1980 or 1981 or so when they said I was crazy. But several years later they got VITASAT going.

"GreenStar is putting up satellite transceivers and little economic development units out in the middle of nowhere so people get the equipment in exchange for GreenStar being their sales agent—it's venture capitalism. GreenStar takes a percentage of the business; they can pay back for their equipment by selling their music or art that don't cost a whole lot [to produce] through the Internet. So this whole idea of computer communications as a development tool was pioneered through CARINET, now owned by CGNET. Back then, there was a general hostility toward technology by development professionals in developing communities. Largely they were trying to stay away from it. Now, it's there, but I have to tell you they were hostile to it at first.

"Partnership for Productivity [PfP] in which CARINET was created—intrepreneurship—was the pioneer in microcredit. We set up the first USAID money for microcredit systems in Africa and other countries. We were known as the smart kids on the block on how to make poor economies work. So I added into that the idea of computer communications as part of that tool. There are management techniques, and credit and communication are very important for an economy to survive. Eventually, CARE bought PfP International, but didn't see any value in CARINET, so a group of five other development organizations bought it, and in turn sold it to CGNET. CARE bought up PfP because it wanted to get involved in economic development.

"CARINET felt like having a little electronic baton running around third-world countries and causing all these smiles to occur. We would plug a jack right into the telephone company's switchboard with Whisper Writers, which could get through airport checks because they looked like electric typewriters rather than computers—and god forbid—computer communications devices; at that time what we were doing was against the law because we were a common carrier and Cable & Wireless—held monopoly agreements in most developing countries, and they'd say, *Who are you with a communications device?* Our acoustic broadcast went right into the air so it wasn't touching their electronics, so technically we were not breaking the law. When I would get caught, I would simply tell them that we weren't putting in a network, that we were simply testing the equipment to see if it would be possible."

Glenn went on to write a book titled *Future Mind: Artificial Intelligence, The Merging of the Mystical and the Technological in the 21st Century* that addresses humans augmenting their capabilities with nanotechnology in and on their bodies and the external environment. A philosopher and futurist by training, Glenn tackles some very heavy duty subjects when he meets with others from all over the world who have the same goal in mind; peace. Peace in convergence with technology.

"The biggest prejudice of all time between all cultures is the prejudice between the mystic and the technocrat," says Glenn. "The mystic says something and the technocrat says, *Baloney, I don't read that stuff,* and vice versa. They both ignore each other, yet we are all part mystic and part technocrat—one just dominates the other—and it seemed to me we could make a healthy civilization if we get the mystic half and the techno half in concert and get them working together.

"Then it hits me that it's going to have to happen anyway because as we increasingly make technology sentient and we ourselves become augmented with artificial technology, those two trends are going to blur, and to make this blurring intelligent it would force a conversation between the two. This concept of conscious technology as a post-information-age concept would help to reduce a lot of other prejudices in its wake. The idea of having neurons attached to silicon is now a big thing. Technology like a VCR is becoming more intelligent, almost sentient—it remembers your programming—you tell it what you like, and it goes out and finds it. Next people will do more complex things that could become information warfare.

"The only real solution to terrorist stuff—and the farther into the future I looked with the complexity of the technology and information warfare—is that we're just going to have to make a full-court press on how to make enlightened human beings. That's the design requirement—you're Silicon Valley, your next application is making enlightened human beings. Not more information. We've got that—mission accomplished,

A+. Done. The next thing is wisdom and wise use, because the ability for one human being to screw up the system is going to be so much easier in the future than it's been in the past. Obviously the airplanes [WTC] are an example. It's a very big deal, I can give you scenarios that'll make you nervous."

And with that, and because I'm very interested in what the future holds; I baited him on. What I found was that my concern for this planet went up a notch on my private Richter scale.

"Do you believe that you can get 100 martyrs?" Glenn asked. As recent events have shown, there are certainly those who can. I nodded my head. "Do you believe that whoever can recruit these martyrs has enough money for 100 airplane tickets to 20 of the top airports in the world?" I nodded once again. "Do you think they can buy their way into the Congo to get some Ebola?" Anything is possible with enough money. "So you get these martyrs, you give them Ebola virus two weeks ahead of their scheduled flights, then they all go to 20 airports, five of them for each of the airports, and they hang out. In two weeks the skin starts to burst a bit, and slowly but surely they've been infecting people over a 24-hour period and those people are off in many different directions."

I then realized that it wasn't a matter of getting anthrax into an airborne situation—we probably do have enough Cipro to cure people (if caught in time, and the CDC is making it a priority to prepare all medical outlets about the symptoms), at least if I was Bayer, I'd be cranking it out at double-time to get it to the hands of the panicked Cipro-buying public before Congress decides to make its patent worthless. At least the casualties would be far less than an Ebola outbreak.

"People say, *How are you going to get it in the air-conditioning system? How are you going to get it in the water?* Glenn points out. "You don't. You get it into the body; the body is the bomb. You cut out the middleman and you don't need to send an airplane into a building. In one day you've sent Ebola to the whole world. And the thing is that people won't know for another two weeks . . . and they just keep moving. There's no real footprint. Even in nuclear war, or chemical war, there's a footprint, but not in biological war. You could literally infect major hunks of the world's population where getting quarantines together wouldn't work."

That statement really made me reevaluate the world's priorities. "We don't need more examples," says Glenn, sparing me of any further fodder for my nightmares. "What we need, though, is to challenge the Silicon Valleys of the world to say the next design requirement is enlightenment: it's no longer a religious luxury, or a civil responsibility—it's a survival requirement. I think it's more possible than people think.

"Three hundred years ago, if I went to another country to do business, I would have had bodyguards. The odds are there'd be a mishap somewhere. Now when I go to another country I don't even know who is driving this metal can in the air. I trust my life to someone who meets me at the airport and drives me somewhere. Think of how many people today are speaking nicely to strangers. We have all this trust—this amount of niceness among strangers in the world is really quite extraordinary. We have a reason to be so trusting, just like the little birds that know when to duck the cars and the people.

"People talk about self-organization, what happens if the Internet really is the medium for self-organizing the global brain?" says Glenn, in the way only a true futurist asks. "Brains learn by feedback, bull gets exposed. Eventually it gets defeated, it takes a while. The faster the feedback the larger the focus, and the faster we'll be able to get rid of the bull. Here's a challenge for the applications. How do we make

"*We are living in a far more peaceful, friendly world than ever before. There are six billion people in the world, and how many of them are trying to kill each other? Not that many. When there were a billion people—a hundred years ago, you went to answer your door with a gun in your hand. Let's go back to the Internet, the amount of conversations and human connectedness of like minds, in a positive sense, is extraordinary.*"

—Jerome Glenn, futurist, and director
of the Millennium Project

the global brain healthy rather than pathological? That we are moving forward either metaphorically or anatomically—a globally connected conscious technology, or we're not. If we are, how do we move away from pathology and toward enlightenment? It's that kind of seriousness. I think we have to talk in these terms because some of these negative scenarios are quite real. Can you get down to .00001 percent of the population being nasty? Yeah, I think so, and if you have enough goodness, the rest works itself out."

Bringing things to an historical close, Glenn reminds me of a past that I was never aware of while growing up in Hawaii and California. I was just never aware of prejudice because it wasn't a part of my world; as an adult I am aware of it through hearing of instances and seeing it on a global scale, but it wasn't part of my upbringing. It's amazing what you don't learn if you don't hear it in the household as a child. Civil rights and education have made this country a more tolerant place.

"In the 1950s, in the United States, an Italian marrying an Irishman was a *no-no*. Now it's no big deal. Now it's the Caucasian marrying the Black, and back then, they would shoot you for that. Now, increasingly, you see mixed couples on television—you would have never seen this before. These are major shifts in our lifetimes.

"Remember in Tai Chi, what's called *push-hands*? I do a little push-hands metaphorically with the head futures [futurists in the program] from each nation—and as long as we're balanced we're the best of allies. If we're not, maybe he'll take advantage and we'll see. The two of us are trying to stop the economic and informational warfare between the United States and their own countries—for real. There are also countries that are trying to work things out because they've been at war with each other before. Historians tell us when two tribes fight they usually fight again. It's unusual for one tribe to fight just once and that's it. Especially when one tribe has never been defeated. So is there a reason for them to try again? We know about the momentum of things, we know about the future warfare systems."

Much of this conflict is caused by countries feeling that they are not on an even playing field. Glenn feels that optimism and hope are just as key as diplomacy in matters of war and peace. "Some futurists of the '70s—not me—used to talk about *development triage, Why put any money into India? They will never make it, so why waste the money and effort?* Bull. They were wrong, and unfortunately, it held up a lot of investment decisions. Ideas have to be sold. Look at Bucky Fuller [Buckminster Fuller]. When he talked, people thought he was hopelessly romantic; now his ideas about doing more with less, synergy, all of his concepts . . . now he's all of a sudden a very practical guy. So we have to fight hard with people who say, *Not possible.* That's as much of the problem as bin Laden. They may not be the point on the sword, but for those around who say it's not possible to solve these problems—especially the big ones like the enlightenment of humanity—then, it's less likely to get done.

"So we have to answer the question about the healthy brain. We are starting to answer that question right now *anatomically* and *genetically.* Just the other day they found one of the gene combinations on language. On language, for crying out loud! Will we be able to say to people, *If you want to modify your children to be geniuses, you also have to take this other modification for them to be nice, too?* We don't want to make bad geniuses, we want to make good geniuses. That's part of the bargain to get the genius genetic modification. These are things that were considered to be far out, but now they're decisions. Now back to the question—what's the killer app to make humans enlightened? And I'm willing to bet that, looking back, it will not sound silly. Some will say the killer app turned out to be genetic engineering and not the Internet. Someone else will say that the answer is cyber interactive stuff with the neuro network system in the human brain, where if a wild, crazy thing is thought the whole world network is alerted. Those are applications on the Internet [or what will evolve into the Internet] where you could actually begin talking about making the world better.

"We decided to end slavery when many philosophies said it was in the order of things. People say that war is in the order of things, but I believe it can be ended like slavery was. The battle is won in the mind. And that's where information warfare comes in. You get a Carl Sagan up there saying that a nuclear winter will finish us off—that was very important. Whether Carl was right or wrong didn't matter . . . mission accomplished. Can we get another Carl up there saying there are applications for enlightenment and we're going to peruse them and that's the big Manhattan Project of the future?"

Fini? No, it's just the beginning.

INDEX

Abril, Amadeu Abril, 133
Acceptable use policies, 174
Acquisition, as business strategy, 145
Adobe, and copyright infringement, 83, 84, 89, 105
Advanced Research Project Agency (ARPA):
  early research at, 16, 19–21
  Internet development role of, 34–40
Alexa Internet, 223
Alexandria, library of, 120, 223, 225
ALOHA packet radio, 25
Amazon.com, 32, 127
American Council for the United Nations University, 253
American Express, 185
America Online (AOL), 56–57, 61
Anthrax, as terrorist weapon, 257
Antiterrorism legislation, 78
Apollo space missions, 69–70
Apple Computer, 117, 118
ARPANET:
  AT&T involvement in, 191
  creation of, 17, 20–23
  deployment of, 24–25, 41
  evolution of, 26, 28, 36–37
  function of, 34
  as Internet forerunner, 45, 113
  return on investment from, 148
Artificial intelligence, 212
Asimov, Isaac, 5
Association for Computing Machinery (ACM), 48

Asynchronous Transfer Mode (ATM), 146
AT&T:
  early Internet resistance of, 170, 191
  future research by, 191–192
  and packet switching research, 44
Auerbach, Karl, 133
Augmentation Research Center, 33–34
Avatars (Damer), 65, 123
Avatar technology:
  and copyright issues, 124–125
  function of, 65–74

Baker, Fred, interview with, 173–175
Bandwidth:
  amount per user, 147
  and Internet, 148, 149, 169, 177
  of networks, 173
  personal versus Internet, 143
Baran, Paul, 19, 29
Barlow, John Perry:
  on copyright issues, 124
  on DCMA, 78
  as Electronic Frontier Foundation founder, 60, 112, 127
  on government role in technology, 80, 90, 98, 116–120
  on Internet architecture, 102
  on Sklyarov case, 85
  on the Well, 113–116
Barnes, Doug, 54
Barnes & Noble, 127

263

Bell Laboratories, 43–44
Beranek, Leo, 18
Berners-Lee, Tim, 33, 49
Bhushan, Abhay, 24
Biological warfare, 258
Biotechnology:
    convergence with information
        technology, 165, 172, 240
    in diagnostic tools, 218
    future emphasis on, 200,
        209–210
    human-embedded, 233 (*See also*
        Human-embedded
        technology)
    military interest in, 199
Blair, Tony, 129
Blogger, 63
Blokzijl, Robert, 133
Bluetooth technology:
    function of, 163
    future of, 187–190
    in local area networks, 181
Bolt, Beranek & Newman (BBN),
    18, 23, 25, 41
Bootstrap Institute, 35, 205
Brand, Stewart:
    on computer-human connection,
        196
    on copyright issues, 114
    on current Internet status, 80
    on dot-coms, 53
    on freedom versus privacy, 95
    on global Web, 251
    on new technology, 59
    as Well founder, 57, 60
Brilliant, Larry, 57
Britton, Benjamin, 69
Broadband:
    in Korea, 150
    policy on, 177–178
    support for, 170, 171
    widespread use of, 191
Brush, Heidi, 79
Bush, George W., 80

Bush, Vannevar:
    and electronic archiving, 223
    on human evolution, 31, 203
    as Internet innovator, 10–13, 26

Cable & Wireless, 253, 255
Campos, Ivan Moura, 133
CARE, 255
CARINET, 253–255
Carnegie Institute of Washington, 12
Case, Steve, 56
Caspian Networks, 31, 145
Cell phones:
    applications for, 151, 188
    global roaming with, 159
    Internet-enabled, 164, 174, 190,
        246
    ubiquity of, 246
Censor information technology, 199
Center for the Public Domain,
    99–100, 125, 215
Cerf, Vinton:
    on current Internet issues, 81–82
    as Draper prize winner, 145
    and ICANN, 133, 137
    on Internet evolution, 111
    and Internet protocols, 25, 131
    interview with, 163–167
    on public key infrastructure, 91
    at UCLA, 44, 221
    on URL registration, 135
CERHAS project, 69–70
CGNET, 254–255
Chapin, Lyman, 133
Chat rooms, 229–230
Child Online Protection Act, 109
China, cyber cafés in, 5
Chouinard, Joe, interview with,
    183–185
Cisco, 47, 145, 173, 175
Civil liberties:
    versus national security, 78–79
    protection of, 112, 119
Clark, Wes, 22

Client-server architecture, 35
Clinton, Bill, 79, 109, 129
Clinton Administration, and
 telecommunications legislation,
 79, 80
Cohen, Danny, 25
Cohen, Jonathan, 133
Cold War, and Internet origin, 8
Communication Nets (Kleinrock), 16
Computer crime, 116–119. *See also*
 Hackers; Sklyarov, Dimitry
Computer graphics, development of,
 19
Computer networks. *See also*
 ARPANET, CARINET
 as development tool, 254
 early research in, 17, 19, 22,
  28–29, 31, 34, 39–41, 46–48
 infrastructure of, 146–147, 173,
  174
 national, 45
 during World Trade Center
  attacks, 29–30
Computer programmers:
 from India, 247
 nature of, 86
Computers:
 access to, 245
 compatibility of, 21–22, 159
 early research in, 18–19
 educational role of, 245–252
Contact Consortium, 65
Cooper, Alan:
 interview with, 233–237
 on technology evolution, 75
Cooper Interaction, 75, 233
Copyrights:
 and archival information, 123
 drawback of, 215
 duration of, 100
 future role of, 152–155
 infringement on, 120–121
 international view of, 128–129
 legislation on, 104–106

protection of, 80–82, 84, 88, 101,
 118
Corporation for National Research
 Initiatives (CNRI), 169
Crack magazine, 116
Craigslist, 50–52
Crocker, Steve, 24, 25, 44
CSNET, 25, 45, 46
Cyber cafés, 5
Cybercash, 154. *See also* Micropay-
 ment systems
Cyberspace:
 avatar technology as, 65–70, 72
 culture of, 116
 as global village, 252
 legislation in, 79
 property rights in, 120–121

Damer, Bruce:
 and avatar technology, 65–74
 on intellectual property issues, 123
DARPA:
 Bob Kahn at, 169
 return on investment to, 148
 role in Internet evolution, 17,
  44–46
Databases, origins of, 35
DayPop, 64
D-Day, 6–7
Dead Heads, 113
Defcon, 83
Defense Advanced Research Projects
 Agency. *See* DARPA
Defense Communications Agency,
 25
Dense Wave Division Multiplexing.
 See DWDM
Developing countries, technology in,
 254–255
Digital books, 206–207
Digital Equipment Corporation
 (DEC):
 early computer from, 18
 Research Center, 24

Digital integration, 161
Digital Millenium Copyright Act
    (DMCA):
  and encryption, 98
  freedom versus security issue with,
    77–80
  future of, 106
  government support for, 101–103,
    110
  and hackers, 105
  and Sklyarov case, 82, 84, 89, 90
  technologist view of, 104
DigitalSpace Corporation, 65, 70
DoCoMo, 150–151
Domain Name System (DNS):
  administration of, 132–134
  development of, 25
  internationalization of,
    138–139
Draper, John, 118
Draper prize, 145
Dreyfuss, Richard, 124
DWDM, 191

Ebola virus, as terrorist weapon,
    257–258
EBook software:
  market for, 206–207
  protection of, 83–85
E-commerce:
  early assessment of, 32
  function of, 49
  payment system for (*See* Micro-
    payment systems)
Economy:
  in developing countries, 255
  postwar effect on, 8
  and technology boom, 171,
    189
Education, technology role in,
    245–252
E Ink, 179–182, 231
ElcomSoft, 83–85, 88, 89
Electronic books, 155

Electronic Frontier Foundation
    (EFF):
  founding of, 80, 112, 119
  and Internet architecture, 102
  naming of, 127
  and The Well, 60
E-mail:
  address configuration for, 23, 25
  via cell phone, 151
  as community tool, 75
  encryption software for, 91
  management of, 24
  origins of, 13, 32, 42, 48
  role of, 148, 197
  satellite technology for, 254
  specifications for, 25
  and weblogs, 63
Embedded computing, 187
Embedded connectivity, 187
Encryption:
  detection of, 108
  hacking of, 83, 109
  and national security, 3, 95, 96
  and Pearl Harbor attack, 7, 8
  and radio-based transmissions,
    163
  regulation of, 80, 82, 109,
    111–112, 122
  software for (*See* Pretty Good Pri-
    vacy (PGP))
Engelbart, Douglas:
  influences on, 12–15
  interview with, 203–207
  at Stanford Research Institute, 24,
    33
  technology contributions from,
    34–35
Ericsson Technology, 163, 187–190
Eslambolchi, Hossein, interview
    with, 191–192
Estrin, Gerald (Jerry), 44, 221
Estrin, Judy:
  interview with, 221–222
  on misuse of technology, 92

Estrin, Thelma, 221
Ethernet, design of, 25

Fair use, 80, 81, 88, 119–120
Fano, Robert, 17
Farber, David J.:
    background of, 43–44
    and computer networking,
        45–48
    on DCMA, 110
    on encryption, 98, 108
    at FCC, 106–109
    Interesting People list from,
        62–63, 107
    interview with, 201–202
    on privacy, 105
Federal Communications Commis-
    sion (FCC), 107, 109, 201
File transfer protocols, 23, 24
Freedom:
    of information, 4–5
    Internet as tool for, 252
    restrictions on, 79–81, 112
Fuller, Buckminster, 260
Future Mind (Glenn), 255

Gates, Bill, 48
Gene modification, 261
Get a Single Life (Simpson), 54
Gigabit Test Beds, 47
Gilmore, John, 119
Glass, Bob, interview with,
    229–231
Glenn, Jerome, interview with,
    253–261
Global project management, 73
Goldstein, Emanuel, 115
Google, 64
Gore, Al, 80, 110
Governance:
    of Internet, 138
    as political issue, 80
Government:
    and antiterror technology, 199

    response to computer crime,
        116–119
    role in technology control, 95–98,
        106–108, 110, 112, 177, 209
Grateful Dead, 112, 113
GreenStar, 254

Haartsen, Jaap, interview with,
    187–190
Hackers:
    conferences for, 83, 118
    skills of, 114
    threat posed by, 79, 89, 116
Handheld devices. *See also* Cell
    phones; Wireless technology
    displays for, 180–181
    interconnectivity of, 190,
        216–217, 246
Harper's magazine, 113
Hatch, Orrin, 78
Heart, Frank, 23
Hertzfeld, Charlie, 20
Homes, wireless applications for,
    164, 190, 198
Honeywell 516 minicomputers, 23
Host-to-host protocol, 24, 41
Human-embedded technology:
    desirability of, 226
    drawbacks of, 199–200
    evolution of, 211–212, 233, 256
    as futuristic, 201
Human enlightenment, technology
    applied to, 256–261
Human factor:
    effect on Internet, 50
    in technology development,
        256–257
Human Interface Technology (HIT)
    Lab, 200
Human-machine interface, 196, 233,
    243
Human population, sustainability of,
    204
Hush Communications, 91

Hyperlinks, invention of, 13
Hypermedia, early research in, 35

IBM, 19, 46
ICANN, 132–139, 163
India, computer education in,
 246–249
Infocom, 19
Information:
 accessibility of, 31, 32
 freedom to transfer, 4–5
Information Processing Techniques
 Office (IPTO), 17, 19, 21, 24
Information technology (IT):
 elitist aspects of, 221, 260
 emphasis shift from, 200
 future of, 240
 origins of, 12
Inmates Are Running the Asylum, The
 (Cooper), 75, 233
Instant messaging, 57, 68
Institute for Global Futures, The
 (TIGF), 239
Institute for the Future (IFTF), 197
Intellectual property. *See also* Copyrights; Patents
 in Cyberspace, 120
 international view of, 129
 protection of, 82, 110–111,
 125–126
 tangibility of, 100
Interactivity, future role of, 150, 229
Interesting People list, 62–63, 107
Interface Message Processors (IMPs),
 23, 24, 40
Internet. *See also* World Wide Web
 access to, 221, 237
 architecture of, 41
 and Cold War, 8
 commercial transition of, 26, 47
 community on, 50, 52–54, 57–58,
 60, 61, 66, 75, 113, 142, 230,
 259
 copyright issues with, 81

cultural influence of, 121, 225
device connectivity of, 163, 165,
 172, 179, 246
evolution of, 16, 19–20, 22–23,
 26–27, 165, 234, 242–243 (*See
 also* ARPANET)
function of, 221, 248–250
future of, 149–150, 165,
 169–170, 174, 197, 231,
 239–240
as global village, 5, 175, 251,
 252
growth of, 38, 42, 43, 49, 81,
 143, 147–149, 151–152
impetus for, 36–38
infrastructure for, 146–147, 236
nanotechnological role of, 241
and national security, 3–4, 79
as news source, 3, 26, 28, 59
 61–64
number of users of, 164, 169
as partner source, 54–55
security infrastructure for, 97,
 172
smart technology for, 211
standards for, 137–139
during terrorist attacks, 2–3,
 29–30, 50–52, 171, 172
transactions on, 82, 143,
 152–155, 159, 183–185
wireless applications for, 191,
 205
Internet Archive, 120–123,
 223–225, 227
Internet Assigned Numbers Authority (IANA), 132
Internet Corporation for Assigned
 Names and Numbers. *See*
 ICANN
Internet Engineering Task Force
 (IETF), 173
Internet protocols:
 development of, 25, 41, 132,
 163

proprietary versus open, 131
and speech processing technology,
165
and switching technology, 146
Internet service providers (ISPs),
evolution of, 47
Internet2, 173–174
Internic, 134–135
Interrupt Culture, 69
Intrapreneurship, 255
IP:
development of, 132
dominance of, 191
function of, 25, 30, 198
version 6, 166
Iuliano, James, interview with,
179–182

JCB, 185
Joint Research and Development
Board, 11
Journalism, Internet effect on, 59

Kahle, Brewster:
and copyright issues, 101
and Internet Archive, 100,
120–123
interview with, 223–227
on open versus proprietary protocols, 131
Kahn, Bob, 23–25, 37, 44, 45,
47
as Draper prize winner, 145
and Internet protocols, 131
interview with, 169–172
Kamikazes, 8
Kapor, Mitch, 60, 102, 118
Katalov, Alex, 83
Kleinrock, Leonard:
and ARPANET, 23, 24, 37
on computer networking, 39,
41
as Draper prize winner, 145
on encryption, 94, 97

influences on, 15–16
on Internet creation, 36, 42
interview with, 157–161,
211–213
Knowledge:
evolution of, 242
increasing, 204
Internet tools for, 74
power of, 4–5
Korea, broadband use in, 150
Kremen, Gary, 134–136

Leahy, Patrick, 77, 78, 101–103
Libraries:
digital, 224 (*See also* Internet
archive)
traditional, 225
Library of Congress, 227
Licklider, J.C.R., 12, 16–20, 31
Light technology, 175
Lincoln Labs (MIT), 20
Linking, early research in, 35
LiveJournal, 63
Local area networks (LANs), 44,
191
Lynn, M. Stuart, 137, 138

Magaziner, Ira, 137
Mainframe computer, 18, 31
Manila software, 63
Marimba, 177, 209
Massachusetts Institute of Technol-
ogy (MIT):
in computer evolution, 10, 16, 17,
20
in Internet development, 37
MasterCard, 185
Match.com, 56, 134, 135
McCarron, Pat, 65
MCI, commercialization of Internet
by, 26
McLuhan, Marshall, 58
McQuillan, John, 25
Memex, 12–13

Metcalf, Robert, 25
Mickapetris, Paul, 25
Microcredit systems, 255
Micropayment systems:
  and copyrght issues, 152–154
  deployment of, 183–185
  and Napster, 143
Microprocessors, effect of, 187,
  197
Microsoft, 128, 175
Military:
  Internet use by, 27
  sensor use by, 199
  technological research for, 12, 17
Millennium Project, 253
Minicomputer(s):
  DEC PDP-1, 18
  Honeywell 516, 23
Mitnick, Kevin, 79
Mobile devices. *See* Wireless technol-
  ogy
Mobile house network, 164
Mobile payment industry, 185
Moore's Law, 151, 233–234
Mouse (computer), invention of, 13,
  35, 203
Multi Communicator Link (MC
  Link), 188
Multitasking, 67

Nanotechnology:
  convergence with information
    technology, 165
  evolution of, 241
  human-embedded, 256
  and Internet applications, 205,
    231
  medical applications for, 172
  robotics using, 235–236
Napster, 88, 143
National Defense Research Committee, 11
National Nanotechnology Initiative,
  239

National Research and Education
  Network (NREN), 46, 47
National Science Foundation (NSF):
  and ARPANET support, 45
  early networking at, 25, 46, 253
  research funding by, 171
National security:
  versus civil liberties, 78–79
  Internet role in, 3–4, 79
  and technology research, 171
Network Associates Inc., 91
Network Information Center (NIC),
  35
Network Measurement Center
  (UCLA), 23, 24, 40
Network Solutions, 134–136
Network Working Group (NWG),
  24
Neuromancer (Gibson), 199
Newmark, Craig, 50–51
New Prometheus League, 117,
  118
Newsgroups, 42, 93
Next Generation Internet (NGI),
  165, 169, 173
Nichols, Trey, 142
Nomadic computing, 41, 158
Nomadix, 157, 158, 211
NSFNET, 25
Nuance, 164

Office of Scientific Research and
  Development, 11
1–click shopping, 127
ONLine System (NLS), 34, 35
Open source software:
  and development competition,
    130
  Internet protocols as, 131
  virtues of, 99, 128
Optical networks, 174, 191
Ornstein, Severo, 23
Ostman, Charles, interview with,
  239–243

Packet Radio Net, 25
Packet switching:
    advantage of, 28
    origins of, 16, 22, 44, 160, 211,
        253–254
Papyrus, use in archiving, 225
Partnership for Productivity (PfP),
    255
Partridge, Craig, 25
Patents:
    drawback of, 215
    filing of, 126–128
    on future technology, 230
    as political issue, 80, 82, 106,
        125
    protection of, 118, 126
    on software, 129–130
PDP-1 computer (DEC), 18
Peace programs, technology role in,
    252, 253, 256–261
Pearl Harbor:
    effect on technology, 199
    Japanese attack on, 7, 193
Pentagon, terrorist attack on, 2
Personal computers, 31
Personal computing, windows-style,
    13
Pew Internet & American Life Proj-
    ect, 52, 53
Phone networks, versus computer
    networks, 29–30, 40
Pisanty, Alejandro, 133
Plug-and-play capability, 158, 159
Polese, Kim:
    on encryption policy, 110–112
    interview with, 177–178,
        209–210
    during terrorist attacks, 2–3
Postel, Jon:
    and file transfer protocol, 24
    and ICANN, 137
    and Internet protocols, 25, 132
    and packet switching research,
        44

Powell, Michael, 109
Pratury, Lakshmi, interview with,
    245–252
President's Information Technology
    Advisory Committee (PITAC),
    171
Pretty Good Privacy (PGP),
    90–96
Privacy:
    future role of, 233
    protection of, 80, 82, 105, 111
Process management, future role of,
    241, 242
Project MAC, 17, 19
PSI Network, 47
Public key infrastructure, 91

Radio transmission technology, 163,
    165, 169, 187–189
Rainie, Lee, 53
Rand Corporation, 19, 39, 43
Rave Awards, 84, 131
Raytheon, 12
Red Hat, 99, 215
Research:
    computer networking for, 46
    government funding for, 171
    industrialization of, 199
    patents on, 129–130
    time study of, 18
    at universities, 11–12
Rheingold, Howard, 69
Rickey, Branch, 36
Roberts, Lawrence:
    and ARPANET, 19–25, 28,
        31–32, 34, 35, 39
    and computer networking, 16
    on encryption, 96
    on Internet function, 26–32
    interview with, 145–155
Robotics, in nanotechnology, 236,
    240
Roddenberry, Gene, 5
Roosevelt, Franklin D., 6, 7, 11

Routing:
  distributed, 160
  evolution of, 25
Ruina, Jack, 16

Saffo, Paul, interview with, 197–200
Sagan, Carl, 261
Satellite technology, 254
SATNET (satellite network), 25
Scalability:
  and centralized control, 160
  importance of, 38
  improvement of, on Web, 63
  of Internet, 152
Schools Online, 245–252
Schweickart, Russell, 70
Science, role in war, 4, 256–259
Science fiction:
  and digital information, 75
  influence of, 5, 6
Scientific Data Systems, 40, 43
Scripting News, 62, 63
SDS 940 computer, 24
Search engines, limitations of, 223
Self-organization, 258
Semiconductor technology:
  future of, 241–242
  for wireless applications, 181
Sensors:
  military applications for, 199
  proliferation of, 198
September 11, 1991:
  Internet impact of, 29, 30, 51–52,
    64, 172
  and national security, 171, 253
  personal impact of, 1
  and privacy rights, 80
Sex.com, 134
Shatner, William, 6
Sigma 7 computer, 24, 40
Simpson, Liz, 54
Sklyarov, Dimitry, 77, 82–89, 108,
  119
Sky City avatar project, 72–73

Smart technology, 211, 256
SMTP, 132
Snow Crash (Stephenson), 201
Software:
  developers of, 247
  for encryption, 90
  as intellectual property, 82,
    129–130
  proprietary versus open source,
    99, 117, 130–132
  self-evolving, 242–243
  universally embedded, 235
Software agents, 212, 213
SONET, 191
Spam, 61
Speech recognition technology, 164
Spottiswood, John, 56
Stanford Research Institute (SRI),
  15, 24, 33, 39
Star Trek, 5
Sun Microsystems, 230
Sutherland, Ivan, 19, 20
Synchronous Optical Network. *See*
  SONET
Syrian Library, 225
System Development Corporation,
  39

Taylor, Robert:
  and ARPANET, 20, 22, 34, 35
  and IPTO, 24
TCIP, 131
TCP:
  development of, 132
  function of, 25
TCP/IP, 163
TechNet, 177, 178
Technology:
  craftsmanship in, 235
  cultural effect of, 143, 175, 201,
    226, 256
  in developing communities, 255
  economic downturn of, 171
  educational role of, 245–252

environmental effect of, 203–204
future of, 195–196, 200,
    217–218, 229–231
and industry consolidation, 103
innovative, 59, 161, 198
as intellectual property (*See* Copy-
    rights; Intellectual property;
    Patents)
oversight of, 9–10, 101, 178
in peace mission, 253, 258–261
promotion of, 177
restrictive legislation on, 78,
    101–110, 122
smart, 211, 256
and user intentions, 92
in war on terrorism, 3, 199
women's relationship with,
    221–222, 245
Technology Transfer Institute Van-
    guard (TTIV), 157
Terminal Interface Processor (TIP),
    early use of, 24
Terrorism:
    effect on technology, 10, 171, 199,
        256, 257
    Internet as medium for, 79
Tomlinson, Ray, 23
TTI Vanguard, 211

UCLA, 23, 24, 37–40
Universities. *See also specific universi-
    ties*
    computer networking at, 46, 173,
        174
    computer science programs at, 45
    research at, 11–12
University of California at Santa Bar-
    bara, 39
University of Utah, 39
Unmanned Aerial Vehicle (UAV), in
    Afghan war, 199
URLs:
    disputes over, 133, 135–136
    registration of, 132

U.S. Department of Commerce,
    133, 134
U.S. Department of Justice (DOJ):
    in Sklyarov case, 87–89
    in Zimmermann case, 94
U.S. Patent and Trademark Office,
    130
User groups, population of, 53
UUNet, 166

VBNS network, 166
VeriSign Inc., 133–134
Video conferencing:
    failure of, 67
    future of, 150, 229–230
    origins of, 13
Videophones, 5, 217
Virtual conferences, 67
Virtual reality, 65–66, 124–125
Visa e-commerce channel, 183
Visionaries, 194
Visual Basic, 233
VITASAT, 254
Vittal, John, 25
Voice over Internet, 150, 169
Volunteers in Technical Assistance
    (VITA), 254

WAIS, 120
Walden, Dave, 23
War companies, 8
Warfare, technology role in, 7–8, 11,
    199, 256–259
Webcams, drawbacks of, 67
Webex, 67
Weblogs, 62–64
WebPersonals.com, 54
Well, The:
    community on, 58, 61, 113
    copyright issues on, 114
    creation of, 57–58
    influence of, 60
    as news source, 59
    as opinion outlet, 118

Wide area networks:
early research in, 17
mobile access to, 188
Windows technology, 13, 158
Winer, Dave:
on future of technology, 195
on intellectual property, 129–132
weblog from, 62–64
Wireless Application Protocol
(WAP), 189
Wireless technology. *See also* Bluetooth technology
applications for, 164, 166, 170
bandwidth for, 151
display technology for, 181–182
effect on Internet, 169–170
encryption issues with, 97
evolution of, 216
as investment, 171
links for, 160, 163
standards for, 191
transactions using, 183
ubiquity of, 246
WorldCom, 163, 166
World Internet Center, 195
World Trade Center, terrorist attacks
on, 1, 3, 29, 50, 171
World War II, technology in, 7–8,
11, 199

World Wide Web (WWW). *See also*
Internet
archive of, 120–123, 223–225,
227
browsers for, 33
effect of, 58–60
effect on Internet, 49
function of, 55
growth of, 48
resources on, 226
Wozniak, Steve, 118, 119

Xerox Palo Alto Research Center
(PARC), 24, 25, 67

Yamamoto, Isoruku, 7
YesNet, 173
Young, Bob:
on copyright issues, 99–106
on encryption, 122
on freedom, 81
interview with, 215–219
on open source software, 99
on patent ownership,
125–129
on Sklyarov case, 88

Zimmermann, Phil, 83,
90–96